WRITING ROMANCE FICTION.. FOR LOVE AND MONEY

WRITING ROMANCE FICTION ♠♠ FOR LOVE AND MONEY

Helene Schellenberg Barnhart

Edited by Susan Whittlesey Wolf

 Cincinnati, Ohio   ♠ ♠ ♠ ♠ ♠

Library of Congress Cataloging in Publication Data

Barnhart, Helene Schellenberg
   Writing romance fiction—for love and money.
   Bibliography: p.
   Includes index.
   1. Love stories—Authorship. I. Title.
PN3377.5.L68B37   1983   808.3'85   83-10585
ISBN 0-89879-105-7

Design by Linda Huber

Permissions Acknowledgments

The ruled quotations throughout the book were contributed by Rosemary Guiley, author of *Love Lines* (Facts on File, 1983); Vivien Lee Jennings, Editor of *Boy Meets Girl* romance newsletter; the author; and the editor.

Excerpts from *P.S. I Love You* by Barbara Conklin, copyright ©1981 by the Cloverdale Press and Barbara Conklin, and *A Love for All Time* by Dorothy Garlock, copyright ©1983 by Dorothy Garlock, are both used by permission of Bantam Books Inc., All Rights Reserved.

Excerpts from *Her Decision* by Irma Walker, copyright ©1982, used by permission of Ballantine Books; from *The Marriage Contract* by Virginia Nielsen, copyright ©1980, and *Glory Land* by Dorothy Dowdell, copyright ©1981, both used by permission of Fawcett Books, which are published by Ballantine Books; All Rights Reserved.

Excerpts from *Contract for Marriage* by Megan Alexander, copyright ©1982 by Harlequin Enterprises Ltd.; *Music of Passion* by Lynda Ward, copyright ©1981 by Lynda Ward; *Windward Crest* by Anne Hampson, copyright ©1973 by Harlequin Enterprises B.V.; and author's guidelines by the editors of Harlequin Superromances, copyright ©1979 by Harlequin Enterprises Ltd., all reprinted by permission of Harlequin; All Rights Reserved.

Excerpts from *This Calder Sky* by Janet Dailey, copyright ©1981 by Janet Dailey, reprinted by permission of Pocket Books, a Simon & Schuster division of Gulf & Western Corporation; from *Winter Lady* by Janet Joyce, copyright ©1983 by Janet Joyce; *Kate Herself* by Helen Erskin, copyright ©1981 by Helen Santori; *Bitter Victory* by Patti Beckman, copyright ©1982 by Charles & Patti Boeckman, Inc.; *Golden Girl* by Helen Erskin, copyright ©1982 by Helen Santori; *Amber Wine* by Fran Wilson, copyright ©1982 by Fran Wilson; *Renaissance Man* by Stephanie James, copyright ©1982 by Stephanie James; and the author's guidelines by the editors of Silhouette Romances, all reprinted by permission of Silhouette Books, a Simon & Schuster division of Gulf and Western Corporation.

Excerpts from author's guidelines by the editors of Rapture Romances, used by permission of the New American Library, Inc.

Excerpts from *Passion's Price* by Donna Kimel Vitek, copyright ©1983 by Donna Kimel Vitek, *The Black Swan* by Day Taylor, copyright ©1978 by Day Taylor, *Call It Love* by Ginger Chambers, copyright ©1983 by Ginger Chambers, *Lover from the Sea* by Bonnie Drake, copyright ©1983 by Bonnie Drake, *Wagered Weekend* by Jayne Castle, copyright ©1981 by Jayne Castle, *Spanish Masquerade* by Jane Peart, copyright ©1980 by Jane Peart, and author's guidelines by the editors of Dell Books, are all used by permission of Dell Publishing Co., Inc., a subsidiary of Doubleday and Co. Inc., All Rights Reserved.

With love to the men in my life:
Barney, my husband; Carl, my son; and
Stanley, my brother

Acknowledgments

Writing Romance Fiction—for Love and Money is my way of saying thank you to my colleagues in the California Writers' Club, whose continued support over the years has greatly enhanced my teaching and my own writing. Many of them have contributed their advice, experience, and romance fiction for use in this book.

In writing it, I have had the faces, questions, and concerns of my students before me—students from many classrooms and from the Writer's Digest School, whom I've known through the mail. I am grateful to them for allowing me to be part of their dreams, and I am proud to include some of them among the stories of successful romance writers in chapter 17.

My deepest appreciation goes to the staff at Writer's Digest Books for making my own dreams come true through the publication of this book. Carol Cartaino, Howard Wells, Jo Hoff, Nancy Kersell, Kirk Polking, Doris Fannin, and many others over the past ten years of my association there have given me not only the benefit of their editorial expertise, but also their friendship as well.

A special thanks to Susan Whittlesey Wolf, my editor on this project and my friend, for her excellent suggestions and for her constant support through the days of writing and rewriting.

Susan Whittlesey Wolf is a former editor of *Reader's Digest* Condensed Books. She is a writer and freelance editor, specializing in romance fiction.

Special thanks also to Florence Feiler, my agent, and one of the first to see the need for and potential in this book; her faith in me never wavered.

CONTENTS ◢

Introduction
AT LONG LAST, LOVE *by Vivien Lee Jennings* 1

Chapter 1 / WHY WRITE A ROMANCE NOVEL? 11

Chapter 2 / VARIETIES OF ROMANCE — PAST, PRESENT,
SWEET, SENSUAL: *Which Type Could You
Write?* 19

Chapter 3 / ROMANTIC BOOK LOVERS' LEAP —
FROM READER TO WRITER: *How to Analyze a
Romance Novel So You Can Write One* 31

Chapter 4 / SETTING THE MOOD: *Making Your Office Romantic
(and Efficient)* 43

Chapter 5 / THE GIRL OF HIS DREAMS... HER KNIGHT IN
SHINING ARMOR: *Your Heroine, Hero, and Other
Characters* 55

Chapter 6 / WHERE LOVERS MEET: *Romantic Settings and
Professional Worlds* 71

Chapter 7 / THE COURSE OF TRUE LOVE: *Plotting Your
Romance Novel* 89

Chapter 8 / FROM THE BOTTOM OF HER HEART. . . OR HIS?
The Question of Viewpoint 105

Chapter 9 / THE HARSH AND TENDER WORDS OF LOVE:
Creating Lively Dialogue 119

Chapter 10 / WILL THEY OR WON'T THEY? *Writing Sensual
Sex Scenes 141*

Chapter 11 / HAPPILY EVER AFTER: *Planning Carefully for a
Satisfying Ending 163*

Chapter 12 / FINAL TOUCHES: *A Last Check for Perfection 173*

Chapter 13 / YOUR PASSPORT TO PUBLICATION:
The Editorial Package 181

Chapter 14 / THE KNOT IS TIED—*Between You and Your Editor
195*

Chapter 15 / SUSTAINING ROMANCE: *Next Steps in Your Career
203*

Chapter 16 / ANY MORE QUESTIONS? *What Beginning Romance
Writers Most Frequently Ask 213*

Chapter 17 / THE GLORIOUS GLOW OF SUCCESS: *Romance
Writers Tell How They Did It 225*

Chapter 18 / TO YOU, WITH LOVE 245

Appendix 1 / READING TO PUT YOU IN A ROMANTIC MOOD
251

Appendix 2 / ROMANCE NEWSLETTERS TO SUBSCRIBE TO
253

Appendix 3 / ENDURING ROMANCE TITLES *254*

Appendix 4 / RESEARCH SOURCES *257*

Appendix 5 / ROMANCE PUBLISHERS *259*

Index *263*

WRITING ROMANCE FICTION .. FOR LOVE AND MONEY

Introduction
AT LONG LAST, LOVE
The coming of age of
romance fiction

*"He wrote Hollywood scripts to improve his finances and kept on drink-
ing. When they cleaned out his office after he had left Warner Brothers,
they found only an empty bottle and a sheet of yellow foolscap on
which he had written, five hundred times, 'Boy meets girl.' "*
Donald Hall on William Faulkner in The Oxford Book of American Literary Anecdotes. *(Oxford University Press, New York, 1981.)*

Boy meets girl, boy loses girl, boy and girl are reunited and live happily
ever after. The love story is one of the oldest forms of literature. Some trace it
back to prehistory and up through the era of troubadours' ballads and
songs. Some point to the love stories of the Bible as evidence that romance
is an ancient and enduring category of writing. Others find its beginning in
twelfth-century Europe, or even earlier in the Far East.

Our modern romantic fiction owes much to the works of Jane Austen in
England and books like *Forever Amber* and *Gone With the Wind* in this
country. But it wasn't until 1957 that the "category romance"—today's
popular fare—was introduced in the United States. Today it has become a
business whose gross sales are believed to be worth half a billion dollars at
the retail level, and whose top authors enjoy earnings which rival the in-
comes of television, film, and sports superstars.

Like TV and movies and professional sports, romantic fiction is now a
major part of the entertainment business. It is generally acknowledged to be
the single largest segment of the publishing business in America today, con-

stituting nearly half of all the paperback books sold in the United States month after month. Little wonder that insiders in the publishing industry refer to the romance fiction boom as "the phenomenon."

It is more than just a sales phenomenon, however. The demand for romance fiction has made publishing companies aggressively seek new authors, advertising in magazines and newspapers and send their senior editors to regional conferences and on nationwide publicity tours in hopes of finding fresh talent. Have fiction writers ever been so much sought after?

For a 55,000-word, two hundred-page manuscript from a newcomer with a good story, publishers offer an advance against royalties which may go as high as $10,000, as well as an attractive percentage of retail sales. For many, an exclusive multibook contract may follow, which a talented and prolific writer can turn into an annual income of professional proportions.

But as Faulkner proved in Hollywood, not every good writer can capture the special essence of the love story. Though the boy-meets-girl formula seems simple enough, increasing competition has forced a demand for better and better quality. As more love stories are written, the requirements for originality, freshness, and believability increase.

It is easier to be original when you are aware of what has already been done. In post-World War II America, especially during the Eisenhower Era, "nurse novels" were the favored form of women's paperback fiction. Harlequin Books in Toronto launched a line of formula romances bearing such titles as *Nurse with a Dream, Next Patient, Doctor Anne, Hospital on Wheels*. These doctor/nurse love stories continued to be a part of the American romance reader's diet well into the 1960s, with competition from such titles as *Walk Softly, Doctor* and *Dude Ranch Nurse* (Ace Books, New York). This theme was suitable for that time, when a woman's highest professional achievement was usually in a field that was a natural extension of her "proper" role as mother and nurturer.

In 1957, Harlequin began to publish love stories about very young, very pretty, and very straitlaced, usually British, women who were swept off their feet by tall, dark, handsome strangers from foreign lands. The Harlequin formula was described by the publisher as "hardcore decency." There was no sex outside marriage. In fact, there was no description of sexual activity as such. Harlequin romances were sweet and simple, guaranteeing a happy ending, and that happy ending was almost always delivered as marriage or plans to marry. Most of the Harlequin monthly titles were reprints of books acquired from Mills & Boon, London, a publisher that has since been acquired by Harlequin.

During the 1960s, the gothic romance also found favor with the American audience. These stories, often set in England, followed the tradition of

Jane Eyre and *Rebecca* and featured spirited heroines who were governesses or innocent brides, brought to live in large gloomy mansions that were staffed by strange servants and owned by dark, handsome men with mysterious pasts.

By the mid-1970s, hefty, spicy historical romances were catching the attention of the public, romances with such smoldering titles as *This Loving Torment, Savage Surrender*, and *Love's Wildest Fires*. The press dubbed them "bodice rippers." Rich in historical detail, the formula often included the abduction and rape of a young heroine who was described as "feisty" and "spirited." The heroine's struggle against the strong hero's sexual domination was blatantly physical. She kicked and screamed and pounded his chest with her fists before she surrendered.

Throughout this period, the Harlequin "sweet romance" remained virtually unchanged and continued to dominate category romance. At this time, too, the English author, Barbara Cartland, began her prolific production of romance novels. Their style and stories were quite similar to Harlequin's, though most were set in Regency England (between 1811 and 1820).

During the 1970s, thousands of American women were steeped in these romance novels, and by 1983 there were an estimated 2,000 working romance writers in the United States. Most had begun as avid readers in the genre. Janet Dailey, the most productive and well-known American romance fiction writer, who has sold 100 million books worldwide since 1976, began her career in a fashion typical of many of today's successful romance writers. She relates: "After reading so many of them, one day I said, 'I can do this!' To which my husband, Bill, responded, 'Well, then, stop talking about it and do it!' "

In "doing it," Janet was among the first to introduce contemporary American settings to the romance novel, which until that time was essentially British. She recognized the appeal of local settings and heroines to American women, and methodically proceeded to write romances set in each of the fifty states; this achievement qualified her for, among other things, mention in the *Guinness Book of World Records*.

American settings and American heroines now dominate the contemporary category romance. Roughly eighty percent of all category romance titles published today are properly classified as "American contemporary"; "contemporary" refers also to the modern mores, attitudes, and situations which now characterize these stories.

It is change for the better. The category romance of a few years ago was often little more than a retelling of the Cinderella story. The heroine was pretty, but somehow found herself in reduced circumstances. The hero was handsome, rich, and powerful. As Prince Charming, he rescued her from some peril, such as an evil stepmother or a disagreeable suitor or a life of tedium. It was a sweet little fantasy, but hardly one that rang true.

By the 1980s, the category romance was also well on its way to becoming liberated from traditional male domination. Women began to be depicted as able to think for themselves, often with careers that matched those of the male protagonists. The men began to be described as more sensitive, more capable of displaying a broad range of emotions, and even, in some of the best recent romantic fiction, as vulnerable as the heroines. The escapist fantasy became "fantasy within the realm of possibility," which was ultimately displaced by "romance within the realm of reality," or, as some say, "reality with rose-colored edges."

In growing up, the heroine, naturally enough, was also depicted as older than in earlier romances. No longer a trembling nineteen-year-old, the heroine of today's contemporary romances is most often between the ages of twenty-five and forty-five, and acutely aware of her sexuality. Now she chooses a man not to acquire an identity, but to have a partner with whom to share her future. Mr. Right is not Prince Charming. Prince Charming could never exist in the real world. Instead, Mr. Right in today's romance fiction is the best of several reasonable choices. The heroine may even have made the wrong choice along the way, according to some of the most popular executions of the formula. But her emotional suffering and sexual experience serve her well, and she finds true love at last.

An older, more mature heroine will elect to sleep with a man she is not married to. This is hardly a revelation, but it caused a revolution in contemporary category romance in the 1980s. The day of the virginal heroine is over.

How did the new heroine come into being? Until 1980, Harlequin books had been distributed in the United States by Pocket Books, a division of Simon & Schuster. In that year the two companies ended their relationship, and Pocket Books created its own line of romance novels, Silhouette Books, originally intended to be a duplication of the Harlequin formula. These books were advertised as featuring "fresh, young heroines and strong, responsible men, who play out their lives in exotic places, with happy endings. Romance the way it used to be."

But then something happened to shake up the industry. A new brand appeared in January 1981, offering readers something different. It was called Dell Candlelight Ecstasy Romance, and it did not deliver romance the way it used to be, but romance the way you wish it *could* be. Dell Ecstasies were boldly sensual. The stories contained sex, even premarital sex, as enjoyed, in fact, by modern American women in their twenties and thirties. With virtually no advertising, Dell Ecstasies quickly became the first choice among romance readers. At the time, many observers believed that this success was due entirely to the comparatively high level of sensuality in these books. In retrospect, though, we see that Dell's success was probably due to something more important—to a more realistic depiction of today's woman in *every* facet of her life.

In the same year, the Second Change at Love line was launched by the Berkley/Jove Publishing Group. As its name implied, Second Chance took the view that modern women don't always find the perfect match in their late teens. Sometimes they have to keep trying. As in the Ecstasy line, Second Chance heroines were more mature, sometimes widowed or divorced, and the stories were also more sensual than the sweet romances still being offered by Harlequin and Silhouette. Second Chance was not the overnight sensation that Ecstasy was, but its audience continued to grow at a steady pace, until by early 1983 it was the only category contemporary line whose sales continued to increase during a virtual explosion of new romance fiction lines.

These two lines, it is now agreed, changed the industry forever. Their editors, two mature fiction professionals based in New York, understood their audience. They knew that romance fiction is almost exclusively women's territory. In fact, most of the readership is the female half of the famous postwar baby boom.

These readers have survived the sexual revolution of the 1960s; the liberation movement of the 1970s, with family and career conflicts that precipitated the highest divorce rate this country has ever seen; and the economic recession of the 1980s, which brought women into the American work force at every level. They see the modern American woman as both romantic and realistic, as she makes a place for herself in a world previously dominated by men. Romance fiction in the early 1980s reflected the values, the expectations, and the newly acquired self-image of some twenty-two million women who were now in their peak earning years.

Sigmund Freud once lamented, "The great question, which I have not been able to answer, despite my thirty years of research into the feminine soul, is, 'What does a woman want?' " The answer must lurk somewhere in the new form of romance fiction. These books, written, edited, and read by women, obviously fill some basic needs.

"We all felt that tastes were changing," one editor told me in the summer of 1981. "We all felt that some needs had never been met. None of us ever liked love-at-first-rape books, heroines who were wimpy and victimized, and we felt uncomfortable about the violence and degradation we found in a lot of the historicals, especially. Our new guidelines now call for a heroine who is spirited, intelligent, involved, and caring, who often initiates the story's action, rather than simply reacting to it."

Research conducted among romance readers in the spring of 1982 confirmed the editor's view. The great majority of women surveyed said they preferred to read about a woman with a career. They didn't mind if the hero wasn't rich. They preferred that the love story result in a true partnership. They preferred that the heroine not be a virgin, and they were adamantly opposed to the use of physical violence against the heroine.

They identified with heroines who were intelligent, independent, spirited, confident, witty, capable, and sensual. They liked heroes who were intelligent, confident, tender, considerate, sexy, tall, witty, handsome, and powerful.

The publishers responded to these insights with such a proliferation of brand-name category romance that by the end of 1982, the consumer had more than 100 new titles to choose from every month. In addition, great numbers of single-title releases were published as trade paperbacks and lead titles, or "bestsellers."

Inevitably, and fortunately for the authors, the demand for skilled writers far outstripped the supply, and as the demand for their talents increased, so did the level of payment. During this period the so-called "standard advance" doubled, and, in many cases, doubled again. At the same time, many of the editors who had proven their ability to shape a hit category romance series for one publisher found greater opportunities and rewards among their competitors.

Consider this short chronology of events in romance fiction publishing from January 1981 to January 1983 alone:

January 1981. The first Dell Candlelight Ecstasy titles appear on the shelves. *Gentle Pirate* by Jayne Castle features an obviously imperfect hero, a man missing one hand.

February 1981. Harlequin introduces Superromances, longer, more sensual romances. These are described as "sophisticated and in keeping with today's lifestyle." Superromances are such a departure from traditional Harlequin fare that the publisher decides to delete the Harlequin imprint, and uses its Worldwide Library name instead.

March 1981. Richard Gallen Books, a packager of historical romances for Pocket Books, announces that it will add two contemporary titles to its monthly output. Jove announces the pending introduction of Second Chance at Love, novels that "begin where happily ever after ends." The *Saturday Review* discovers to its amazement that two of the five bestselling authors in the world are romance novelists, Janet Dailey and Barbara Cartland.

April 1981. Demand for Dell Candlelight Ecstasy romances is so great that consumers stand in line to receive books pulled directly from the shipping cartons.

May 1981. National sales figures credit romance fiction with twenty-five percent of all paperbacks sold. (Our own surveys show that it's almost forty percent.) Silhouette prepares for the introduction of Silhouette Special Edition, a longer, more sensual book, designed to compete with Harlequin's new Superromance.

June 1981. The New York Times declares romantic fiction "paperback's liveliest genre." ABC's "20/20" prepares a network feature on "the phenomenon," as does "NBC Magazine."

July-August 1981. Silhouette says that it will introduce a "short and sexy" line (Desire). Harlequin and Dell announce price increases from $1.50 to $1.75. Janet Dailey publishes her sixtieth book. Harlequin and Silhouette each advertise for American authors.

September 1981. Two former *National Enquirer* executives try to cash in on romance with a supermarket tabloid called *Rhapsody Romance.* Vivian Stephens, creator of the Dell Candlelight Ecstasy series, joins Harlequin Books as senior editor for a new line of American romance. Dell announces that it will increase its output of Ecstasy Romances from four to six titles a month. Jove's Second Chance at Love plans a similar move. Bantam and Silhouette introduce teen romances. Harlequin, Warner, Pocket Books, and others phase out their Regency romances.

October 1981. Ace Books begins a search for authors of teen romances. Anne Gisonny, former editor-in-chief for MacFadden Romances, takes over the Dell Candlelight Ecstasy line and actively seeks new authors. *Good Housekeeping* magazine confirms that it will publish condensations of current romance fiction in every issue. Jove research shows that romantic fiction accounts for forty-five percent of all paperback books sold.

November 1981. Bantam Books prepares a new romance series called Circle of Love.

December 1981. Harlequin announces that it will increase its Harlequin Presents series (slightly more sensual than Harlequin Romances) from six to eight titles a month. Phil Donahue pits critic Anne Douglas against Janet Dailey in a debate that characterizes romantic fiction as "anti-feminist, pornographic trash." Comworld begins development of a daytime TV series called "Romance Theater," with the endorsement of the Romance Writers of America.

January 1982. Ballantine Books prepares to launch Love & Life, aimed at a mature (over-30) female audience, with heroines from thirty to forty-two years old in situations that focus on realistic conflicts and midlife crises. New American Library announces plans to offer a "more sensual" line (Rapture), featuring "a heroine who has her own job and makes her own way, and who meets a man who eventually discovers he wants a strong, capable woman." Harlequin announces that Mills & Boon editor Jacqui Bianchi will travel from London to the United States to conduct a series of workshops for American authors. Avon begins development of a series called Finding Mr. Right, whose formula "strikes the right balance between reality and romance." Silhouette Special Edition arrives at bookstores.

February 1982. An American category romance makes the bestseller list in the United Kingdom for the first time. New American Library begins to explore romances for senior citizens.

March 1982. Forbes magazine credits romances with $250 million in annual sales. Harlequin research puts the figure at $493 million. Bantam Books hires Carolyn Nichols, creator of Jove's Second Chance at Love line. Vivian Stephens, now at Harlequin, asks for stories that feature "real people, normal people, which means fat people, tall people, short people, thin people, and bald-headed people." Pocket Books announces plans to produce its own line of historical romances (Tapestry) after its separation from Richard Gallen Books.

April 1982. Consumers turn thumbs down on Bantam's Circle of Love, when books prove to be outdated "sweet romances." "The line," according to a wholesaler, "has been a total bomb." Doubleday seeks authors for a hardcover romance series called Starlight.

May 1982. Jove reveals plans to prepare a new romance series featuring married women in love with their husbands (To Have and To Hold). Silhouette Desire arrives on the bookstands with what some find to be "an overdose of sex."

June 1982. Teen romances from Bantam and Silhouette continue to grow in popularity. Dell's Anne Gisonny announces plans to travel across the U.S. looking for writers. She offers advances up to $10,000. In Germany, romance fiction is published at the rate of one title a day.

August 1982. Jove's senior editor Ellen Edwards observes, "There are simply not enough professional writers with experience to meet the needs of all the new lines, so all of us are having to develop new writers." Harlequin romances and Harlequin Presents add ten new American authors. Zebra

Books introduces a new series called Leather & Lace, in which "the historical romance weds the adult western."

September 1982. Superromance says it is "the fastest growing romance line in the industry." RCA picks up Second Chance at Love for subscription distribution. Most of the major romance publishers have women in charge of their product.

October 1982. According to a spokesperson for Waldenbooks, if category romances were included in bestseller lists, "they would take up the major portion of the Top 10 titles. Few things would push them out." Bantam's Carolyn Nichols predicts, "The 1983 version of the love story will contain humor and wit, with almost no limit to the level of sexuality, if it is not separated from romance."

November-December 1982. Dell begins to acquire manuscripts for a new line called Temptation. Harlequin announces a price increase. Avon has plans to produce a new line of romantic suspense stories. Bantam releases a sample of its first six Loveswept titles, and every one's a winner.

January 1983. Dell announces plans to develop a new series called Ecstasy Supremes, "containing more non-category elements." Harlequin begins its introduction of Harlequin American Romances. Historical romance sales slip. Various publishers prepare eight more new lines for introduction over the next eighteen months.

So it has gone, and so it goes. Romance fiction is a big and volatile business, where it seems nothing is constant but change.

The simple theme—boy meets girl—continues to evolve, as it always has, into new and different forms.

When the current boom wears itself out, as all booms do sooner or later, some books will survive, and some writers in the ranks will continue to produce what editors want, i.e., what readers will buy. These will be the writers whose skill and originality elevate the theme into the mainstream of fiction writing by creating the best love stories of the day.

By Vivien Lee Jennings

President, Rainy Day Books (R), Inc.
Editor, BOY MEETS GIRL (R)

Silhouette Romance

57213-X
$1.75

#213

JANET DAILEY

Separate Cabins

Chapter **1.**
WHY WRITE A ROMANCE NOVEL?

You and I haven't met, but I feel that I know you quite well. I've met your think-alike in my writing classes, in my workshops on various college campuses, and as an instructor in the Writer's Digest School of Writing over the past ten years.

Many of you have yet to sell your first novel, and you're curious about this relatively new, definitely booming romance fiction market. You've heard exciting stories about beginning writers who have sold their first romance novels. You wonder if you could learn to write one.

Maybe you have published one, two, or more romance novels—either contemporaries, historicals, or young adults. Now you want to branch out and try another type, as so many other successful romance writers have done.

Or maybe you are not yet seriously interested in writing romance fiction. You're at work on the Great American Novel, a long book with a powerful theme of great social significance. Perhaps it's a serious historical tome like *War and Peace*.

That is all well and good. But it will take you a long time to write it, perhaps years. It's hard work. And when you are finished, it may be tough to find a publisher for your masterpiece.

Meanwhile, news of the money to be made in writing romance fiction has seeped through the cracks in the walls of your ivory tower. You're curious. *Maybe you could write one and earn some money while you're working on your "serious novel."*

Whichever niche you fit into, you want to know more about writing a romance before you invest your time and energy in trying to write one, or before you try another side of the game. Sound thinking! Whether you write for love, money, or both, this book will answer your questions about the exciting world of romance fiction, and how you, too, can reap profits from this bountiful field.

I'll answer some of these questions in this book, but first I'd like to make a few suggestions you may find helpful.

First, if you have never read a romance novel, waste no time. Run to your nearest supermarket or bookstore and buy a few. Scan the titles and read the blurbs, those teasers on the back covers. Then choose only the novels that arouse your curiosity and interest. At this point, you're going to read purely for pleasure. (In the next chapter, I'll show you how to read analytically to learn exactly how a romance is written.)

As you browse among these romance paperbacks, you may be surprised at the art on the covers, pictures of lovely heroines and handsome heroes caught in a moment of romantic bliss. You'll also observe the provocative titles: *Playing for Keeps, Fortunes of Love, Terms of Surrender.*

Whether you're already addicted to reading romance fiction or completely uninitiated, you can learn a great deal just by studying the titles and blurbs on these books. They give you clues to the type of characters, the kind of backgrounds (foreign or domestic), and the essence of the plots. You can be sure these were carefully approved by experienced romance editors and it is likely that they are fairly close to the sorts of stories those editors are still looking for.

As you return home with a romance novel, or two, or three, tucked into your shopping bag, another question haunts you. How long will the romance balloon fly without bursting and falling to earth? Will the market hold up until you've had a chance to start your novel, much less finish it?

Believe me, romance is here to stay. As you saw in the introduction of this book, romantic fiction has been around a long, long time. I assure you, it will continue to warm our hearts and nurture our fantasies as long as there is girl to meet boy, and love to be fallen into, hazards to be overcome, and ultimate happiness to be found. The details may change over the years, but the romance novel will always exist in one form or another.

The following facts will convince you that romance fiction is worth considering seriously, whether you are a beginning writer looking for a market or an established writer who knows how important it is to stay versatile and flexible and to stretch your talent in new directions.

1. It's an Open Market.

You don't have to have a well-known name to break into the romance fiction market. Many writers who now have published one or more romance novels were unknown three, two, or even *one year ago*. You'll meet some of these newcomers in the pages of this book.

2. The Financial Returns are Excellent—Even on a First Sale.

You can earn anywhere from $1,500 to $10,000 as an advance on the sale of your first romance novel depending on what kind it is, with royalties to follow at 6 to 8% of the cover price, which could be anything from $1.75 to $3.50. The print run, or number of copies published, could be as high as 300,000. Simple math will show you the possible profits.

3. It Doesn't Take Forever to Write a Romance Novel.

After you've studied this book and applied these lessons to the idea in your head (or your typewriter), you could finish your first romance novel in six months or less. When you become proficient at writing romance, you'll cut this time in half. Many writers with word processors turn out one romance novel a month, and those who still use the typewriter often finish one in two months. That is six a year.

4. You Can LEARN to Write Romance Fiction.

While it might take you years to learn all the intricate techniques needed to write the Great American Novel, any writer with a measure of creative talent and a determination to succeed can learn to write a saleable romance.

This is no blithe statement. Students in my classrooms have made their debuts as novelists in this way. Chapter seventeen is filled with stories of romance writers who applied their talent to this genre and found swift success.

5. Learning to Write Saleable Romance Fiction Will Improve ALL Your Writing.

This statement is absolutely true. When you learn to write romance fiction, you will learn to write sensuously, creating vivid pictures with words. You will learn to build solid plots. You will develop understanding of motivation, so that your characterization takes on depth and dimension. Finally, to make your way in the increasingly competitive romance marketplace, you will learn to be fresh and original, at the same time disciplining yourself to stay within the established format of a given type of romance fiction.

These skills will make you not only a better romance writer, but will also pay off when you return to other types of writing.

6. There Are No Special Educational Requirements.

Education is good for a writer to have, of course. The more you know about the world—its past, its present, and its future possibilities—the more you'll have to write about. But as a writer, you don't have to fill out an employment application with endless questions on your education and past employment. Editors in general, and romance editors in particular, are interested in the words you put on paper—romantic words that take the reader away from it all into the lovely world of romance, where dreams always come true. If you've ever been in love, you have the background you'll need in this field.

The lessons and suggestions given in this book will help you develop your romantic style. But if you're already a romantic at heart, all you'll need is a little encouragement to get you started.

7. There Are No Geographical Requirements.

As a writer of romance fiction, you may want to create exotic, faraway settings. But there's no need to withdraw your life's savings and travel to the corners of the earth. Through your imagination and careful research, you can stay right at home and still write of faraway places.

You don't even have to be within shouting distance of New York publishers to attract editorial attention. If you come up with an exciting idea for a romance novel, and demonstrate that you know how to write, the editor will hear your voice, no matter where you live.

The successful writers in chapter seventeen live in all parts of the United States; some, like Alla Crone, who writes historical romance, came originally from other countries. (Ms. Crone was born in Russia, lived in China, and now resides in California.)

Janet Dailey, perhaps the most successful romance writer living today, writes on wheels. She has traveled through all fifty states in her trailer, collecting background material for novels set in each.

8. There Are No Age or Sex Requirements.

In spite of the efforts of the Women's Movement, women still find it difficult to reach the top in many professions because of sex discrimination. Not so here. Romance writing is particularly well suited to a woman's imagination and experience. She can pursue it when she must be at home with small children and later, after the children are grown and gone from the nest.

Romance fiction writing is not off limits to men, however. In fact, a few have been very successful. Jennifer Wilde is really one Tom Huff, for example. Patti and Charles Beckman are a prolific husband-and-wife writing team. You'll find their romance novels under the Silhouette Romance label, as well as others. Charles happily uses *Patti* as his byline for his romantic creations, retaining his own name for other types of writing.

Patricia and Clayton Matthews have been called "the hottest couple in paperbacks." They are successful historical romance authors, both individually and as a team. They collaborated on *Midnight Whispers* (Bantam); Clayton wrote *The Harvesters* and *The Power Seekers;* and five of Patricia's historical romances have sold over one million copies each.

Your age doesn't matter either. England's Barbara Cartland, often called "the queen of romance writers," with over three hundred titles to her credit, is now in her eighties.

9. You Have a Guaranteed Readership.

"Lines" of romance novels sell each month to the same readers. Historicals have a steady following, and the young adult romance audience is growing all the time.

While your Great American Novel might long be hidden on crowded

---

"I don't smoke. I don't drink. I don't play golf. If I want to buy romance novels, I owe it to myself. It's a cheap safe way to forget your problems." **A romance reader**

---

bookshop shelves, you can be sure that your romance novel will find its way speedily into the hands of readers who will enjoy it. Publishers and booksellers skillfully promote romance novels to a known and, by now, well-developed readership.

10. Romance Is Here to Stay.

In an age when independence and equality are more important to women than ever, romance fiction is being read so hungrily that publishers find it difficult to match the supply to the demand. Many explanations are given for the enormous popularity of romance fiction, but whatever the reasons, this message is loud and clear: People read to ESCAPE from the constant pressure and stress of modern-day living.

The romance market, like all others, is sensitive to the response of its readership. For this reason, there will be continuing changes; new lines come along to replace those that didn't make it. Editors and publishers spend a great deal of time and money to test the market before they announce and promote a line of romance novels.

There will be variations, changes in the way the love-conquers-all theme is presented in romance fiction. But the theme itself will endure.

"If all the Harlequin books sold **in a single day** *last year (1981) were* **stacked one on top of the other, the pile would be 16 times as high as** **the World Trade Center."** **Walter Kendrick in The Village Voice**

So come with me through the workshop chapters of this book. Meet romance writers who have carved out exciting and profitable careers for themselves writing romance fiction for love *and* for money.

If you haven't sold a novel yet, there's no reason to hang back. You have just as good a chance as many of the successful romance writers who were in your shoes a year or two ago. I'll teach you how to analyze their techniques and how to use them.

I've given you ten good reasons why you should consider learning to write romance fiction if you haven't already, and I've pointed out that even if you have published in one type of romance market, it's wise to learn all you can about other kinds of romance fiction.

I will show you how to test your idea, and then how to develop that idea into a saleable romance novel. I'll also show you how you can determine which line of romance fiction is best for you.

Many of my students have sold their first books to the romance market,

---

"This is not a business for amateurs. There was a day when a house-wife could sit down and write a manuscript, send it off without knowing how to submit a manuscript, and then be transformed into a writer, but that doesn't happen anymore. Forbes did a survey in 1982 which estimated the income from one of these books at $30,000. Some of us are writing 10 books a year, and with that kind of income at stake, we're not going to leave any room for amateurs." Maura Seger, author of contemporary and historical romances

---

and you can, too. And you'll want to follow up sales in one line of romance with sales to several other lines, as most of these students have.

After you read a few chapters in this book, you won't be asking "Why should I write a romance novel?" You'll be shouting, "When do I start? I've got this great idea!"

The time to start is *now!*

Turn the page and let's go!

Harlequin American Romance

1

Tomorrow's Promise

SANDRA BROWN

VARIETIES OF ROMANCE – PAST, PRESENT, SWEET, SENSUAL: Which Type Could You Write?

Now, back at your bookstore, you may be overwhelmed at first. Rack after rack of erotic and exotic paperback covers gleam out at you, bordered in purple, pink, or gold. Where do you start? What do you read? How do you discover how these books differ from each other, who publishes which kind of romance, and last and most important, how do you figure out how you might apply your writing talent to this booming genre?

You have a right to be confused. There are hundreds of romances to choose from, at least a dozen different publishers, and twice as many "lines." And the words used to describe and discuss these books are often blurry and confusing.

On your way in, you'll probably pass small cardboard stands holding the latest *bestselling* romances, possibly by Danielle Steel, Janet Dailey, Patricia Matthews, Rosemary Rogers, or Kathleen Woodiwiss. These may be either contemporary—set in today's world—or historical—set against backgrounds of times gone by—but in either case, these books are potential *crossovers* into mainstream fiction. This means that their themes are broader than just a central romantic story; that they are not part of a "line;" and that they are intended to be read not just by romance readers but by a more general audience.

A nearby stand may hold a few other romances by less well-known authors, as well as single-title releases. These are what publishers call their *midlist* books, which are neither *lead titles* for the month (i.e., bestsellers)— on the one hand, nor category fiction on the other. Occasionally a midlist novel will take off unexpectedly, but for the most part, publishers are reluctant to publish an unknown quantity in these shaky times. The number of midlist books on the stands seems to be declining.

Now walk over to the section labeled "Historical Romance." Here the covers are graced by handsome men in velvet waistcoats and beautiful women dressed in low-cut, frilly gowns, their hair in ringlets. A careful reading of the blurbs on their back covers will show you some of the distinctions here.

The long (500 pages or more), highly erotic stories, set against some period of history in America, Europe, or elsewhere, are the *erotic historicals* or so-called *bodice rippers*. (That last term came from the hero's rough approach to the heroine's garments.)

Others may be *family sagas*, generational tales of a single family's fortunes over several decades. Some volumes are installments in *historical series*, sequences of novels written to explore the development of a part of this country or another from early days to the present.

Mixed in among the historicals, or perhaps on a separate rack, you will find other romances set in times past: *gothic romances*, not so popular right now, but still around and bound to return, their covers eerie with haunted mansions perched on dark English moors. There may be Regency, Victorian, or Edwardian romances, set in those periods of English history. All of these are apt to be relatively "short reads."

Now, turning the corner, you will find the biggest rack and the hottest-selling romances of the day—the *contemporary category romances.* You may have heard these referred to as "category brand romances," "line romances," or "formula romances." (Also, don't confuse the general term "category fiction" with "category romance." The former is the standard umbrella word used for stock novels, such as mystery, science fiction, westerns, action and adventure, and romance *as a genre.)*

Most other romance novels are single-title releases, that is, books which stand on their own, but contemporary category romances, or, as some call them, *category romances,* are published as part of a line of romances. All of these carry the same imprint or line name, which usually appears on the cover above or near the title.

The same logo or pictorial symbol often appears on each book, and there is usually a number on the spine to indicate the book's place in the line. All novels in a given line will be the same length (give or take a few pages) and the same price, and will be issued monthly. Some houses release as few as two a month; some as many as six.

Another distinction here will interest you as a writer. Category romances have been written, for the most part, by authors who followed specific *guidelines* or *author tip sheets* put out by the publisher. The content, tone, and direction of all the novels in a given line are similar, and when the reader buys the book, she knows the kind of story she can expect to find on its pages.

Just to make this more confusing, there are a few lines in which the books do NOT follow similar plots. They attempt to be more realistic than the category romances, which are written to a formula. Some people refer to these as *contemporary series* rather than as lines. We will discuss them shortly.

There are other important distinctions among category romances. If you scan the covers, you will notice that lovers on some appear to be *sweetly* embracing. Others are more *sensuously* involved. As you learned in the introduction, category romances do indeed come in two flavors—*sweet* and *sensual.*

Pick up a sampling of these titles and you'll notice something else. They come in two sizes. Some are short (180-200 pages); some are longer (250-400 pages or more), with more complex plot lines and bigger casts of characters.

The blurbs on the back covers will show you that heroines differ too. In the sweet romances, the heroine is virginal and innocent. In the more sensual ones, she is rarely a virgin, though she is probably single. In some cases, she is widowed or divorced, possibly finding love for the second time. She may be older, over 35 or even 40; in one line, heroines are married and find true love with their spouses. Most heroines are Caucasian, but some are American Indian or Hispanic or black. Settings vary widely too. Some lines prefer American settings; others offer romance set in exotic distant places.

On a separate rack, perhaps, or mixed in with the category romances, you may find a few *romantic suspense* novels. This type of romance is not new, as fans of Victoria Holt, Mary Stewart, Phyllis Whitney, or Barbara Michaels could tell you. The stories have some elements of the gothic novel, but they are present-day tales that may be set anywhere in the world. The heroine is usually a spunky woman who is involved somehow in a mysterious and frightening situation. In the course of her terrors she meets the hero and emerges free of fear, the mystery solved, and in love.

Although these books have lost popularity during the rise of other types of romances, at least one major publisher plans to start a line of romantic suspense, and there may be a real return of interest in these stories.

Now go over to the rack holding *young adult paperbacks*. You will see covers featuring a teenage girl and boy—often a photograph—looking up at you over a frothy pink ice-cream soda. The blurb may imply that they are trying out "first love." These books are the *young adult romances,* written expressly for a teenage audience, and are definitely sweet rather than sensual.

Depending on the size and scope of your bookstore, further careful search might turn up other varieties of romance such as inspirational (religious), occult, or even lesbian romances. As this fast-growing genre expands, you might find just about anything!

If you brought along the titles of a few specific category romances and hoped to find them here, you may be disappointed. Though mainstream romance is available as long as it is in print, category romances have a very short shelflife. They appear in a bookstore or supermarket in the week in which they are released. A few weeks later, they are replaced by the next month's offerings. You will have to go to your local library or *used paperback bookstore* to find titles even a month or two old. In fact, if you don't already have a good library of romances, I recommend a weekly trip to your local dealer in used paperbacks. This is an economical way to collect these books so you'll have them on hand for quick reference. If you are searching for titles not available second hand, you can write the publisher directly to see if the book is still in print.

You may have come to your bookstore with another specific mission— to find all the romances, historical and contemporary, sweet and sensual, written by one author. Some authors do write more than one type. Both you and your bookseller may run into a brick wall on this. Although your author may have written ten or even twenty romances, it is more than likely that she used a different name for each type, and may have used a different publisher each time. To round up a collection you will have to know *all* her pen names and then look for them at the library or used paperback store, or try writing the publishers.

Now let's look broadly at these types of romance, and what each one requires. Keep your own talents and interests in mind to see where you might fit.

The Category Romance—Sweet
Dell Candlelight Romance, Harlequin Romance, Silhouette Romance

Sweet romances are usually 55,000 to 65,000 words and somewhere between 165 and 187 printed pages (roughly 220 mss pages). The plot line is simple, with the emphasis on the meeting of the heroine and hero and the complications arising between them to keep them apart while they yearn to be in one another's arms. Although the sexual attraction is strong between them and exciting to read about, physical contact is restricted to breathless kisses, tender embraces, and yearning sighs. Hands do not wander to touch "intimate places," as they do in the more explicit romances.

In spite of today's openness where sex is concerned, a large readership still prefers virginal heroines and tender rather than explicit descriptions of physical love.

But just as in other types of romance, *sensuous* writing is a must in the sweet romances. Description of characters, places, clothes, food, flora and fauna, and weather must appeal to the five senses.

The ability to write sensuously, that is, to create vivid word pictures that evoke emotional response in the reader, can be developed with practice and by studying the styles of various romance writers. Most of these writers have developed their ability to write sensuous description into an art form. Study successful writers of Silhouette's sweet romances, such as Dixie Browning, Patti Beckman, Brooke Hastings, and Phyllis Halldorson.

Among the many fine writers with a good sensuous style in Harlequin's sweet romances line are: Anne Mather, Lilian Peake, Anne Hampson, Roberta Leigh, and Violet Winspear.

Many writers served their apprenticeship writing sweet romances. Then, having developed skill and sensuous style, they moved on to write the more lusty type of romance. Could this be the route for you?

The Category Romance—Sensual

Short: Ballantine Love & Life, Bantam Loveswept, Dell Candlelight Ecstasy, Harlequin Presents, Jove Second Chance at Love, Jove To Have and To Hold, New American Library (NAL) Rapture Romance, Zebra Hourglass. Longer: Avon Finding Mr. Right, Dell Ecstasy Supreme, Harlequin American Romance, Harlequin Superromance, Silhouette Intimate Moments, Silhouette Special Edition

Short or longer, these more sensual romances are characterized by explicit descriptions of lovemaking between the hero and the heroine, with no restrictions placed on the author's imagination. Typical editorial guidelines state, "Plenty of foreplay and afterplay should be described in such a way as to give the reader a vivid picture of what is taking place, what the lovers are feeling, during each phase of the sexual encounter."

In these more sensual stories, little is left to the reader's imagination. We see the heroine's nipples grow turgid under the hero's expert caressing, and vicariously experience her arousal, perhaps described as "a warm melting sensation which pervaded her being."

The heroine hungrily clings to the hero as his tongue "invades her mouth," and she trembles "as he demands more and more of her."

Do you think you could create such passion and ardor? (Because writing strong sex scenes can be difficult for the new romance writer, or the one who feels inhibited, chapter ten will discuss the subject in depth.)

As you consider your interest in writing the category romance, remember that any contemporary romance novel—category or mainstream— must reflect *today's world*. The writer must enjoy keeping up with the times, antennae constantly alert to catch the nuances in the ever-changing social and economic scenes. It is important to keep up with changes in thinking regarding relationships between men and women; newspapers and magazines must be this writer's constant companions.

Subjects that were taboo yesterday are openly discussed today, on talk shows such as Phil Donahue's, for example. These topics can provide fresh plot situations for romance novels, ideas for heroines troubled by truly modern problems.

For example, Megan Alexander explored the idea of motherhood without wifehood, in *Contract for Marriage* (Worldwide Library Superromance). The heroine, Christy Steele, confronts the hero, Mark Brandon, with a "deeply personal and intimate request." She wants him to father her child under an impersonal contract agreement. Christy feels responsible for the death of her sister's child, and to add to her sorrow, her sister can have no more children. Christy feels that she herself must have a baby to give to her sister. When she meets Mark Brandon and realizes how much he looks like her deceased nephew, she turns to him in desperation to help her make amends to her sister, who is crushed with grief over the death of her son.

This type of dilemma is also good grist for the mill of the more realistic category romances, such as Ballantine's Love & Life or Avon's Finding Mr. Right. These two are really "series" rather than lines; books under these imprints are less similar in theme and structure than are the line romances.

In writing sensual romances, you'll need a heroine who stands on the threshold of tomorrow's world. She must be attractive, courageous, capable of independent thought; a high achiever. Often she has made it up the corporate ladder to sit as vice president on the board of directors of some big business. She may head a veterinary clinic with a D.V.M. (doctor of veterinary medicine) degree tucked into her white pantsuit pocket. She may own a string of exclusive women's dress shops, or direct the operations of an exciting, dangerous, and challenging underwater research project.

But even beyond an ability to create a heroine bursting with courage and independence, you must be able to portray her as a woman with a woman's needs for love. There is a void in her life which she wants to fill, but only a special man can make her life complete.

You must come up with an attractive hero, a man with an aura of sexuality about him that causes feminine heads to turn. He, too, is independent and sure of himself, often seeming arrogant until the heroine knows him better. Usually he is a man of importance in whatever occupation or profession he has chosen.

Then, most important of all, when your heroine and hero meet, you must charge the scene with instant sexual attraction that runs like a high-voltage wire between them. At the same time, you must create an explosive clash between these two potential lovers by putting obstacles in the path of their true love, obstacles which are not removed until the final pages of the book.

While secondary characters in the shorter category romance are kept to a minimum, several may be needed to thicken the plot in the longer ones, and are usually cast so as to provide added conflict.

And readers of category romance are not only seeking emotional escape; they also want journeys to interesting or colorful places. When you write this type of book, you need an ability to convey your setting vividly, whether it is a wheat farm in Kansas, the streets of San Francisco, a neighborhood in your own home town, or a romantic foreign setting that you create with the help of research. And whatever profession you choose for your hero and heroine, it must also be well researched and fully presented.

Because modern woman is evolving into quite a different person from her ancestors or even her own mother, traditional roles and lifestyles are giving way to experimental ones. Would you like to explore these in your writing? Then perhaps the more sensual contemporary category romance is for you.

Historical Romances
Jove Regency, NAL Signet Regency, Pocket Books Tapestry Romances, Zebra Leather & Lace

Although most contemporary category romances are published as part of a line or series, most historicals are not. With the exception of the four specialized lines listed above, guidelines do not exist and historicals are published as single title releases.

To be a successful writer of historical romance, you must love history in general, or at least have an absorbing interest in a particular period. You'll need the patience to do exhaustive research, as well as a vivid imagination that allows you to project yourself back in time to the days of Napoleon, Queen Victoria, or the War Between the States.

As a writer of historical romance, you must also have an eye for detail, so that you *see* the clutter in that Victorian living room or the ravaged and warn-torn streets of a Southern town in the wake of enemy boots. You need to know as much as possible about the era of your story—what foods were eaten, the mode of travel, the morals and manners, the clothes and houses and furniture; and the feelings and thoughts of people living then must be as familiar to you as those of your own time.

In writing historical romance, nothing can be left to chance. Somewhere out there is a reader who is a history buff, a reader who will be deeply disappointed in your errors.

In the more erotic historical romances, the writing is highly sensual and vividly graphic. We see "the flickering torchlights" and taste the wine forced between the heroine's lips, and then feel her thighs being nudged apart. Rosemary Rogers described this scene in her bestselling historical romance, *Wicked Loving Lies,* which sold three million copies in one month.

Lush descriptions of the heroine abound in historical romances. She is exotically beautiful, and nature has favored her with a full bosom, a slender waist, shapely legs, and trim ankles. Her hair is lustrous, usually long, and, of course, smooth as velvet or silk to the hero's touch.

The hero is described in such a way as to leave no doubt in the reader's mind as to his sexual prowess. Dominic in *Wicked Loving Lies* is "a savage dangerous animal with steely muscles, his eyes like shards of splintered glass and a contemptuous conviction that all women are whores at heart."

In spite of occasional gloomy predictions that these bodice rippers are on their way out, good writers in the genre, such as Beatrice Small, Valerie Sherwood, Rosemary Rogers, and Patricia Matthews, continue to sell well. To join them, you must have an ability to produce richly sensual and highly erotic prose.

Historical Sagas

Historical sagas usually cover three generations, beginning with the grandparents when they were young, very poor, and often living in a small village in Europe, as in Belva Plain's *Evergreen*. The immigrants leave the poverty of the old country for the New World, only to find themselves struggling against the privations of tenement life. Through their determination and talent, they gain wealth, power, and position.

The story moves on to the next generation, the sons and daughters of the original immigrants, and then down to *their* children. The family becomes a dynasty, and the reader learns about a particular world, such as the lumber industry in Dorothy Dowdell's saga, *A Woman's Empire* (Fawcett Gold Medal).

Medicine, architecture, oil, and railroads are a few of the other colorful backgrounds against which historical sagas have been set. The plots always revolve around the part played by each generation in the founding, and sometimes the final disintegration, of the family holdings.

The plots in such sagas may take us all over the world, but the family is always the core of the story. Many subplots enrich the story as various family members play out their individual lives, giving these sagas richness, color, and added dimension.

Characters are drawn in depth, with a strong central figure emerging for each generation. Family ties are strong, but violent conflict frequently arises when jealousy and greed flare up between the members of the second generation, as they struggle to gain control of the family enterprise.

The older heroine in a saga is a strong matriarchal figure whose influence reaches beyond her generation into the second and third. Often a strong tie exists between her and a granddaughter or grandson. Even after her death, her presence is still felt in the bosom of the family, and she leaves a rich heritage of tradition and moral values for the third generation to pick up and incorporate into their lives.

Sagas usually run 150,000 words or more. It is probably wise to try your hand first at the shorter, easier-to-write romance novels before you tackle an historical saga with its complex characterization, subplots, and multiple viewpoints.

Historical Series

Here we find the so-called historical series, novels such as *Wagons West* by Dana Fuller Ross, describing in vivid color and with page-turning drama the "continuing saga of dauntless men and women united by a single vision—a dream of a land bursting with the promise of gold, and other treasures."

Sagas and series are difficult to write unless you've served your apprenticeship writing less demanding types of romance novels. Even with considerable writing experience behind you, you can't succeed in the arduous task of recreating history without a willingness to dedicate yourself to hours, weeks, even years of research.

Young Adult Romances

Ace Tempo, Bantam Sweet Dreams, Dell Young Love Books, Dutton Heavenly Romances, NAL Signet/Vista, Scholastic Wildfire, Scholastic Windswept, Silhouette First Love

The *young adult,* or *teen* romance is an exciting, relatively new subgenre. These novels are stories of the problems connected with *first* love specifically and with growing up generally, written for the eleven- to fourteen-year-old or slightly older reader. Boy-girl relationships are treated tenderly and with sensitivity, and expressions of physical love are held to shy kisses, hand-holding, and starry-eyed gazes. Most teen romances are short, approximately 40,000 to 55,000 words, or from 156 to 186 printed pages, broken into ten to fourteen short chapters. The writing style is simple and clear, with fairly short sentences and paragraphs, and pages broken up with plenty of dialogue.

The conflict in young adult romances evolves out of the everyday problems experienced by most teenagers—the confusion of first love, finding one's identity, and the struggle toward maturity. Heroines are usually at least sixteen years old, and the heroes are seventeen or eighteen. The stories are usually set either at home or at school, with short visits to the beach or a mountain cabin, or possibly to a relative out of town.

To write this popular kind of romance successfully, you should have a good rapport with today's young people. You can't use nostalgic memories of how things were when you were sixteen. You'll need to talk to teenagers today, or, more important, listen to them.

These stories require great sensitivity on the author's part. To be suited for this kind of writing, you must have a keen interest in this age group and an ability to understand the subtleties of emotional growth and the complexity of inner problems.

So, Which Type of Romance for You?

You've had a bird's-eye view of the romance field. Do you already have an idea which type you might like to try? The chapters that follow will give you fuller opportunity to see what is involved. If you are already a published romance author, you might want to consider branching out and trying a new type. In the writing game, it's always wise to stay flexible and to keep opening new doors, so that if one market suddenly blows away, you have another to which you can turn.

To keep things as clear as possible in discussing the multifaceted subject of today's romance novel, I will talk about techniques and requirements for writing three types of romance:

(1) *Category romances*—contemporary romances published as part of established lines

(2) *Historical romances*—with some reference to sagas, series, gothics, Regencies, etc.

(3) *Young adult romances*

Now that you understand some of the subtle differences among the romance novels on the market today, what is your next step in deciding whether or not you could write these books? How can you find out if you really WANT to write one?

The true test will come when you devote time to reading and studying the kind of romance that interests you. Reading and analyzing romance novels is as important to your success as your inborn writing talent.

Writers who succeed in this field read hundreds of romance novels before they sat down at the typewriter and tried to write one. You must do this, too.

The next chapter will show you how to read romance with the eyes of a romance writer.

BY KAREN HARPER

ZEBRA/0-8217-1177-6/$3.95

Chapter **3.**

ROMANTIC BOOK LOVERS' LEAP — FROM READER TO WRITER:
How to Analyze a Romance Novel So You Can Write One

Now that you have read at least a few romance novels, have you enjoyed one type much more than the others? Have you said to yourself, "*I could write one of those*"?

Then it is time to study seriously the techniques that successful writers use to create these books. You have read romance for pleasure; now you will learn to read it *analytically.*

The best way to do this is to choose one romance novel, the kind you most want to write and preferably your favorite of those. You will learn more from a long, close look at this one book than from a less thorough survey of ten.

As you analyze this book, you are going to write down everything you discover about the techniques the author used, as well as your observations and feelings about the story. The very act of dissecting fiction in this way and organizing the results on paper will help you think analytically in all your future reading.

This exercise will help you remember how this author handled plot, dialogue, sex scenes—all the workings of the story. Like taking apart an alarm clock, disassembling this book will teach you something about the opposite process—the putting together of a work of romance fiction, piece by piece. You will learn to see *technique in action.*

Before you settle down to your study, assemble the other things you'll need: colored pencils or pens in various shades (at least eight); a sturdy three-ring notebook with at least seventeen dividers; and, for future use, a supply of three-by-five file cards and a box to keep them in.

Label your seventeen notebook sections as follows:

1. Title page
2. Reader Reaction
3. Overall Structure
4. The Beginning
5. Characters
6. Plot
7. Complications and Conflict
8. Setting
9. Professional Background
10. Viewpoint
11. Dialogue
12. Sensuousness
13. Sex Scenes
14. Author's Style
15. Synopsis
16. Miscellaneous
17. Ideas for *My* Novel

Then write each of these headings in the top right-hand corner of seventeen separate sheets of paper. In the upper left-hand corner of each, write a key word from the title of the book you are going to study. Then insert each in your notebook behind a page tabbed with the same heading.

"The best thing you can do for yourself is to know your market. One of the best ways to do this is to read current books in your bookstore in whatever subcategory interests you. And despite what we all hear of overnight successes in this business, the only real way to achieve success is by hard work. You may have to do a lot of writing before you achieve that level of writing which sells." Andrea Cirillo, literary agent

---

As you fill in all these sections in the process of analyzing your favorite romance novel, ideas for your own book will certainly come to you. As they occur, write them in section 17.

1. Title page

Write the title, author, publisher, date of publication, the name of the specific romance line (if any), and the type of romance novel this is; i.e., category, historical, young adult.

2. Reader Reaction

Now you're ready to go to work. When you read this book the first time, you read for pleasure. If the story held you in its grasp, you probably didn't notice how the author was putting it together. But now you will go back and imagine yourself sitting in an editorial chair. Ask yourself the following questions and write your answers in the Reader Reaction section of your notebook. Answer on the basis of your *feelings* as you read.

A) Did the novel hold your attention throughout? Did it seem to drag in places? If so, where?

B) What facet of the novel interested you the most? Background? Characters? Plot? Style?

C) What is outstanding about the author's work? Plot twist? Memorable characterization? Sensuous style? Unusual background? Clever dialogue?

D) What do you think you will remember about this novel weeks from now?

E) What was your emotional response? Did you cry? Laugh? Feel anger? At what points?

F) Did you like the heroine? Why?

G) Did you fall in love with the hero? If so, what did you like about him? If not, what turned you off?

H) Did the author arouse sensual reactions in you? If so, how did she do it?

I) How would you grade this novel for pure enjoyment on a scale of one to ten?

J) Would you want to read other romances by this writer?

In answering these questions, you are analyzing *reader response*. This is just what an editor must evaluate in a manuscript before recommending it for publication. Looking at this book in this way will help you later as you judge your own writing. A good book will bring a "yes"—or the equivalent—on all ten points.

"I'm ashamed to admit that when friends in the business suggested that I read one of those short romances called category contemporary, I turned up my nose in disdain. Not for me the helpless heroine, the obnoxious hero, and the kiss on the last page. But when I read the first one and saw the state of the art, I knew that creating a line was going to be nothing but fun." Robin Grunder, romance editor

---

You have noted your first response to the romance novel you're studying. Now you're ready for phase two, a deeper study of the specific writing techniques that made this a saleable romance novel.

Be ready to write your answers in the third section of your notebook.

3. Overall Structure

How many pages were there in the novel? How many chapters? What was the average page count per chapter?

Record this information carefully. If this is a category or young adult romance, the page count and number of chapters are probably fairly standard for that line. If it's an historical romance, it will at least be representative of this type of book.

Next, note the number of paragraphs per page and the length of the sentences. In the short category and young adult romances, which are fairly fast-paced, you'll notice that the paragraphs are relatively short, an average of six to eight sentences per paragraph. In the longer ones, such as Superromances, and in historical romances, the pace of the book tends to be slower. There is more space for the story to develop, and paragraphs can be longer, perhaps, allowing for slightly longer passages of description.

4. The Beginning

Reread chapter one. Ask yourself the following questions and write the answers in the next section of your notebook.

- A) How did the novel begin? What was the situation? How did you learn about it? Through thoughts in the heroine's mind? Through dialogue? In dramatic action?
- B) Were you drawn immediately into the story? How?
- C) If the book did not open in the heroine's mind, how soon did the reader get into her thoughts? What was her prime concern?
- D) How soon was the hero introduced?
- E) How soon did conflict begin between the hero and the heroine?
- F) How was the conflict revealed? Through characters' thoughts? Action? Dialogue?
- G) How did the author present the personal history of the hero and heroine and events that took place before the story began? Was the information given in flashbacks? If so, were the flashbacks given as interior monologue—i.e., in the mind of the heroine or hero? In dialogue? Were they worked into the story in passages of narration? Were they long or short? Did they slow down the story? (Suggestion for later: you might want to read the first chapters of ten or twelve romances, to compare techniques used by different authors to pack this crucial chapter full of information and interesting action.)

5. Characters

Turn now to the section of your notebook labeled "Characters" and write the heroine's name, her age, her profession, her position in that profession, her dominant character traits, and a brief physical description. Write a paragraph stating everything you are told about her background—her family, her education, special experiences.

Now write a paragraph on what you know about her *psychologically* and *emotionally* at the end of chapter one. Add any other information that you think is important.

Study the hero next, allotting him a page of his own, and make the same notations about him as you made for the heroine. (If you need more than one page for either character, by all means keep going.)

For important secondary characters, a paragraph or two should do nicely. Take each of these in turn and tell a) all you know about each, physically and factually, and b) all you know about each, emotionally and psychologically.

6. Plot

In this section of your notebook, number a separate page for each chapter in the novel. (You may need to use more than one page per chapter.)

Now you will go through the book page by page, and write out exactly what happened in each chapter. Record the physical action in this chapter. Did the heroine have her first date with the hero? Did they go sailing? Did he give her certain information about himself? Briefly, write out the events as they occurred in the chapter.

Next, go back through the chapter in search of everything that happened in the *emotions* of the hero and heroine. How did she feel about him when the chapter opened? Did her feelings change in the course of the chapter? How did he seem to feel toward her? If you don't know (because *she* doesn't know and the story is written from her viewpoint), how did he act toward her?

7. Complications and Conflict

In a romance novel there is usually a strong feeling of ambivalence when the heroine first meets the hero. She is physically attracted to him at once, but she has an equally strong feeling of doubt about him. In some situations, she may even feel hostile because of something she's heard about him, or because she misinterprets his actions or his words.

This barrier of doubt and uncertainty between hero and heroine is an absolute *must* in the plot of every romance novel. It is the misunderstanding in the beginning of the novel that gives rise to complication after complication as the story unfolds. Each further misunderstanding helps to heighten the emotional conflict felt by the heroine and the hero. Even though they yearn to be in each other's arms, they struggle to keep emotional distance between them.

On the basis of your current knowledge of the book, can you summarize the major complications in the story?

1) What things actually happen to keep the lovers apart and cause misunderstanding? In this section of your notebook, first list just "external complications." These complications evolve from differences of opinion on important issues, from conflicting approaches to her career or his, or because of events in the story.

2) Now list the inner conflicts of either the heroine or the hero that keep the lovers apart. These include any emotional reasons why the heroine can't let herself go, such as residue of grief from death of a former husband, a traumatic broken engagement, her conviction that the hero is a playboy.

It is useful to distinguish between external complications and inner conflict in your analysis of this book, because you will want to have plenty of both in your own novel.

Now, to get a better understanding of the heroine's inner conflicts, take two pencils, red and blue, and go back to the novel.

Underline in red every phrase that shows the heroine's physical and emotional attraction to the hero. Then underline in blue each phrase that shows her negative feelings toward him: doubt, suspicion, fear, or anger.

By marking these passages in different colors, you will soon realize that every time the heroine is motivated to fall into the hero's arms (or bed, depending on the type of romance), there is an equally powerful reason for her to pull back.

This tug-of-war within her, attraction versus rational resistance, is what makes a romance novel work. Without this push-pull in the heart of the heroine, no romance would last 100 pages, much less 187 or 350. She would simply fall into his arms and be done with it.

Everything that contributes to the "yes-no" between the lovers, the "will-they? won't-they?" in the mind of the reader, builds sexual tension in the romance novel. We will discuss this key ingredient later, in chapter ten.

8. Setting

Describe the setting fully in the section under that heading in your notebook. Tell how the setting added to the sensuality of the story. Did the descriptions of the people, food, art, foliage, weather, and topography seem accurate? Was the setting presented in such a way that you could hardly wait to go there if you haven't already gone, or in a way that recalled happy memories if you have?

Was the setting romantic by nature, or did the author make it *seem* so in plotting her story? If so, how did she accomplish this?

Now, to get an idea of how much and what kind of information you must have for your setting, underline all passages in the book which describe the setting in, say, green. Then study these sections carefully and imagine what sources the author used to gather all these facts and images.

9. Professional Background

What professions were the heroine and the hero involved in? How much of their professional background was established in the novel? Record this in section nine of your notebook. Then underline in orange the information on professions that the author must have researched. This will give you an idea of how much of this type of research was or was not necessary.

Were the heroine and hero working in the same profession, or in different ones? What specifically was the professional role of each?

If the heroine (as often is the case) was in a prestigious position, did this complicate the romance in any way? What was the hero's attitude toward the heroine's professional life? Write answers to these questions in your notebook.

Professional backgrounds are most important in contemporary category romances. In historicals, the heroine usually wields power through her great beauty, her cleverness, or her social position.

In a young adult romance, the heroine and the hero are usually both still in school, or have just graduated, and have not yet reached a professional level. However, they dream of the time when they will be working in a certain profession, and already know something about it.

In whatever type of romance you're studying, think about how the author handled the professional background or social world, and summarize how this added to the story.

10. Viewpoint

Was the novel written from the heroine's viewpoint? Was it *single-viewpoint?* That is, did the story stay entirely within the thoughts of one character only—heroine, hero or another?

If this book was written from the heroine's viewpoint, was there ever a brief change into the hero's viewpoint? This happens more and more, particularly in love scenes. The heroine's feelings toward the hero are shown and then we jump briefly into the hero's thoughts and find out how he feels toward the heroine.

If there was a change in viewpoint from one character to another, what was the author's purpose in changing?

Or, was the book written in *multiple viewpoint?* Was the story told through the thoughts of several characters, usually changing at chapter breaks, but sometimes even within a scene?

Did the changes in viewpoint confuse you? Do you think the novel would have been better had the author used a single viewpoint? Write your thoughts on viewpoint in section ten of your notebook.

11. Dialogue

Scan a sample of chapters in the book you are studying—say the first three, then the last three. Estimate what percentage of each chapter is dialogue. In most romance novels, the proportion of dialogue to narration is quite high.

Now take four colored pencils—maybe brown, purple, yellow, and black—and in the same chapters, *bracket* sections of dialogue to show what each section accomplished.

For example, underline in yellow the passages in which the dialogue *moved the story forward* by presenting or hinting at an upcoming event.

Bracket in brown any dialogue that *reveals the character* of the speaker. Then bracket *sensual dialogue* in passionate purple. In black, bracket *dialogue* that shows conflict between the lovers.

Dialogue should always accomplish something in a story. Study these bracketed passages well. Record a few passages of the most effective dialogue in your notebook.

12. Sensuousness

How *sensuous* was this novel? Did the author make frequent use of all five senses? In portraying sex scenes, were strong sensual images used? Was the author's vocabulary rich in words that made you feel sensuous as you read?

Now use your purple pencil again to *circle* words in a few chapters in the middle of the book, words that created the sensual mood of the story. When you have done this, go back and list these words and phrases in your notebook here in section twelve. Then, beside this list, try to make another one showing words *you* might have chosen instead. You can use this as the beginning of a general list of sensuous words to which you will be adding constantly.

By listing words of this kind, you will increase your awareness of sense imagery. When you see a potential heroine's beautiful hair, for instance, you'll automatically think of how you could describe it sensuously. Does it *shimmer?* Is it *silky soft?* Is it the color of amber wine?

13. Sex Scenes

How explicit were the sex or love scenes in this novel? On what page did the heroine and hero touch each other for the first time? How soon did they kiss? Was the sexual act consummated in this book? If so, how soon, and how many times? Chart in your notebook under this heading the specific chapters in which sexual intimacy occurs, and how many pages were allotted to each sex or love scene. How far apart were these scenes spaced? Can you draw a graph to show this?

How would you generally describe the sex or love scenes in this novel? Gentle? Tender? Passionate? Somewhat explicit, or *very* explicit?

Did you enjoy the sex or love scenes, or did they turn you off? Were they in good taste?

14. Author's Style

No two romance writers are alike. Each has an individual style, even though she or he follows closely the particular requirements of the romance line for which she or he publishes.

What do you think was special about the style of the author in the book you are studying? Was the plot unusual? Was it a fresh treatment of an old plot? Was the character development unusually good? Was the heroine different from the heroines you've met in similar novels? Were unexpected bits of humor injected into the plot situations or into the dialogue? Was

---

"Women about 46 or 47 make good romance writers. They straddle two worlds. They remember life as young girls, before the sexual revolution, when girls talked about whether a boy was a good kisser or not. And they've lived through the sexual revolution in which young women talk about whether or not a young man is good in bed."
Vivian Stephens, romance editor

---

anything special about the way this author used words?

Summarize what you liked best, with examples, in a few paragraphs under "Style" in your notebook.

15. Synopsis

As briefly as you can, write out the plot of the novel you've just analyzed. Tell how the novel begins. Describe the major problem that kept the lovers apart and what exactly happened to resolve the problem. Finally, tell how the novel ended. How were the initial misunderstandings cleared up?

You will find the ability to write a short, informative synopsis very useful when it comes both to plotting, and later selling, your own book.

16. Miscellaneous

Add in this section anything you thought of that I haven't mentioned here.

17. Ideas for My Novel

By now, have you filled three? five? twenty? pages in this section of your notebook? If you are not already bursting with ideas for your own romance novel, I'm sure you will be by the time you have finished this book.

Keeping File Cards

Do you remember at the beginning of the chapter I suggested that you own file cards and a box? This is what they are for. Now that you have thoroughly analyzed one romance novel, you won't have to do it again so completely, on paper. You will be able to read much more analytically because you have done it once so thoroughly.

But do keep a file card for each book you read from now on. (You are going to keep reading and reading! There's no better way to learn about writing.) List the title, author, publisher, type of romance, and name of specific line, if any. Then summarize the plot briefly and record your feelings about the book. This will make you evaluate every book you read and help you to keep reading *analytically*.

One other use for your three-by-five cards: If you are like most writers, you read on the run—in the dentist's waiting room or waiting at the garage while your car is tuned up. Along with the ever-present romance novel in your hand, you might want to carry file cards in your purse. Use them to jot down any immediate impressions of what you are reading. If your notes are extensive, you may want to transcribe them later into your notebook. If they are brief, you can keep them in your file box. Also, as you read, ideas may come to you for other books of your own. You don't want to let those escape! Keep file cards handy to capture them. File them at the back of your file box.

Now you are ready for the big question:

Could You Write This Type of Romance?

Now that you have given time and serious thought to all the techniques used in this romance novel, you're ready for an honest evaluation of yourself. *Could you write this kind of book?*

Be completely honest with yourself. Each kind of romance novel requires a special talent and temperament. If strong explicit sex scenes are distasteful to you, you'll never be able to write them successfully. If long historical novels bore you, you shouldn't try to write them. If you don't empathize with young people, leave the young adult romance field to someone else.

Ask yourself these questions and answer them as honestly as you can.

1. Would I be proud to have my name on the dust jacket of such a book?
2. Will the idea I have for my (next) romance novel fit into the requirements for this particular kind of romance?
3. If that idea doesn't fit, can I change it so that it will follow the editorial guidelines or the formula as illustrated by the novel I've just studied?
4. Having made a study of this one novel, and having read many others like it, do I have a good understanding of the writing techniques required?
5. Having studied this one novel closely from beginning to end, am I *excited* about this kind of writing?

Perhaps the last question is the most important. If you feel uncontainable excitement and urgent impatience to get started, you may have found your calling. If romance gives you that certain feeling, if you hear a voice within you whisper, "Hey! I could write one like this!" you're ready to begin. You can't wait to get to the typewriter or word processor! The next chapter will show you how to organize your material, your office, your life, so you can start writing.

AVON
81810
$2.95

ADMIT DESIRE

CATHERINE LANIGAN

HE PROMISED HER LOVE.
BUT DARED SHE GIVE HER HEART TO A
MAN WHO HAD BROKEN SO MANY?

Chapter **4.**
SETTING THE MOOD: Making Your Office Romantic (and Efficient)

No matter how limited your writing space is, making it look and feel romantic will put you in the proper mood to write sensuously. You can wave your magic wand over the dining room or kitchen table, a corner of the bedroom or porch, and presto, it becomes a special place where love reigns supreme and conquers all.

A few pictures depicting romantic scenes, or photographs of your favorite movie stars who may resemble your heroine or hero, can do wonders to create the atmosphere you need. A bouquet of roses, or even a single bud in a silver vase (or jelly jar), can change a prosaic work space into something special. And you can be inspired by placing the beautifully illustrated covers of your favorite romance novels where you can see them when you look up from the typewriter.

If your work place is the kitchen table and your family objects to staring at Robert Redford over their cereal bowls, tape the photo to the wall while you work and remove it later.

You'll meet with few objections, however, if you're professional in your attitude toward your work. Whatever you need to keep you in a romantic mood as you write should be considered a tool of your trade; a doctor usually has a not nearly-so-romantic picture of the human anatomy pinned to *his* wall, doesn't he?

To interest your family in your work, you might install photographs of *them* in your work area—wedding pictures, graduation photographs, and such. I have a picture of each of my granddaughters on my wall, placed so that when I look up, I see their fresh young faces over and over again.

The two older ones, eighteen and twenty, are on the threshold of perhaps the most romantic time of life. One is brunette with lustrous dark hair and big brown eyes; the other is a honey blonde with deep blue eyes. The way they dress and talk, and their views on life, keep me in touch with today's world so that I don't unknowingly date my novel with yesterday's fashions, speech, and values.

From whatever source, it helps to have visible images of your heroine and your hero near your typewriter. Hunt through pictures in fashion and women's magazines, in men's periodicals, and the newspapers, until you find pictures that will help you bring your characters to life.

When you have chosen your setting, find pictures which could be that landscape or city, your hero's mansion or cottage in the woods, and the rooms inside. These will lead you gently into the world you are creating and keep you there while you write.

Even when you step out of your imagined world into that other one in which you have to think about laundry and groceries, keep gazing through romance-colored glasses. Wherever you go, watch for the girl or woman who could be your heroine, and for the boy or man who could be her hero.

"People have asked me who influences my work, and I like to tell them that everyone does. Having met me, no one is safe! You never know when you'll turn up in one of my books. So you just have to keep reading them." Carolyn Thornton, author of contemporary romances

You never know when he or she will appear on the television screen, in a newspaper ad, or on the street. When you do see a look-alike for your heroine or hero, or for some other character in your book, memorize features, hair style, clothing, manners, voice, and figure or physique. As soon as you step back across that magic threshold into your special work place, make notes on what impressed you, if you weren't able to do so at the time.

Pictures. Notes. You are beginning to accumulate more background material for your book than you can tape to the wall. It is time to buy your first batch of file folders.

When you have decided which type of romance novel you are going to write—or if you need help in making that decision—you may want to label your first folder "guidelines." Write to the appropriate publishers for their tip sheets or editorial guidelines. All houses which publish category romance, and some others as well, give out specific instructions stating their special requirements for an acceptable hero and heroine, secondary characters, setting, plot, and even sex scenes.

More about editorial guidelines later. For now, it's enough to mark your folder and start your collection. A list of publishers' addresses appears on page 259 of this book. When you write them, be sure to include a long SASE (self-addressed stamped envelope) with each request.

Now get ready to mark and fill many more folders as you gather material for your romance files. As you do your research, you will come across things that spark ideas for future books, as well as for this one. You may want two folders for each of the following headings—one for material for the book you are about to write, and another file of more general information on these topics, which will be waiting for you when you are ready to begin your next book.

Characters / You'll need several folders to hold the information—everything you invent or learn about the character, description, and experiences of your hero, heroine, and supporting cast. Label these folders *"hero," "heroine,"* and *"secondary characters,"* and add their names as soon as you know what they will be.

Your character folders are probably the most important, and the better you get to know these people, the fatter these files will become. The crucial entries in your first two folders will be the *character biographies,* full narrative descriptions of every aspect of your hero and heroine from their faces to their psyches. In chapter five we'll talk about these and other things that go into your character folders. For now, file any pictures reminiscent of your characters that you haven't tacked up on the wall, your preliminary notes on your characters' personal pasts and current problems (if you've come that far), and maybe possibilities for their names.

Clothing / We all know that what a woman wears contributes greatly to her attractiveness and to the aura of romance which surrounds her. Women of all ages are interested in fashion, and since most readers of romantic fiction are female, you should be keenly interested in the appropriate clothing for your heroine.

Whether your novel is set in today's world or in the past, or is written for young adults, your reader wants to know what your characters are wearing as they head for the executive suite, the Regency ball, or the junior-senior class picnic.

Here again, pictures in magazines can help you, as well as mail-order catalogs, department-store brochures, and newspaper advertisements. Clip pictures of models in various types of dress, casual to formal, and drop them into your folder labeled *clothing.*

If you have decided to write an historical romance, consult the research librarian at your local library. He or she will help you gather an armload of books on the subject of dress in the period about which you're writing. You can photocopy many of these for your files

Career Information / In most contemporary romance novels, category and otherwise, both men and women have careers and work for a living. In historicals, heroines are involved for the most part in their domestic responsibilities and their social duties while their heroes wage wars, run estates, and conduct family businesses. If you are writing this type of romance, you'll need background on the latter.

In young adult romances, the heroines wonder what they'll do when they graduate from college or high school, or they may already know and be preparing for that career in after-school jobs. The reader of these books has career choices very much on her mind, and likes to pick up information on various professions even while she reads a romance.

Researching professional or career backgrounds is important for all types of romance novels. So whichever kind you are going to write, you will need a folder labeled "hero's professional background" and, for a contemporary story, one labeled "heroine's professional background" as well.

Food / Dining out is a favorite pastime of romance characters, and readers like to know exactly what was on the menu when the hero gazed into the heroine's eyes and said, "Do you mind if I order for both of us?"

To give authenticity to a dining-out scene, whether it takes place in a castle on the Rhine or in a bistro in San Francisco, you can't rely on your memory or your imagination alone. You will need to serve both mouth-watering and—if foreign—authentic dishes at your elegant restaurants.

Several romance writers I know collect menus from posh places they visit on special occasions. I've found this helpful myself, and now have quite a collection of menus not only in English but in French, Italian, and Spanish as well. Keeping your cookbooks handy is a good idea too, especially ethnic and regional ones.

Read the gourmet food column in your local newspaper and borrow a stack of food magazines from the library. For your food folder, copy descriptions of dishes that would be appropriate—depending on the locale—for your hero and heroine to enjoy together. Keep a more general folder for other exotic or interesting taste sensations which might go better in a future book, perhaps set in a different part of the country. (You might try serving a few of the dishes to your own special hero or heroine, to show him or her that he/she won't be forgotten as you plunge into your writing!)

"On days when the words refuse to come, I start typing anything so that I'm not confronted with a blank page. Make something happen *is one of the mottos I keep taped to my bulletin board. Sometimes I make lists of situations and try to imagine how my characters would react to them—a thunderstorm, a death in the family, sudden wealth. One thing I know, I must begin."* **Phyllis Taylor Pianka, a.k.a. Winter Ames, romance author**

Setting / A single manila folder might not hold all the information you will need for the place in which you set your novel. Use a folder for hasty clippings on possible future locales, but buy yourself a sturdy envelope-shaped file for material on your current setting. Into this you'll slip Chamber of Commerce pictures, articles clipped from magazines, postcards from your globe-trotting relatives and friends, maps and brochures obtained from your automobile club or travel organization, and all the notes you gather from books and other sources.

In addition, it's a good idea to have a few travel books and a good atlas at your elbow. I find the automobile and travel club guides and Fodor travel books indispensable. To save money, I buy the editions that are a year or two old and sold at a discount. The slight changes from year to year don't make any difference when you are creating a fictional background.

Furnishings / Not only are you about to become a novelist, but you can try out your skills as an interior decorator in the process. Choosing furniture, rugs, and wallpaper is up to you as you furnish a career-girl apartment or the drawing room of a grand estate or a teenager's bedroom. Browsing through such magazines as *House Beautiful, Better Homes and Gardens, Sunset, Woman's Day, Family Circle, Ladies' Home Journal, Good Housekeeping, Vogue, Town and Country,* and *Architectural Digest* will give you ideas for up-to-date decor of various kinds.

Antiques Magazine, Antique & Collectors Mart, Antique Monthly, and Antique Reader Weekly will give you plenty of information on period furnishings. And of course your reference librarian can point you toward many scholarly books on the subject.

Keep in mind that romance readers are well versed in such matters as period furniture. They know the difference between traditional styles and Danish Modern, and are quick to spot an error. Check and double check your information.

You must be accurate in all your research. *Never* guess. Look everything up. Planting a certain kind of tree on a hillside in a climate where it could never grow will bring you scathing letters from the many experts in flora and fauna in your audience. So, while you're at it, label another folder "plant and animal life," and collect those facts to help you learn your chosen setting down to the last detail.

Chapter Folders / When you decide what type of romance you are going to write, you will find out how long it must be. The examples you read will show you how many chapters are required. Label a folder with a number for each of your chapters. (If you need more than one folder for a chapter, you can add others later.) As you think of plot ideas, drop notes into the appropriate folders. If you change your mind later and decide an event or a scene you have given to chapter five would be better in chapter seven, you can easily refile it.

You will need other folders labeled with headings to satisfy the special needs of your novel, but those I have mentioned will get you started. Let's review them quickly:

- Characters—heroine, hero, others
- Clothing
- Hero's Professional Background

- Heroine's Professional Background
- Food
- Setting
- Furnishings
- Plant and Animal Life
- Chapters

"Writing is a skill, a craft, a commitment. Too many writers today think of romance as a contract to get money. A good book will endure for a long time. The well-written romance requires a delicate balance of spontaneity and hard work—spontaneity in feeling, and hard work to deliver the words with clarity, urgency and simplicity. A plot should develop in a manner that is inevitable, in retrospect. To keep your reader turning pages, relate what happens next as fast and as simply as possible." Jacqui Bianchi, romance editor

---

You and Your Office

There is nothing romantic about clutter and disorganization. Even romantic writers must have some order and system. Once you start your research, you'll need a place to keep the material so that you can get to it quickly and conveniently.

Think of yourself as a business person. Wherever you work, even if it is a broom closet, that place is your *office.* In addition to a typewriter and a telephone, an office needs a file cabinet. Yours need not be the Cadillac of the line. A sturdy cardboard two-drawer file will do just as well as an expensive metal one, at least for now. Later you can expand and upgrade, as the need arises. Set your file cabinet near your typewriter and work table. You won't want to waste precious time running into another room to get a file folder.

Your File Cabinet / You may have, or prefer to invent, your own way of sorting and filing. The important point is not *how* you set up your files, but that you *do* organize them and stick to one method. Here's a system that works for me and for many of my colleagues and students.

1. Bottom Drawer

Label this drawer with the title of your novel and the word *"Research."* Place your chapter folders at the front of this drawer. Then file the other folders on clothing, career, background, and the rest behind them in alphabetical order, or in any order that works for you. Leave room for additional folders. This is all you'll put in the bottom drawer for now.

2. Top Drawer

Label this drawer, too, with the title of your novel in progress and with the word "Business." This drawer will house all correspondence during and after the sale of your book. Much of this will come later, but thinking ahead will encourage your professional attitude. For now, label folders as follows:

A.) *Editorial Correspondence* Each time you submit your manuscript to an editor, make up a file folder with that person's name on it. It's important to keep all the letters you write and receive, stapling a copy of your letter behind the editor's reply. Then, if that editor should call (which *can* happen), you will have both letters in front of you.

   I find it convenient and efficient to file all editorial correspondence in chronological order, with the most recent correspondence at the front of each folder. Correspondence concerning a novel can become voluminous and cover a long period of time. A great deal can happen between the time you type "CHAPTER ONE" and when you happily type "THE END."

   If you have to submit your novel to a second editor, a third, and so on, make up a new folder for each of these editors and keep them together so that you can compare editorial responses.

B.) *Your Bibliography* If you want to save yourself a lot of trouble, keep track of all sources of information you use in your novel as you find them. If the item came from a book, type out the title, publisher, author, date of publication, and the exact page where you found the information, as well as the name of the library and the room in which you found the book. Also include the library call number, if there is one.

   Having this information at your finger tips can help in two ways. 1.) If your editor later wants to know your source, you can easily supply it. 2.) If you want to refer to the item again, you will save searching time if you know exactly where to find it.

   You can jot down this information on index cards if you are working in the library to begin with, but eventually you should have a typed sheet headed *Bibliography,* filed in this folder.

C.) *Drafts* You may think you will sit down at your typewriter and emerge a month or two later with a finished novel after the first go-around. But if you are like most writers, your book will actually pass through several incarnations before it takes its final shape.

   It will help to have different colored folders for the various drafts of your novel. Date these folders as you complete each draft, which will save the wear and tear on the nervous system that can occur when you're not sure whether the blue folder contains the fourth draft or the fifth. Noting the date and indicating whether this is the first, second, or third draft also reminds you of the passing time and acts as a good kick in the pants!

D.) *Agent Correspondence* If you are just starting out, this will come later. But after you have published one or two books, you may be fortunate enough to acquire a good agent. When you do, you will need a folder with that person's name on it. Keep this correspondence separate from your correspondence with an editor. When you receive a telephone call from your agent, it saves your time and his if you can dip into a file and immediately find the relevant folder, instead of frantically digging through a fat general file while he dangles long distance.

If you're a comparatively new writer, telephone calls to and from the editors and agents can turn you into a babbling idiot. All the questions you've been saving up for days, weeks, months fly out the window. If you're expecting a call from an editor or an agent, or intend to make one, write out your questions. Put them in the appropriate file folder—the one with your editor's or agent's name on the label—and when the telephone rings, or when you dial the magic number, you'll be ready. You will also want to take notes during these conversations, so you'll remember what was said. Date and file these notes too.

E.) *Editorial Guidelines* The top drawer is also a good place to keep your editorial guidelines. Since these are frequently changed, replaced, or updated, be sure to write for new ones every six or eight months.

F) *Articles on Romance Writing* Clip and save all articles you read about romance fiction. You'll find such articles not only in trade magazines such as *Writer's Digest,* but also in the *The Wall Street Journal,* your local newspaper, *Time* magazine, and in romance newsletters such as *Romantic Times* and *Boy Meets Girl.* Separate articles into two groups: a) articles on *how to write* romance, and b) articles *about* romance publishing.

G) *Ideas for Future Novels* Even while you're completely absorbed in writing your present romance novel, ideas for future novels will pop into your head now and then. Label one folder *Ideas* and file it at the back of your top file drawer.

H) *Ongoing Business* If you're a selling writer already, you'll be in the midst of much correspondence about books you have already published, and about other manuscripts out for consideration while you are at work on your current book. Use available space in your top drawer for this material so that it is within easy reach, but keep it separate from the folders concerning your *current* work.

Eventually, as your writing business grows you'll need headings for the other folders in your top drawer, so keep those spare folders handy. The way you file and what you file is a very personal matter—as personal as the way you like to arrange your clothes closet. Use the suggestions given in this chapter in the best way for you. Modify them to suit your own purposes, and add as many other folders to your files as you need.

On Your Desk

Addresses and Telephone Numbers

Of course you will need a Rolodex or some other handy list of the names, addresses, and phone numbers of people you will contact frequently, such as:

    a. Publishers—address and phone; the name of each *line* put out by romance publishers whose guidelines you want to keep up with.
    b. Your agent, or the names and addresses of agents you are interested in pursuing when you are ready.
    c. The names of companies and people you will write and/or phone in the course of doing research for your current book.
    d. The phone number of your local reference librarian, who can solve small problems for you as you write.

Small Index File / You may or may not want to bother with another file, but I personally find it very handy to have a small file box on my desk; I like the bigger five-by-eight size better than three by five to reach for while I am writing. I make a card for my heroine, my hero, each of their careers, each of my secondary characters, and various aspects of the setting. I may have a card for each house or place where important scenes will take place.

"I'm at work by 6:30 in the morning, and I write until about 2 in the afternoon. . . . I don't believe in inspiration as the way to break writer's block. I just force myself to sit at the typewriter until I get the juices flowing again." **Jayne Castle, a.k.a. Stephanie James and Jane Frentz, author of contemporary romances**

    This can save time while you are writing. For example, you don't have to go back to your bulging file folders if you want to find out what color the rug is in the heroine's bedroom or what kind of trees are growing along the road to an old estate. If you think a file would help you, list key details like these on cards and keep them at your finger tips.

Using A Steno Pad / One other item I find indispensable is a steno pad. The moment I get an idea for a novel, I begin jotting down rough bits and pieces of my story. The red line down the center of each page makes a great organizer. For example, you can write the heroine's name on the left side of the line—or several names, if you haven't decided which suits her best.

Then, on the right side, you can begin to fill in facts about her: age, height, problems, and other details.

In describing her physically, you might want to write "hair," for example, on the left side and describe it fully and sensuously in a few phrases on the right.

You can head a page "setting"—let's say it's Washington, D.C.—and write on the left side of the line places you will need to research, such as the White House. On the right, jot down ideas for where to get that information.

If one scene takes place on the Delaware shore for example, write that on the left; on the right, list names of towns on the map that might serve the purpose, whose Chambers of Commerce you could write.

And so on. A steno pad helps me organize my first thoughts on a book, and you might find it useful too.

File Tray or Basket / The last essential item in my office is a file tray or basket, which I keep on top of my file cabinet. On some days you'll be so inspired at your typewriter that you won't want to take even a minute for such mundane tasks as sorting and filing. An item may come in the mail that you think you can use later in your novel. Or you may think of a terrific idea for your ending. Drop these into your basket for the time being. Later, when the cover is on the typewriter and you have a few minutes to spare, you can go through this catchall and file the accumulation in the proper folders.

I've discovered that the kitchen counter makes an excellent place for sorting and sifting. It's the right height, and I need the expanse! Make sure you wipe it dry, though. There's nothing useful about a clipping so soggy you can't read it.

Setting up a convenient, simple filing system and having those two—for now—all-important file drawers near your typewriter will save your sanity. Surrounded by order, you will be free to give your precious time to the creation of vivid, sensuous scenes, which will transport your readers across the magic threshold into the world of romance.

DELL • 12858 • $1.95

159

A Candlelight
Ecstasy Romance ®

A FLIGHT
OF SPLENDOR

Joellyn Carroll

Chapter **5.**

THE GIRL OF HIS DREAMS... HER KNIGHT IN SHINING ARMOR: Your Heroine, Hero, and Other Characters

One of the nice things about being a romance writer is that you get to meet such fascinating people. Your heroine is beautiful, intelligent, and talented. A hush falls over the room as she pauses in the doorway, and heads turn as she walks by.

And then there is your hero—a handsome, virile devil who has the charm and power to quicken a female pulse with a mere glance or a sudden smile. As you write your novel, you will live with these charming people and their supporting casts, as they pursue their hopes and dreams and finally find love.

Where do they come from, these beautiful people? As a romance writer, you create them, drawing upon your own dreams and fantasies. Your reader wants to imagine what it would be like to be one of the beautiful people, a jet setter, a movie star, the only woman to sit on the Board of Directors of some huge corporation, or perhaps just someone other than who she is in real life.

It is your job to offer your reader her fantasy, to make her dream world seem real. One of the best ways of doing this is through *good characterization*.

While readers love thrilling plots in which the heroine is transported to a castle on the Rhine or to a remote archaeological dig amid ancient ruins where she meets the man of her dreams, it is the characters themselves who will linger in the reader's mind and heart and make your story memorable.

A beautiful face or a rugged build are not enough to give substance to your heroine and hero, however. Of course physical description is important. But it is the sum total of your characters—body, mind, and spirit—which will touch your readers' hearts. You must convey the total personality of your heroine and hero.

Heroes and Heroines In Category Romances

If you are writing a category romance, study carefully the guidelines for the kind of characters that line is looking for. Remember that editors base these requirements not on their own personal tastes, but on careful surveys of the readership. If sales suddenly dip, for example, or if reader questionnaires show boredom with one type of heroine, you can be sure the editorial guidelines will be revised in a hurry.

Guidelines for a line of contemporary romances—in this case from Dell—tell clearly what is expected of heroines presented for consideration there:

The heroine *is dynamic, self-assured, young (19 to 34) with uncommon intelligence and drive. She is shrewd and mature, with good sense, but never manipulative. Not generally a virgin, but no hussy either, our heroine is sensuous and sensitive . . .*
 While she need not be a beauty, the heroine is trim, fresh and attractive . . . Most likely, she will be employed in work she enthusiastically enjoys and is able to adequately—or even handsomely support herself . . . In short, the heroine, should be a credible, contemporary young woman with whom the reader can identify.

And *the hero* for the same line may be one of two types—conventional or an antihero. The conventional hero is described as:

 . . . self-confident, decisive, with an intensity both intellectual and physical. Most often in his late 20's to late 30's, the hero is able to arouse the heroine's passion as no other man has done in the past.
 He is irresistibly attractive—well-built and frequently tall—though not always conventionally handsome. At any rate, our woman is as much drawn to this man's character as to his looks. His strength translates to professional success and he's wealthy enough to amply provide for the heroine's material comfort. He can work in any field appropriate to an acceptable story line and be either a self-made man or possess inherited power and riches. Only his kindness and warmth equal his toughness and force. But forget about true-grit—our hero's never an unbearable macho type or a devil who needs taming.

This is the conventional hero in today's contemporary romance novel. He is the epitome of masculinity, dynamic and sexually attractive. Whether he is dressed in a black dinner jacket, a business suit, or hip-hugging, tightly fitting jeans, he is devastatingly handsome, and is apt to be characterized by such words as *rugged, strong, firm, muscled, trim.*

"I try to write tender, sensual stories with a hero who is strong enough to be gentle and a heroine who is not afraid to take responsibility for her own life and achieve her fullest potential."
Maura Seger, romance author

However, not all romance lines are sticking to this traditional type of hero. In fact, Dell's guidelines offer the author the alternative of making the hero for this line atypical: what they call the "antihero."

> *It takes our heroine a while to appreciate [the antihero's] particular charms, which may include 'flaws' such as being short, skinny, bespectacled, pudgy or just not gorgeous . . . Our lady is drawn to this man's character, more than his looks. He may be quiet, studious, poetic, clownish, a little insecure, you name it, as long as he's not portrayed as a bum, rake or drifter.*

Secondary Characters in Category Romances

The purpose of secondary characters, not only in the contemporary categories but in historicals and young adult romances as well, is to support the story of the hero and heroine. They may function as sounding boards for the heroine—as might her business colleague, lady's maid, or best friend at school. This gives you a convenient way to air the heroine's thoughts, as she readily confides in this secondary character.

An enemy, a rival, or another woman can make trouble for the heroine by spreading rumors or conniving against her in some way. In a young adult romance, there might be a teacher or a person in the profession the heroine hopes to enter, who inspires her toward her goals.

"There are certain kinds of stereotypes that readers are sick and tired of seeing—the Other Woman, for example. But you can do some original things with her; develop her into more of a real person so that she's not a black-and-white villainess. You can turn her into a confidante, or someone the heroine may have reason to be jealous of, not because she's an outright witch, but maybe because she has a close relationship with the hero." **Ellen Edwards, romance editor**

Every secondary character must serve the story in some significant way, either by advancing the plot or as a vehicle for deeper characterization of the hero or heroine.

Dell's guidelines for this read as follows:

Other Characters

> *At least one other character should have features similar to the hero and heroine. But remaining characters may differ from these in*

any way the author sees fit. We want to see friends, rivals, lovers, sisters, brothers, mothers, fathers, children. Virtually anyone will fit as long as they're "round" believable people . . .

Before you go to work on the living, breathing hero and heroine who will dominate your story, be sure you understand the guidelines, if they exist, for the type of book you want to write. If they don't, be sure you feel comfortably familiar with the character types you are going to create. Remember—I repeat—if you are following the suggestions of guidelines, be sure you have the very latest ones. If they are a year old, they're probably outdated.

Heroes, Heroines, and Other Characters in Historical Romances

Since most historical romances are single-title releases, there are not many guidelines for these books. The major consideration, of course, is that the hero and heroine be a man and a woman of their time. The heroine is usually younger than in contemporary romances; women in times gone by did not go to college or prepare for careers. At a tender age they were looking for husbands. The heroine is usually breathtakingly beautiful and often has a fiery temper, a spunky nature, or a streak of independence that needs to be tamed. Often she is in a vulnerable financial position because her fortune has been lost, or because of her station in life. She usually starts off a virgin, but this condition is likely to change early in the book, often involuntarily, and the change is blamed upon the cruelties of fate. She will discover sexual pleasure when she finally submits to her passion for the hero.

The hero in an historical romance shares many characteristics with his contemporary counterpart—good looks, a virile physique, commanding presence, sexual prowess, and success in his adventures and undertakings. However, he is most often of royal blood or at least of the aristocratic class. Occasionally the hero and heroine are both from fine families traditionally at odds with each other, as in the classic situation of Romeo and Juliet, but the love between them transcends these circumstances.

If he is from a common background, the hero will be or become a man of importance in some way, possessing power and prestige. Or he will be a dashing rake who leads a life of adventure; the better part of his character lurks just under the surface, awaiting the heroine's special touch.

Depending on the complexity and length of the book, the characters may be limited to the families of the hero and heroine, or may include a "cast of thousands." For the best way to learn how successful authors of historicals handle hero, heroine, and secondary characters, you should read and study a good number of these books. Pay close attention to the qualities that go into the personalities of the fetching heroine, the dashing hero, and their supporting cast.

Heroine and Hero in Young Adult Romances

Typical requirements for young adult characters are reflected in these guidelines from the Caprice Romances line of Ace Tempo Books:

> *The girl is fifteen or sixteen and a virgin. Her experience with dating up to this point is the author's choice, but this relationship is the one in which she blossoms.*
>
> *The boy is sixteen or seventeen, not necessarily a virgin, but he respects this girl too much to sleep with her yet.*
>
> *There should be additional developed characters . . . a best friend, possibly an understanding adult (not a parent), a jealous ex-girlfriend or -boyfriend.*

Generally, the teenage heroine is attractive, though she may not see herself as such, and she worries about minor flaws in her appearance. She sees the boy as physically attractive, but, like her older counterpart, the heroine in adult category romances, she is also attracted to his inner qualities—sincerity, warmth, sense of humor—and she has sincere respect for him. Temporarily he may be a source of despair to her, as he seems to be more interested in scuba diving, or worse, in another girl, than he is in her. But in the end these misunderstandings will be cleared away, and communication (as opposed to passion) will conquer all.

The Character Biography

Even if you are following guidelines in creating your characters, it will not be enough simply to pour them into the mold. They will have to emerge as individuals, distinctly different from all the others that began in the same way. They will have to be fully developed, well-rounded characters.

For example, you will have to know your heroine and hero inside and out, from their past love relationships and the childhood influences that color their adult lives to their hobbies, career goals, deeper philosophies.

"I find a man who is interesting. And then I think to myself, wouldn't it be neat if . . . And off I go, pouring my fantasies into each new novel. The setting isn't so important as making the characters come alive. Sometimes it gets so intense that I dream about them. The hero of my novel becomes the hero of my dreams. Then I know I'm on the right track." Aimée Duvall, romance author

---

Minor characters you will not have to know as well, but the more clearly you present them, the stronger your story will be.

In casting your book, begin with the heroine, your central character. First you will write what is called a *character biography* (or bio) of her, supplying information under the following fourteen headings. Until you have easy familiarity with all these facts about her, you are not ready to write. When you have completed her bio, write one for your hero. Then, for minor characters, choose the questions here that seem relevant and write about a page for each character, summing up their major traits.

Here are fourteen basic aspects of your characters and their lives, with which you should be conversant:

1. Name, age, birthday, birthplace.
2. Body type: height and weight; short description of overall appearance; general impression she/he gives.
3. Details of physical appearance: color of eyes; color of hair, and complexion; frequent facial expressions; way of moving and walking; sound of voice. Characteristic mannerisms and gestures.
4. Dominant character traits. Which get her/him into the most trouble? Basic personality: extroverted, introverted, independent, insecure, other.
5. Taste and preference in dress; favorite outfits, jewelry, makeup, if applicable.
6. Personal history and background: are parents alive? siblings? Role in family when growing up; type of childhood.
7. Previous relationships with opposite sex. If married before, describe marriage. If divorced, how bitter? If widowed, describe feelings about deceased spouse. If single, what past love experiences? Attitude toward sex, toward own sexuality, toward opposite sex.
8. Educational background and current profession: skills, responsibilities, goals; daily responsibilities in present job.
9. Personal goals, dreams, hopes, and philosophy of life.
10. Hobbies and talents, outside of professional skills.
11. Problems character is facing as the novel opens, both emotional and practical.
12. Past experience that provides motivation for character's decisions and

actions in relation to problem or problems that arise(s) as the story develops.

13. How will character's decisions and actions complicate the resolution of the problem?
14. Write a paragraph summing up the essence of this character's personality. Now reduce it to one line.

As you mull over the various aspects of your hero's and heroine's characters, remember that one of their dominant traits should get them into trouble, or at least cause problems. For example, a contemporary heroine might be a little too independent, a good cause for conflict between her and her hero. (She can become more soft and yielding as she falls more deeply in love.) The hero may be given to silence when he is angry, a good way to create misunderstanding. (Later we learn of something in his past that makes him behave in this way.)

If yours is an historical romance, the heroine's independence might lead her to stow away in the hold of a clipper ship in order to follow her true love, who has sailed away without her.

If you pick traits that will lead your characters to act in interesting ways and to do things that create problems and complexities in your story, you automatically thicken the plot. But be sure that both the heroine and her hero are always understandable and appealing to the reader. All their faults must somehow be endearing and ultimately forgivable. Romance readers like sympathetic characters, whether they are chic and modern, naive and Victorian, or young and confused.

Making Your Characters Come Alive

Now you know your characters well. You know what they look and sound like; you know their thoughts and feelings. Now comes the challenge of communicating them, physically, emotionally, and psychologically, to your reader—the challenge of making them come alive.

You must accomplish this as soon as possible, preferably starting on page one. If the reader feels nothing about your characters after a few turns of the page, she will probably put the book back on the shelf.

You need to keep several things in mind as you breathe life into your characters. Let's see how one author does this successfully. An in-depth look at *Glitter Girl* (Jove, Second Chance at Love), a contemporary category romance by Jocelyn Day, will serve as illustration.

On page one, heroine Tiffany Harte returns after a seven-year absence to the town where she was once in love with the hero, Clay Gossard. She notes changes—the hardware store with its fresh front, the new office building, the new stoplights. The town has changed. Then the author describes Tiffany herself:

> *The town hadn't changed so much that a champagne-and-silver-streaked blond in a flame-red Jaguar could drive through unnoticed. With wry amusement, Tiffany noted the heads turning to stare at the car—and her. . . . The never-ending breeze whipped through the window teasing her expensively cared for hair in wild abandon.*

Clay is then introduced through Tiffany's recollections of him. Notice the contrast between Tiffany's Jaguar and the car Clay used to drive, paving the way for possible differences between them:

> *Seven years. Was it really only seven years since she had driven along this very same street in Clay's beat-up old pickup, her body pressed tightly against his, his hand tucked around her leg with easy familiarity? Seven years since she had ridden along here in a clam-shaped float as Queen of the Clam Festival. Clam Festival Queen. That funny-sad memory brought a smile to her lips, and yet at the same time, she had to blink back unexpected tears.*

Then she passes the Cougar Plywood mill, and again her memory is stirred:

> *Was Clay still working there, still grading and sorting endless streams of veneer as it came along the conveyer from the machine that peeled it off the logs. That was where Aunt Pru had said he would be all his life, complete with a beer belly and worn-down wife and a handful of bratty kids living in a patched-up shack outside of town.*
>
> *And yet, no matter what Aunt Pru said, somehow Tiffany couldn't quite envision Clay Gossard's lean, hard figure gone all soft and beer-bellied.*

In the first two and one-half pages, Jocelyn Day has given us both a wealth of physical description and many clues to the character of both Tiffany and Clay.

The descriptive phrase "champagne-and-silver-streaked blond in flame-red Jaguar" is a clue that Tiffany is sexy looking. She was Queen of the Clam Festival, and she was crazy about Clay Gossard.

We know that Clay worked hard for a living at the mill. He drove a beat-up old pickup, and Aunt Pru didn't predict great things for him. He was also sexually attractive seven years ago; Tiffany remembers his lean, hard figure.

Such a beginning, setting up sharp, clear pictures of the heroine and the hero, hinting at their personalities, indicating their past involvement with each other, creates great reader suspense. We know the two will meet again. Have they changed? What will happen? Has Clay's hard, lean figure gone "all soft and beer-bellied?" Not likely.

And what happened to end Tiffany's romance with Clay? We feel that she cared deeply and that somehow she was hurt. How?

We don't have to wait long to savor the meeting between them. It comes to us with plenty of emotion on page five. Tiffany is walking on Solitude Beach, one of her favorite places. Again, memories rush back: wiener roasts; walking barefoot in the chill, frothy surf; lying on a blanket in the sand next to Clay's muscular body; feeling the throbbing ache of his desire.

Tiffany sees a lone man walking on the beach. He looks like Clay. It can't be! But he has the same dark hair, the same loose stride. Of course, it *is* Clay.

> *The man was looking at her now, and Tiffany's heart felt as if it rolled over within her chest. But she still tried to tell herself it couldn't be. The coincidence was too great. She was merely seeing Clay in any handsome ruggedly built, dark-haired man.*
>
> *He took a few steps in her direction, stopped again only a few feet away. "Tiffany?", he finally said incredulously.*
>
> *For one whirling moment Tiffany could think only that her ears were deceiving her as her eyes had. But this time there was no mistake. He was standing only a few feet away from her, wind whipping his dark hair, his expression as incredulous as his voice. Tiffany felt strangely lightheaded. Was fate perhaps finally on her side, guiding each of them toward a predestined meeting here on this windswept beach?*
>
> *"Clay! I—I didn't expect to see you here!"*

As Tiffany stares at Clay, she compares her memory of him with the way he looks now:

> *He had been virilely attractive in his twenties, handsome in a reckless, devil-may-care sort of way, with a flashing smile and dancing eyes. He was still handsome, but something had been added now, an intensity, a powerful maturity that was at the same time compelling and a little frightening. Oddly, Tiffany's first thought was that no woman would get away with the way she had once teased and tantalized him, knowing the power his desire for her gave her over him. Her second thought was that Aunt Pru had been wrong. He hadn't acquired a beer belly. If*

anything he looked even harder and more fit than he had seven years ago.

Tiffany felt a strange flood of helplessness as she stood looking up at him. There were so many things she wanted to say. How could she start? I was wrong. I made a mistake.

In these opening pages, Clay and Tiffany are clearly defined. Some of their inner conflicts, emotions, and psychological traits have been shown us, and sexual tension—the sexual attraction that seven years apart hasn't destroyed—crackles off the pages. The reader is hooked and the plot has been set in motion.

Tagging Your Characters

One reason these opening pages of *Glitter Girl* are so successful is that the author has made good use of *character tags*—words and phrases chosen carefully to establish her character in the reader's mind. You tag characters with adjectives and phrases that give clear clues both to a character's appearance and to his or her important inner feelings.

If you are selecting character tags for your heroine, for example, look over the biography you have just written for her. Come up with concrete images that will immediately convey to your reader such things as her body type, her facial features, the quality of her voice, her mannerisms and gestures, her facial expressions, the way she moves when she walks.

Dress her in clothing that gives the reader clues not only to her appearance but to her lifestyle, her economic situation, her image of herself as a woman.

Then choose phrases that will let the reader know as soon as possible her state of mind as the story opens. Drop clues as to what she is worrying about, what she is feeling about the hero—as soon as we know who he is.

After a few pages, certainly by the end of your first chapter, you should have your heroine well tagged. The reader will have a good idea of the kind of person she is and what her problems are.

Let's look at some of the tags Jocelyn Day uses in these opening paragraphs of *Glitter Girl* and in the next few pages of the book, and at what they convey to us.

Tiffany, the heroine

Words and phrases which tag her appearance, lifestyle and character	Words and phrases which tag her emotional and psychological state
champagne-and-silver-streaked blond (sexy)	she feels wry amusement as she notes heads turning to watch her drive into town
expensively cared for hair (no financial problems)	
Clam Festival Queen (image of beauty)	a funny-sad memory of Clam Festival brought a smile to her lips and she blinks back unexpected tears
she ran lightly (implies petite figure)	
tanned wrist (she has time to sunbathe)	
spice-brown silk blouse and cream wool pants (expensive; good taste also implied)	
hooded jacket, casual on outside, luxuriously fur-lined on inside (again, expensive)	longing for a time when the world—when she—was more innocent
	her heart rolled over (when she sees Clay)
	his new maturity (Clay's) was compelling and frightening to her
	she feels a strange flood of helplessness (as she looks at Clay)
	She thinks—I was wrong. I made a mistake.

Clay, the hero

Words and phrases which tag his appearance, lifestyle and character	Words and phrases which tag his emotional and psychological state
Clay's beat-up old pickup (he was hard pressed for money)	moment of open astonishment

his hand tucked around her leg with easy familiarity; the tender yet possessive way he put his arm around her (he is aggressive, yet intimate and tender)

tender and sensitive

devoid of curiosity

aloof, detached look

laughing light in his dark eyes, the husky sound of his voice

cool indifference

the man who had once pleaded, argued, demanded that she marry him (Tiffany's recollection)

lean, hard figure

a lithe, swinging stride

ruggedly handsome features

his body had throbbed with passion—his fiery kisses and caresses had aroused her (also in the past)

loose stride

wind whipping his dark hair

virilely attractive

a hardness, a ruthlessness that hadn't been there (in Clay) before (signaling some change in him)

handsome in a reckless, devil-may-care way

flashing smile

dancing eyes

Jocelyn Day has given the reader an abundance of clues as to the appearance, character, and emotions of her heroine and hero, tightly packed into her opening scene.

As soon as you have written the opening chapter of your romance novel, make a list of the words and phrases you have used to tag your characters and establish them in your reader's mind, physically and emotionally. If the list is too short or somehow incomplete, go over these pages and add more concrete, descriptive tags, which will convey a stronger visual image and clearer understanding of your characters' thoughts and feelings in these scenes.

In tagging your heroine and hero, be sure to use specific words and phrases that carry color, texture, concrete images. Here is a list of phrases taken from a random sampling of contemporary category romances, which effectively tag the heroine and hero in the stories. You will want to think of phrases of this kind to describe your characters:

The Heroine
her long hair fell in a copper braid
her features glowed with vitality
her coltish figure in crisp blue jeans
her mouth expressed vulnerability
her hazel eyes flecked with green; or velvet brown eyes, electric blue eyes
her auburn hair that caught the fire in the sunlight

she had a long, leggy look
there was an animal earthiness about her, a latent sensuality
tossing back her raven-black hair
she smoothed the green sharkskin skirt over her trim hips
her wide brown eyes were fringed with gold-tipped lashes
brown hair shot with gold highlights
her small delicate earlobes
her long dancer's legs
her breasts, high and firm, straining against the fragile material of her blouse

The Hero

the glacial light in his deep-set gray eyes
his briar pipe clamped between his even white teeth
the fragrance of his aromatic blend of tobacco
his wide-legged stance
a smile that didn't reach his eyes
his expensive gray topcoat carried a designer label inside
a smattering of freckles gave him a youthful appearance
he let his lids half cover his coffee-colored eyes
his voice was hypnotic, low, and throaty
his dark eyes, burning with fire
his slim taut body gliding into the water's depths
in his white cotton shirt and tight-fitting pants, he looked magnificent
thick dark brown hair tumbled across his forehead as though begging to be
    smoothed back by a female hand
strongly carved features, yet capable of showing a wide range of emotion—
    love, hatred, indifference . . . gray like the mist over a storm-tossed
    sea
he regarded her with the patience of a king in the presence of a slave

Building Your Characters

You have tagged your characters with strong, memorable images. Your reader has a good idea of what they look like, what sort of people they are, what they are currently feeling and thinking. This is a fine introduction for your heroine and your hero, but your job of characterizing has only just begun.

Think of each of these tags as a foundation stone for one aspect of your heroine or hero. You are going to build on each by *dramatizing*, or showing in action, the characteristics you have said belong to each of them. You will select action—plot events—that will show the intensity of the emotions they are feeling.

For example, it is not enough to show once how your heroine feels about something. You will have to remind the reader constantly of her emotions and inner thoughts and of the kind of person she is, and illustrate this again and again in what she says and does. Show how her spunk, for example, leads her to do certain things; her anger at the hero when he causes her to make regrettable fiery statements.

Like themes in a symphony, each of the characteristics in the early pages of your story will be echoed again and again throughout your book. Well-chosen character tags, those handy descriptive words and phrases, will be woven in and out of the action to keep your reader constantly aware of your characters' thoughts and appearance. *Never slow action with long descriptive passages.* Drop tags into sentences and keep the music flowing.

If you succeed in giving the reader an in-depth portrait of your heroine, showing how her character, thoughts, and feelings motivate her actions, she will be *well defined.* She will be a living, breathing person with whom your reader will easily become emotionally involved, and you will be on your way as a romance writer.

Points to Remember:

1. In tagging your characters, be selective. Choose strong, concrete images. Whenever possible, choose physical characteristics that will symbolize or harmonize with the inner conflicts important to the story. (If your hero has a fiery temper, for example, why not give him red hair? If your heroine is an artist and a dreamer, how about watery pensive eyes?)

2. Go back to your character bios and make sure that in your first few chapters you have introduced the physical characteristics you planned for your heroine and hero. Have you come up with descriptive words and phrases to tag their mannerisms, gestures, body build, quality of voice?

3. Have you hinted at things in each character's past that cause the present inner conflicts motivating their actions?

4. Does the heroine's state of mind at the opening of the book relate to the key complication in your story?

5. Check to be sure that descriptive tags are woven into the flow of your first few chapters. If you have used long narrative passages to describe your hero's or heroine's physical appearance, break them up so you won't slow down the beginning of your story. Later, after the reader is fully hooked into the plot, you can slip in fuller descriptions between scenes of action and dialogue.

6. Are you building on each aspect of your heroine's and hero's personalities, vividly dramatizing their feelings, as well as tagging each of them with key phrases showing their emotions? If your characters are fully realized and well defined, plot events will flow naturally out of their problems and personalities.

RAPTURE ROMANCE • 451-AJ2065 • $1.95
NINA
COOMBS
PASSION'S
DOMAIN
RAPTURE
ROMANCE
#6

Chapter **6.**
WHERE LOVERS MEET:
Romantic Settings and Professional Worlds

If you've ever admired the scenery while on a romantic picnic or when dancing with your own hero on a moonlit night, you know how much the backdrop can add to the heady and sensuous feeling of being in love.

Just so, the setting in your romance novel can not only make the book more colorful and interesting, but intensify the romantic atmosphere considerably. Except for romance lines that specify that you use only American settings, the world is open to you when you choose your geographical setting—countries hot or cold, lofty or flat, near or far. Your only limits are the boundaries of your own interest and imagination. If you are a zealous researcher, you can bring to life settings anywhere on the globe. Or if you prefer to stick to places you know, research and imagination can make just about any place a suitable setting if your story is romantic enough.

But the country and landscape of your setting are only part of the backdrop of your story, if one or both of your main characters also live in the world of a *profession*.

Whether your heroine is a real-estate agent in today's world, an eighteenth-century heiress expecting to inherit and run a cotton plantation in the South of yesterday, or a student of journalism still in high school, you will have to know enough about those activities to make her abilities and responsibilities clear to your reader. And whether your hero is a modern movie star, a cattle rustler on the Western frontier, or a star on the school swimming team, you will have to know a good deal about what movie stars, cattle rustlers, or swimmers do.

It is a definite "plus" for your novel if the reader can learn something about such worlds while wrapped up in your tantalizing love story. Again, your ability to choose an interesting profession and to research it are your only limits.

Either the geographical setting of your story, the professional world of your hero and heroine, or both can provide the reason these two lovers meet in the first place. They each need a reason to be where they are, as well as reasons to do whatever they are doing. You need to choose the country, city, or town of your setting and the work world of your characters with this in mind.

Let's look over some combinations of geographical settings and professional backgrounds used in some recent romance novels. Here are some category romances:

- A cruise to Monte Carlo, Crete, Athens, Cairo, Tangiers, and then a small fictional island southeast of Madeira off the coast of Africa, provide the setting for *Midnight Magic* (Superromance/Worldwide), by Christine Hella Gott. Heroine, Tara Lownes, writer of children's books is shipwrecked on the island owned by world-famous vintner, Jorge Silves, her hero.

- On location at a hospital in the Amazon River Basin of Brazil, documentary film producer Toni Carruthers meets her love, Dr. Luis Quental, in *River of Desire* (Superromance, Worldwide), by Abra Taylor.
- The snowy slopes of Sun Valley lead Felicia Hollingsworth, ski champion and Olympic hopeful, into the arms of her ski instructor, Grant Mitchell, in *Winter Love Song* (Jove, Second Chance at Love), by Meredith Kingston.
- In a cabin in the Minnesota woods in winter, magazine writer Raine Morgan finds rock star Devlin Paige in *Winter Lady* (Silhouette, Desire), by Janet Joyce.
- On a trip on the famous Orient Express, traveling from Venice to London, San Francisco gift shop owner Torey Jensen meets Los Angeles museum art consultant Peter West in *Love with a Perfect Stranger* (Silhouette, Special Edition), by Pamela Wallace.
- The woods of New Hampshire frame freelance writer and gourmet cook Rachel Grant and her hero, novelist Jason Wilder, in *Intimate Stranger* (Silhouette, Special Edition), by Brooke Hastings.
- A Pacific cruise starting in San Francisco and stopping in Hawaii, Fiji, and Australia is the setting for professional bodyguard Sandy O'Hara's assignment to watch over Senator Ken Rexford in *Guarded Moments* (Jove, Second Chance at Love), by Lynn Fairfax.

Notice that some of these stories are set in more than one place. Some are set in glamorous locations and others take place in picturesque but quiet surroundings. Though most romance novels are set in actual cities or towns, it is possible to conjure up a fictitious island or a fictional small town outside of a well-known city, and play out the romance there, as in *Midnight Magic.*

The settings in historical romances are apt to be as glamorous as the heroes' professions. Heroines may or may not have professional interests:

- On a tobacco plantation in South Carolina, left in ruins after the Civil War, heroine Charlotte King meets and falls in love with her adversary in the tobacco business, Clint Develin, in *Embers of Dawn* (Bantam), by Patricia Matthews.
- Harbin (Manchuria), Moscow, and Siberia are the backdrop for the love story between Tatiana Levitina, daughter of an aristocrat, and Prince Paul Veragin, the White Russian Army officer assigned to protect her in the days of the Russian Revolution in *East Lies the Sun* (Dell), by Alla Crone.
- California Gold Rush days frame the story of Irish actress Mara O'Flynn and handsome Louisiana landowner and adventurer Nicholas Chantale In *Tears of Gold* (Avon), by Laurie McBain.

In a young adult romance, the geographical setting is not likely to be so important as in category or historical romances. Romantic beaches and deserted mountain cabins are not so necessary in these less passionate tales. The settings for these stories are most likely to be the teenager's world of home, school, sports, summer camp, trip, or project.

The story is often set against a "professional background," however, as the young heroine or her hero work in after-school jobs or pursue fields that they hope to enter later. In fact, this element of the story often supplies some of the major challenges to the heroine as she grows up in the story:

- *Love Comes to Annie* (Scholastic, Wildfire), by Lucille S. Warner, is set in the world of choral singing. Anne, the heroine, a member of her high-school choral group, is working on her soprano part in a difficult Bach cantata when she meets the hero, Pierre Bouray, the new tenor. Since he is French, that background is also developed.
- In *Golden Girl* (Silhouette, First Love), author Helen Erskine sets her story against a California surfing background. Hero Kirk Conry is obsessed with the sport, and heroine Tobey Lang comes to realize that there is more to life than riding the big waves.
- In *Trusting Hearts* (Bantam, Sweet Dreams), by Jocelyn Saal, a small town in Virginia and the world of veterinary medicine are the backdrops for this story of Kathy McLain's coming of age. As her lifelong friendship with Dean Waters turns into romance, she also finds her future career.

Young adult romances are more often set in small towns than in large cities, perhaps because setting never dominates the mood of these stories. The town should come through as *Anytown, USA,* recognizable to young readers in any part of the country. Though Helen Erskine, for example, uses California beaches for her surfing romance, the story could take place on any beach in this country where there are waves big enough to ride.

And your young adult romance will have an extra dimension if you integrate into your plot material an interesting career—say, in the arts (dance, music, theater), or sports (professional skating, skiing, tennis), or perhaps science (oceanography, space technology, or archaeology). Not only can you enrich your book, but you can stretch the horizons of your young readers in the process.

Researching Your Story

If you're writing about a faraway, exotic place in a category romance, it may be impossible for you to do first-hand research. If you *can* make a journey to that romantic setting, you are fortunate. If you can't, don't despair. You don't have to be a world traveler to write about a villa in the Alban Hills of Italy, the buzz of the busy Tokyo, or even the ski slopes of Colorado. Most romance writers have not been to these places; they *research* their settings.

What you must do, however, is feel the same excitement about and intimacy with your setting that you would feel if you were standing on a balcony in Italy, in a Japanese garden, or on a snowy peak in Aspen.

How do you generate this excitement without actually seeing a place? You can turn yourself on to your distant setting in many ways. If a friend returns from a trip to Australia or Africa and invites you over to see the inevitable slides of, "our vacation," go! Forget that her husband, George, gives the most boring narrations in the world. Concentrate on the slides. Instead of George and Henrietta and their kids sitting beside the safari campfire, picture a beautiful girl and her handsome hero gazing into each other's eyes as the flames burn low.

Ask questions about every aspect of the place they visited. How was the weather? Humid? Dry? Did the air have a special quality to it? What about the food? Did they try exotic dishes? The flowers and trees—what were their names? How did they smell? Could you borrow any of the books or pamphlets they brought back?

Then go to the library and find pictures and articles in books and magazines. If you haven't already decided on a heroine and a hero, maybe they and their story will come to you in your excitement over this setting.

If no friend conveniently supplies you with a romantic setting, go to a travel agency. Where is the jet set vacationing this year? What interesting off-the-beaten-track places are they recommending?

Once you have chosen your locale and are turned on to a place, learn everything you can about it. An encyclopedia will give you a full and accurate account of the trees, plants, and flowers native to the area, and facts about the climate and the people. And you'll learn what enterprises flourish in that part of the world.

Knowing what industrial, commercial, and professional enterprises support the economy may give you the answer to the crucial question "Why did my heroine go to this place, and what was the hero doing there?" If you haven't established their professions, this may help you with those decisions.

The greatest benefit of researching your setting thoroughly is the authority your descriptions will have because they are accurate. You can relax, knowing that you'll never be embarrassed by having some reader write to your editor to point out your errors.

If you are writing an historical romance and can go to the place where that rich past flourished, you'll find plenty of sources for the details you need to build your story. Start at the local library or historical society. County histories, genealogies of large families, newspapers, and documents of the period will probably be available. Talk to the librarian in charge of special collections and ask if you can see old letters, diaries, and books written in your time period. Tell the director of the historical society what you are researching, and ask for suggestions. If your plot is still vague, reading about floods, fires, political scandals, and the daily trials and tribulations of people who actually lived in this place at that time may solve your problems.

If you can't visit your locale in person, you can write or phone libraries, historical societies, and genealogical organizations, and ask them to send you bibliographies or photocopies of information only they can provide. The local tourist bureau will also have packets of information on historical places and landmarks.

It's just as important to create authentic settings and professional worlds in a young adult romance as it is in any other romance novel. In this case, your task is easier. A trip to the local high school may show you what you need to know about your setting. If you have teenagers in your home or next door, you're lucky. Spend time with young people. Listen to them talk. Draw out their ideas on the world as *they* see it, and share their enthusiasm for the future as *they* envision it. If you're going to use a special occupation or avocation as story background, again take the time to talk to a professional or to people who know this area. Watch how they work, listen to them talk, and absorb the details of their environment.

You can't guess about the environment or occupation you want to write about. Young readers are just as sharp as older readers when it comes to spotting something out of place in your book.

Once you've become familiar with the setting for your romance and can see and smell and taste its scenery, flowers, and food, your excitement will mount. And excitement is contagious. When it spills into your writing through vivid word pictures, your reader will be caught up in the flow of your enthusiasm. She'll feel she's *there* and will escape little by little from the confines of her workday world, whether home, office, or high school chemistry class. She'll slip into that other world, where soft breezes blow off a tropical sea and a full moon inches up over Diamond Head or the Taj Mahal, or wherever your lovers are strolling, arms twined around each other.

If you can't seem to find a setting for the plot idea whirling around in your head, here are a few more suggestions.

Make a list of interesting places in your own area, places you've taken guests or would like to take visitors.

Pretend you're a newcomer in town. What would you want to see? What places haven't you seen yet, although you've lived in this area many years? I grew up in La Jolla but never took the time to see the La Jolla Caves, a great tourist attraction, until I moved away and returned home on a visit. Then I used the background for a young adult novel.

Make a list of all the places you've visited away from home over the years. Jot down what you liked about the place and what lingers in your memory. Include for each place the restaurants and the things you did for entertainment, or watched other people do. Does one of these seem an appropriate setting for your plot?

> *"A writer-friend once advised, 'When the going gets tough, you haven't researched enough.' I have found that the more one knows about a setting or profession the easier it is to write about it and to visualize people living in that place or working in the profession."* Dorothy Dowdell, romance author

Where did you grow up? Most of us end up many miles from the place where we spent our childhood. Your home town might have seemed dull in your youth, but if you put on those romance-colored glasses and take another look, you'll be amazed at how differently you view it today.

If you do decide to write about the home town you left long ago, you still have to do your research. Places change. Dirt roads turn into freeways. Old houses are torn down to make room for high-rises. And your memory can play tricks on you.

Take a sentimental journey back to your home town. Explore those places you loved years ago. Talk to your old neighbors. Then, after you return, subscribe to the local newspapers for the next few months.

Bringing Your Setting to Life

You know the population of the area of your setting, the weather patterns, the sixty-two types of flora and fauna, but can you visualize the sweep of the plains and the thrust of the mountain peaks? Can you taste the spicy food and smell the flowers? You must not only be accurate as you describe the place you are writing about, you must also be able to bring it alive, appealing to the readers' five senses.

You are not writing a comprehensive travel book. This is the story of your heroine's romance. From the bundle of facts and figures you have gathered up, you must be selective. You must also be specific. Pull out the views, foods, wines, and gardens that your hero and heroine will need to see, taste and smell as they do what they do and go where they go, in the course of falling in love.

If you can not easily project yourself onto that Hawaiian beach, into the Maine woods, or into a castle in France, sit in front of a picture until you can. If you simply cannot conjure up the aroma of a simmering bouillabaisse from reading the recipe, go down to your local French restaurant and ask to stand over the soup kettle.

Whatever you must do to achieve it, be sure you can *see, smell, hear, feel* your setting as you launch into your novel. If it isn't growing real to you, consider changing scenery. It won't be real to your reader unless it has thoroughly captured your imagination.

Touch each of your reader's senses as compellingly as you can, whenever an opportunity germane to your story arises. If the rancher hero asks the heroine to dance, make the reader feel the beat of the hoedown and hear the squawk of the violins. If your lovers are walking in a thick German forest, let your reader breathe in the fragrance of the tall pines and see the flickering sunlight filter down through dark boughs across the hero's broad back.

The facts you gather in research not only supply your novel with authenticity but also give you the raw material to develop a rich style, filled with delicious details.

A word of caution is necessary at this point. It is easy to become so attached to every bit of research you have collected that you want to include all of it in your book. You don't want to waste a phrase of that hard-won information. But don't get carried away. Everything you incorporate into your story must *serve a purpose* and be relevant to the scene it is embellishing. Nothing should just sit there with no reason, obviously research material you couldn't bear to throw out.

Never let description interfere with the forward motion of the plot. If you cannot naturally weave aspects of the setting into the thoughts, feelings, or actions of the characters on stage, take them out. Remember that beautiful sunsets, in and of themselves, are only clutter if they do not heighten the emotions of the heroine and the hero, or add texture necessary to the scene.

If many details of a bullfight in Spain, for example, do seem relevant to the story and you decide to use them, don't give them to the reader on several continuous and unrelieved pages. Interrupt them with dialogue and action. Scatter the facts along the story's path.

Setting In Category Contemporary Romances

Now let's see how a few romance writers have made good use of their settings in the category contemporaries.

Lynda Ward's *Music of Passion* (Superromance, Worldwide), is set on an old estate in Austria. Here's how she presents the surrounding countryside:

> *Beyond the slender, silver-barked birch trees, massive oaks and beeches covered the hillside, their thick foliage virid, almost luminous under the July sun. Kurt [the hero] could see one arm of the lake glinting through the forest at the foot of the hill, its usually serene*

surface agitated and troubled, a reflection of his own mood. Little whitecaps contrasted sharply with the water that was even bluer than the Austrian sky.

Notice the specifics—the kinds of trees: birch, beech, and oak. Color and light come vividly to mind through such words as silver, virid (green), luminous, glinting, whitecaps, and reference to blue water and sky.

This passage also illustrates a very important point: whenever you can—always, if possible—give description of landscape, cityscape, and even interiors of houses *in viewpoint.* (Chapter eight will discuss viewpoint fully).

Notice here that the countryside is presented *through Kurt's eyes.* And the author has gone a step farther; she has made the agitated surface of the lake echo Kurt's mood. In fact, he is troubled over the impending arrival of the heroine, an American girl he assumes to be a fortune hunter. Lynda Ward has included the landscape in her foreshadowing of the conflict that will explode between the hero and heroine when they meet. The description here is an integral part of the story.

Music of Passion is filled not only with the colors and sounds of Austria, but is rich in sensuous descriptions of food, music, plants, and flowers.

It takes practice to select the best details, convey them sensuously, and weave them purposefully into your plot. But the result is worth it. Never pass up the chance to bring a scene to life and to make it palpably real by including the sensuous accents your setting offers you.

For example, if your hero and heroine are dining in a restaurant in Spain, as they are in Jane Peart's *Spanish Masquerade* (Dell, Candlelight Romance), bring the menu to life. Not only do you whet your reader's appetite for Spanish food, but the elegance of the meal adds to the romantic atmosphere of the scene.

> *When the first course, a subtly spiced gazpacho, was placed before her, Anne (the heroine) realized how hungry she was. She ate heartily of the light omelet which followed, and relished the salad of crisp greens, tiny tomatoes, asparagus, and olives. It was all delicious.*
>
> *At first, when Miguel (the hero) suggested* postre, dessert, *she refused, saying she was too full. But that was before she saw a flan con nata being brought to a nearby table. Miquel saw her glance and laughingly ordered two. Coffee—black and fragrant—and a cognac were set in front of them with a flourish.*

Susanna Collins is a romance author who is especially good at weaving researched details into her contemporary stories. Here are a few passages from *Flamenco Nights* (Jove, Second Chance at Love), also set in Spain. The book opens with:

"You mustn't hold anything against Chip. He was your best friend for too many years!" Rosie threw back her long, honey-colored hair and tried to concentrate on Francisco Goya's famous portrait of his mistress, The Naked Maja. *She was annoyed at her brother Danny for bringing up the subject of Chip and her broken engagement when she wanted badly to forget it and immerse herself in the wonders of the Prado Museum in Madrid.*

But even more disturbing than Danny's comments about Chip was the tall, dark-haired man who seemed to be shadowing them. Had he not been dressed in modern clothes, thought Rosie, he might have stepped down from an El Greco painting with his swarthy skin, high cheekbones and dark, deep-set eyes of a Spanish grandee. With her artistic perception, Rosie had memorized every detail of the man including the casual, rich dark brown suede sports jacket and the rust-colored silk shirt open at the neck.

In two paragraphs, the author has established the existence of Rosie's brother, Danny; of Chip, her former fiancé; and of an intriguing new man about to enter her life. We learn that Rosie has an artistic outlook, which justifies her interest in the Prado Museum and her seeing the dark man as someone out of an El Greco painting. The art work begins to bring Spain alive, as the setting of the story and every detail has been presented to us through Rosie's viewpoint. Already there is a tight blend of story and setting.

Later in the story, in chapter three, see how this author incorporates her description of flamenco, the spirited Spanish dance, into the flow of her story. It is used here as an integral part of Rosie's deepening attraction to the dark hero she saw on page one, Juan De Arevalo.

Before she (Rosie) could utter another protest, she was being propelled onto the floor. After the first few tentative steps, she grew unselfconscious. The music and the hand clapping, the uninhibited pervasive mood engulfed her, did all the thinking for her, and the intricate steps came as naturally as if she had been born dancing them . . .

She whirled around and found herself looking up into the narrow, handsome face of Juan De Arevalo, who had left his guitar to join her in the dance. The music slowed as he clicked his heels, slowly at first, then building speed, the long hard muscles of his thighs controlling the rhythm, his strong back arched like a matador, his sensuous eyes on her.

Someone threw him a wide-brimmed black Cordovan hat that he set at a rakish angle, shading his heavy-lidded, dark eyes. They circled around each other, like a pair of tigers.

Whether she is describing the bullfight, the winding streets of the city of Cordova, or the flowers adorning the houses, Susanna Collins' description is alive with sensuous detail, and always *part of the ongoing action of the story.*

Setting In Historical Romances

Laurie McBain, in her historical romance *Tears of Gold* (Avon), mentioned earlier, makes excellent use of her research material in presenting San Francisco in 1850. The heroine, Mara O'Flynn, has left Ireland for the New World with her brother, Brendan. In these two richly concrete paragraphs the teeming streets of the Gold Rush days come alive, Brendan's character is hinted at, and the reader gets a good sense of what Mara will be up against in her new home.

His (Brendan's) dark eyes had glazed over as he stared longingly at the gambling houses they passed, oblivious to the mud thrown up by the wheels of the coach, as it lurched through the debris-clogged avenues of San Francisco that were little more than quagmires. What couldn't be carried or made use of by the transient townspeople, was no longer desired or valued, was dumped in the streets. Iron cookstoves, crates and barrels full of spoiled goods crowded the streets in makeshift bridges across the mud or ended up in stacks that continued to grow unchecked.

The streets were crowded with people as well as discarded rubbish. The flannel-shirted figures Mara would find so familiar in future months were just part of the crowd of people that surged and loitered in the streets. Every so often the brightly colored satin jackets of Oriental foreigners would flash before her eyes, then disappear just as abruptly behind the ordinary frock coat of another adventurer hoping to strike it rich in California.

Notice that Laurie McBain's setting is part of her story, not just a distant backdrop. The mood of the town and the tenor of the times will shape Mara's future in California. The adventuring hero she falls in love with will spring naturally from this chaotic, greedy world outside the coach windows. The details describing the streets set the stage and pepare the reader for the story to come.

Setting In Young Adult Romances

Though the setting is often used to heighten the romantic atmosphere and to intensify sexual tension in category and historical romance novels, the geographical details in a young adult romance are often unimportant unless they can be used to further the action of the plot or to provide challenges that the young characters must face in growing up.

Such is the case in Helen Erskine's *Golden Girl,* the surfing story I referred to earlier in this chapter.

As they explore the rugged Pacific coastline together, Tobey, the heroine, is beginning to see that Kirk's (the hero's) daring often borders on the reckless. Toward the end of the chapter six, Kirk ignores Tobey's warning not to go over the edge of a very dangerous cliff. Horrified, Tobey watches as he inches his way down. She sees that the small ledges he'd used in past descents had been swept away by the rain. Here the setting is part of the action, definitely necessary to the story:

> *She (Tobey) leaned over the edge again in time to see a shower of dirt and rocks break away from the side of the cliff and cascade to the beach below. Kirk, still on the flat rock, looked down too, and seemed to sway as if from giddiness. Then he tightened his hold on the rocky projection he was clinging to. He could see now how dangerous Satan's Slide was, its soil loosened by recent rain.*
>
> *"I'll be up in a minute!" he (Kirk) yelled.*
>
> *"I'm here, Kirk. I'll give you a hand."*
>
> *Suddenly, there was a groaning sound. She thought for a second it came from him, but it deepened to a roar that was not human. It was the cliff, moaning as if in pain, as a new shower of debris poured from its side. For a moment, it obscured Kirk. His foothold was gone, part of the deadly shower. His feet swung in space, reaching for anything that would hold him. But there was nothing, and still the slide continued, above him, below him, and all around him.*

The cliff itself almost becomes a character here as it moans "as if in pain." Will the cliff collapse completely? Will Kirk be seriously hurt? Use of the craggy coastline deepens suspense and helps Tobey see a crucial aspect of Kirk's character—his recklessness.

The best rule to follow in writing young adult romance is this: develop the geographical setting only if and when such details point up a central theme, or intensify the action or the emotional impact of something important to the plot.

To sum up, if you are writing a lengthy contemporary romance, such as a Harlequin Superromance or a Silhouette Special Edition, or an historical or family saga, you will probably use longer passages to describe your geographical setting and its details than you would in a shorter novel.

In the short category romance, 60,000 words or so, you will need most of those words to build the plot, to set action in motion, and to develop the all-pervading sexual tension between the lovers. Weave in the appealing details of your setting. By and large, readers of the short romances enjoy a fast-paced read, with something happening on every page, more than long passages of description, no matter how well written.

This is particularly true in the young adult romance. The teenage reader has a shorter attention span than an adult, and expects a story to move right along. After all, she was brought up on television drama, where action and dialogue are everything.

Whereas three or four paragraphs of description might be used in a longer romance, and a short paragraph or two in a category romance, description in the typical young adult romance should be limited to a few vivid sentences.

Professional Backgrounds in Your Romance Novel

In the category romance, the world of your heroine's and hero's careers— the professional backdrop of your story—is as important as the geographical setting. Here again, you are not writing a treatise on the role of the chemist in the world of pharmacology. But you need to know enough about chemistry—should your heroine be a chemist—to make her work believable, interesting, and above all, an integral part of your story. Your reader will appreciate a behind-the-scenes view of the world of music, academia, or high finance as long as your story is always in the forefront, and all the information seems relevant to the fate of the heroine and hero.

For your contemporary heroine, be sure you choose an appropriately current profession. Women have come a long way professionally. They are no longer languishing at the bottom of the ladder, or working only as nurses, as flight attendants, or in the steno pool. Today's woman can hold the top position in a company, or be the director or producer of a film. Make her an exciting, highly-motivated, talented, and thoroughly contemporary creature.

In choosing professions for your hero and heroine, avoid such cliché situations as the heroine hired to catalogue a famous writer's library, or a photographer taking pictures for a famous journalist. Too many recent heroines have been owners of chic boutiques. To learn what other professions have been overdone, read the blurbs and titles currently on the stands. If two, three, or more titles refer to a certain profession, back off—unless you can come up with a fresh twist.

Instead of an everyday journalist, make your hero a deep-sea explorer and your heroine an *underwater* photographer. Instead of placing that exclusive boutique on Fifth Avenue, Rodeo Drive, or Palm Springs Avenue, what if you located it in one of the countries of the Far or Near East? The heroine is an American designer called upon to furnish a wardrobe for some member of the local royalty, and thereby meets her prince.

The "something different," the original twist, is what enchants editors and readers.

How are you going to learn about different and intriguing professions? Listen for them as you hear the TV news or as you meet new people at a cocktail party. Watch for them as you read the newspaper and magazines. Call up the career advisor at a high school, college, or university and ask about new careers in certain fields. You'll be surprised at how many unusual jobs exist, once you are actively looking for them.

Think about careers you dreamed of as a child. What would you like to do if you had your life to live over again? Give your imagination its head and see where it goes.

Once you've selected an occupational background for your heroine and hero, start your research. Collect articles on and pictures of archaeological digs, if that's your hero's profession, and get first-hand information by writing to and talking with archaeologists. Don't know any? You'll find one on the faculty of your nearest college or university. That goes for just about any profession. And don't forget your friend the research librarian.

One way or another, you can probably manage to interview people working in the profession you have chosen and to see them in those surroundings.

"For a first attempt at a researched historical work, choose a limited period of time that contains one or two great climactic events—a great battle with far-reaching results is a convenient device. This simplifies research, gives adequate scope for individual adventures for the heroine or hero, and limits the amount of historical explanation that you must give the reader. If the battle has a name, and most have, you have a specific word to look up in encyclopedias and the indexes of historical texts and biographies to pinpoint which books will be useful to you." **Roberta Gellis, author of historical romances**

Must your hero and heroine be involved in the same field? Often these two lovely people do work in the same office, or meet over a desk in the middle of a big decision or transaction of professional concern to both of them. But just as often, they will be involved in professions that have nothing to do with each other at all. Consider the category romances I mentioned at the beginning of this chapter and see what the hero and heroine do in each case: a children's book writer finds a vintner; a film maker finds a doctor; a magazine writer finds a rock star; a gift shop owner finds a museum art consultant; a freelance writer finds a novelist; and a bodyguard finds a senator.

The gift shop owner and the art consultant, the freelance writer and the novelist have fields that overlap. But not so for the others here. Obviously, there are no set rules. You may or may not need the hero's and heroine's work to bring them together. Perhaps they are going to meet when they sit next to each other on an airplane. Only you can decide how professional factors will be used in your plot. You may want to play them to the hilt in creating conflict between your lovers. Think this all through carefully when you make your basic decisions.

Remember that whatever she does, your heroine's profession in a category romance is definitely a part of who she is, of her identity, of her self-confidence. Her accomplishments in this field make her more than just a pretty girl who is waiting around for a man to find her and make her Mrs. So-and-So. She takes pride in who she is and what she does.

Whatever professions you choose, be sure you can show your heroine and hero as *romantic figures*. Their occupations are dignified, dashing, fascinating or at least reasonably interesting. Their daily doings provide you with appropriate backdrops for one sensuous scene after another. Even if your heroine is sitting at her desk in a sterile office, be sure the motion of her shapely legs, the way she is dressed, the way she talks, make that office *seem* romantic. This is not a career handbook. Remember! This is a *romance.*

Your reader may be coming home after a long, hard day at a real-life job. She knows what that's like. Give her a dream job to escape into. Both the geographical setting and professional world in a category romance are part of the fantasy world where lovers meet and fall in love. Spin the tale. Weave the fantasy. Give your reader a romantic escape.

Professional backgrounds in an historical romance are quite another thing, and will depend largely on the exact period in which your story is set. Be sure that your swashbuckling hero could really have been doing what you chose for him. Get help from history books, research librarians, even professors of history, if you need to.

If you want your heroine to do something beyond looking absolutely gorgeous, your choices will not be so wide as your imagination must be. Our great-great-grandmothers were heavily restricted in their opportunities for activities outside of their homes. In the three historicals I mentioned at the beginning of this chapter the heroines were in the tobacco business, the endangered daughter of an aristocrat, and an actress.

By making the heroine an heiress to the fortunes of a powerful family, you can give her a career in the endeavor which sustains that fortune. You might want her to be employed as a governess to the children of some aristocratic or royal family, if you can use that common situation in an inspired way.

As I have said, her power often lies simply in her beauty and well-endowed figure, which place her in a position to be the power behind the throne.

If yours is a young adult heroine, remember that she is on her way to becoming the kind of woman you see in the adult category romance. She dreams of becoming not the assistant in a veterinary clinic, but the doctor; not a dancer in a chorus line, but the choreographer. Think of the doors that are open to her, that were not open to her mother. She can look forward to becoming a plastic surgeon, to running her own multinational corporation, to becoming a hot-air balloonist, for that matter. The sky is the limit.

Whatever settings and professional backgrounds you choose for your romance novel, be sure that your reader will yearn to go to that place; will dream of, or even seriously consider, doing professionally whatever it is your heroine does; or will wish she could have lived back in the days of your historical heroine, so that she could have been alluring to a hero as dashing as yours.

"Every book is different in terms of how I get the idea for it. My second book, **Forever My Love,** *came to me while I was at a production of* **Brigadoon.** *A lot of mist was rising over the Scottish Highlands. The orchestra was playing the overture and bagpipes were wailing, and the plot came into my head. I never once deviated from it while writing it."* **Rebecca Brandewyne, author of historical romances**

Points to Remember:

1. Fit the setting to the specific editorial requirements for your particular market. Contemporary novels require contemporary settings. Historical

romance settings should be true to the chosen period, and young adult settings should depict home, school, and family vacation sites.

2. Avoid packing absolutely everything about a place into long passages that read like travelogues. If your heroine arrives in London for the first time, show her visiting one or two places such as the Tower of London and Saint Paul's Cathedral, to give a general impression of the setting. Later, have her visit other places of interest with the hero in scenes of action and dialogue, and always with romantic overtones.

3. Make the setting an integral part of the plot. The romance could only take place in this particular setting because . . . (finish the sentence).

4. Instead of using an overworked geographical area (California wine country, New York City, Miami Beach), find some place off the beaten path. People fall in love everywhere, after all.

5. Weave your descriptive passages into scenes of dialogue and action. If the description stops the story, revise it so that it becomes only the incidental background against which the story is unfolding.

6. Unless you have a good reason, let all description of your setting flow through character viewpoint. Let the reader see, smell, taste, touch, and hear through the eyes, nose, lips, finger tips, and ears, as it were, of the heroine or viewpoint character.

7. Use character response to the setting to give insight into the kind of person the heroine is; do the same for the hero and other characters if using multiple viewpoint.

8. Be generous with the time you allot to research. If possible, go to the scene of your story. When using secondary sources, check and double-check information.

9. Rely heavily on sensuous words and phrases to create a thoroughly romantic world for your lovers to inhabit.

10. In choosing professions for your hero and heroine in a category romance, keep in mind how, where, and why they will meet. Will you need to use professional problems to create conflict between them?

11. Be sure your heroine holds a modern and responsible job—nothing menial.

12. Enrich your young adult romance with glimpses into a professional world or the world of a hobby or sport, if these blend well with the central problem of the book.

13. Always keep the story line the primary focus of your book. Use all researched background as you would gold thread in the weave of a fabric, to highlight the solid stuff of your story.

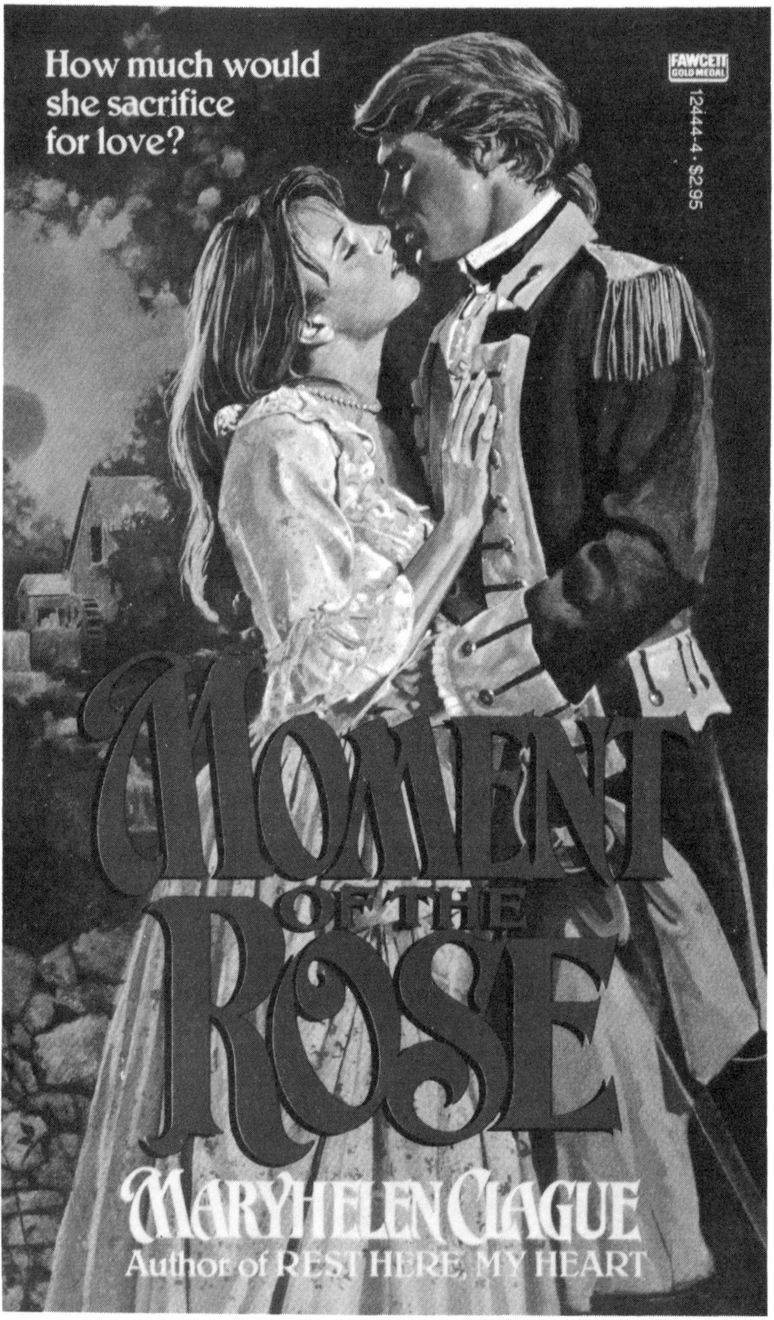
How much would she sacrifice for love?
FAWCETT GOLD MEDAL
12444-4 · $2.95
MOMENT OF THE ROSE
MARYHELEN CLAGUE
Author of REST HERE, MY HEART

Chapter **7.**
THE COURSE OF TRUE LOVE: Plotting Your Romance Novel

Think of yourself as an omnipotent Cupid with magic powers that allow you to see into the past, the present, and the future, and you'll take most of the pain out of plotting your romance novel. You have chosen two attractive people of the opposite sex, you have placed them in an exotic foreign setting or in an interesting American city or town, and now, with a wave of your wand, things will begin to happen.

The first thing that happens, preferably in chapter one, is the meeting between your heroine and hero. They exchange glances, and pow! the sexual chemistry starts to work between them.

But if they fell into each other's arms and escaped together into the moonlight or the boudoir, your novel would end right here. *You must not allow this to happen.*

In all fiction, there is always a central problem. In romantic fiction, the central problem is, by definition, the attainment of love. Neither the heroine nor the hero has found true and lasting love, and they cannot solve this problem until the final pages of the story. So, what do you do? You wave your wand again, and instantly dark clouds appear on the horizon in the form of *complications.*

Complications

The complications in romantic fiction are the obstacles placed in the lovers' path that keep them, for the time being, from the attainment of lasting love.

The first complication should be obvious in the moment your heroine and hero meet. Thereafter, as one complication appears to be almost solved, another raises its head, until the final scene in your novel, when they are all resolved.

"Ideas just fall on me! The idea for **A Promise to Cherish** *arrived while I was waiting for my luggage at the Jacksonville, Florida, airport. A suitcase like mine came by and I instinctively grabbed for it, then re-alized it wasn't mine. I thought, was a neat way for a heroine and hero to meet! I could set the tone of the whole book by what I put in the mixed-up suitcases."* **Lavyrle Spencer, author of contemporary and historical romances**

What kind of complications stand in the way of true love? The heroine might have heard rumors about the hero that put him in a bad light. It is said that he is a male chauvinist, or it is whispered that he is seriously involved with another woman. The heroine may misunderstand something he says, or he may simply appear to be arrogant, cool, and distant. Later, of course, she will discover that there was an understandable reason for his manner, or that she herself unknowingly caused his response to her. Or perhaps he is suffering the trauma of divorce, or grief over the death of his wife.

Complications can arise from within the heroine herself, such as crippling memories of a past love that ended badly, leaving her wary of becoming involved again.

Complications can evolve out of differences of opinion between the lovers on some subject of great importance to both of them, such as differing attitudes toward his or her career.

Some of these complications have been used over and over again. To interest an editor, make your complications new and exciting by giving them a different twist, or come up with something not usually used by other romance writers.

Whatever problems you give your hero and heroine, make this test. Basic sexual attraction is pulling the lovers together. For each complication, ask yourself, *is this complication really strong enough to push them apart?* If not, take it out and find a better one.

Sexual Tension—Plot Necessity

Perhaps the most essential ingredient in your plot is the element known as *sexual tension.* It must be present the moment these lovers meant for each other meet, and must remain throughout the book, even when they are not together but only thinking about each other. The sexual tension between them must be so strong that your reader can *feel* it. In fact, sexual tension is the fuel that must propel your plot from beginning to end.

What does this term mean? In analyzing your favorite romance novel, you underlined in red your heroine's attraction to the hero. You underlined in green her negative feelings about him. You saw the tug of war in her heart between the force of strong sexual attraction and the equally strong opposing forces of caution, fear, and reason. The passionate yearning of her heart came up against the cool dictates of her head.

This unresolved attraction between the hero and the heroine, which has not yet found peace in commitment, *is sexual tension.* It is in the air when they are in the same room; everyone can feel it. It is the forceful pull of sexual attraction.

The lovers are *pulled* together as if by a giant magnet. They are *pushed* apart by problems and complications. Will we be together forever? wonder

---

"An editor once said to me, 'The stronger the conflict the stronger the story.' To get over a hump, an author should analyze what would cause genuine conflict between two characters. When you deliberately pit two contrasting characters against each other, you develop conflict. Think of the **Odd Couple:** *the slob versus the very neat orderly man— and a story naturally comes."* Dorothy Dowdell, romance author

---

the hero and the heroine. Will they or won't they get together in the end? wonders the reader. Suspense keeps a mystery story going. Sexual tension keeps a romance novel going.

Now, *how do you create the push-pull of sexual tension?* The *pull* of that giant magnet is comparatively easy to create. What woman in her right mind wouldn't fall in love with your handsome, virile, and charming hero? And what normal red-blooded man wouldn't want to make love to your lovely heroine?

Pushing the lovers apart, however, requires some hard thinking. The sex drive is not easily turned off. To be convincing, this part of the equation must be as strong as the powerful attraction the hero and heroine feel for each other. Otherwise, it will seem contrived.

The best way to understand how this works in romance writing is to see it in action. The following scenes will illustrate it.

In *Wagered Weekend* (Dell Candlelight Ecstasy), a fast-paced contemporary romance by Jayne Castle, watch to see how this highly successful romance writer establishes the *pull* of attraction and the *push* of complication to come up with all-pervading sexual tension.

> *Savannah Emory was aware of him the moment he entered the room. Everyone was. It wasn't just his sheer size, although Cordell Harding's six feet, four inches of lean height and massive shoulders made him easy to spot in a crowd. Nor was it the surprising thick, uncompromising red of his hair. It was the fact that he was the boss and everyone at Mell North's party that night worked for him, including Savannah.*

This is the first glimpse we get of the hero, and immediately we feel his physical attractiveness and his importance. Savannah feels the *pull* of sexual attraction.

Cordell makes his way to Savannah's table, and the author takes us into her mind, giving us her conflicting feelings. (Notice how the author weaves in physical description at the same time.)

With casual deliberation she (Savannah) gave the cards in her hand one more shuffle, tilted her neat head of sleekly knotted seal-brown hair, and flashed her familiar smile at the others around her.
Out of the corner of her eye, she could see Harding was clearly en route to the card table. She wanted to be out of there fast.

The other card players try to dissuade her, but she replies,

"I always thought the best time to quit was when one was ahead."

We begin to wonder why Savannah allows her attraction for Cordell to be *pushed* away. More physical description follows, woven into the action as Savannah makes her way from the table. She is tall and elegantly proportioned, and moves with smooth coordination, but at just under six feet, she thinks of herself as an Amazon.

On page three of this opening scene, we see the motivation for Savannah's emotional conflict. A slightly tipsy card player pipes up with the beginning of the familiar proverb, "Unlucky in love. . . ," then stops abruptly when an embarrassed silence falls. Savannah tries to cover it up with a light quip, but her thoughts give us her true feelings.

You can't lose what you never had, she lectured herself for the hundredth time, and tried to ignore the argument that she'd come close to having Jeff Painter for her own. If she'd only had more time. But time was something denied her, thanks to the arbitrary business decisions of Cord Harding.

Then we learn that Cord has transferred Jeff to San Diego, where he fell for another woman and broke off his relationship with Savannah. For her, the *pull* of attraction meets the *push* of her anger.

Cord catches up with Savannah, and the pull against the push results in immediate sexual tension between them.

The characteristics that make Cord sexually attractive are described briefly but sharply (see capital letters), and Savannah's equally strong negative reactions to him are woven in (see boldface type).

"I understand you left the card table as the undisputed winner of the evening," said a DEEP, RICHLY MASCULINE VOICE behind her.
Savannah turned in surprise, seeing the WARM GOLD EYES narrowing in deliberation. **He was the last person she wanted to see tonight.** *Up close Cord Harding's RUGGEDLY CARVED FEA-*

> *TURES were dominated by a pair of* **ruthlessly** *PERCEPTIVE GRAY-GREEN EYES,* **arrogantly** *HIGH CHEEKBONES, A FORCEFUL CHIN and lines that reflected his thirty seven years of hard work and driving will fit together in a face that no one in his right mind would call handsome. Handsome implied SUPERFICIALITY and that was TOTALLY LACKING IN THIS MAN.*

Later Savannah plays the game of twenty-one with Cordell. She wants more than anything to win; she loses. Cordell says he'll give her one more chance, but the terms of the game are *his.*

> *"If I win," he said, making each word count heavily, watching her face to see the effect, "You'll spend the weekend with me. Beginning with dinner tonight."*

Savannah is shocked, but she agrees to the terms. Again she loses. How could any reader fail to turn the pages to the next chapter to see what happens when these two attractive but independent romantic characters are confined together for a whole weekend?

"For me, the hardest part is coming up with the plot—taking an idea or a character and creating a whole story. Plotting is like putting a puzzle together: You have to find the beginning, the middle and the end, and be sure all the pieces fit." **Shannon Harper, one half of Anna James, romance author**

You can be sure that as the novel continues, the sexual tension mounts when Savannah, against her better judgment, finds herself falling in love with Cordell.

Glory Land (Fawcett Gold Medal), a historical saga by Dorothy Dowdell, also begins with a scene that paves the way for the central complication in the love story to come.

Garnett, the heroine, is standing beside Roy Kingston, the man she plans to marry, aboard the clipper ship *North Star.* She is worried that her future father-in-law may not approve of her. He is the great Edward Kingston, builder of the transcontinental railroad over the Sierras. Perhaps Edward Kingston has chosen another woman for his son, Roy, to marry.

The *push* element in what will *really* be the central love story—Garnett will fall in love with Edward himself—has been cleverly established. Garnett fears that Edward Kingston won't approve of her, and he is her future father-in-law—two definite obstacles to the positive *pull* of her unexpected attraction to him.

When Garnett comes face to face with Edward Kingston for the first time, first we see his reaction to her:

> *King couldn't blame his son for wanting to be alone with this dazzling beauty who, in her innocence, had no idea what effect she had on a man. As he swallowed the last of his wine to dampen his dry throat, he felt a pang of regret that he was forty-three. Oh, God, if he were only twenty years younger.*

Then we learn of Garnett's feelings:

> *As she sat across the table from King thinking how handsome he was in a white dinner jacket and black cravat, she dared not exchange glances with him for fear she would give her feelings away like a gawky fourteen-year-old in the throes of her first infatuation.*
>
> *She turned to Roy and nodded at something he was saying, not actually hearing him. How colorless her fiance seemed in comparison with his father, like gray wool made drab by the wrong kind of light. His father's magnetism drained all his spark and personality, leaving him insecure and defensive.*

The room is alive with the sexual tension created by the push-pull of attraction versus complication (he is the father of the hero, after all), and it fuels the story right up to the final pages.

In most young adult romances, sexual tension, or the unresolved push-pull, is handled quite differently.

In the first place, as I've said, sexual encounters in these romances are generally very innocent, mostly hand holding and breathless sighs. The complication in the mind of the heroine usually arises from *secondary problems* in her life, such as being an only child, the middle child (as in the example that follows), or the youngest: or from family crises such as divorce, death, or moving away.

In other words, characters in the young adult romance are not involved in complex, passionate relationships with each other. Instead, both the heroine and the hero are involved more generally in the problems of growing up. These problems are usually worked out, or at least lightened, in the course of their romance. They each grow up a little. Usually secondary problems, rather than sexual tension between the hero and heroine are at the core of the plot.

In *Kate Herself* (Silhouette, First Love), a sensitive young adult romance by Helen Erskine, we see a good example of this.

We read on the back cover blurb that "Kate's an in-between girl. Not as sweet as her big sister, not as cute as her little one." Kate Fleming feels like a third bookend. That's why she's surprised when Ross Barrows, one of the most popular boys in school, asks her out.

In a tightly written scene, Helen Erskine sets Kate's inner conflict in motion.

> *"A movie?" she said.*
> *She still wasn't sure there was not some mistake.*
> *She'd hoped for a miracle with the beginning of her junior year—that she'd somehow attract the attention of a really exciting boy. But could it have happened so soon, the second week of school? Maybe he'd said he was going to a movie Friday night, and her imagination had done the rest. Her fantasies could be very real. Had he actually said, "Would you like to go to a movie Friday night?"*

The pull and the push—Kate's attraction to Ross versus her lack of self-confidence—are clearly illustrated in this scene. Kate wants badly to be Ross's girl, but she feels unsure of herself, like "a third bookend"; the middle-child syndrome. This type of conflict serves as the equivalent of sexual tension in the young adult romance.

Plot Climax in Romance Novels

Every plot must have a climax, and the romance novel is no exception. The climax is the point of highest dramatic intensity in your story, and usually the major turning point that brings on the resolution, or ending.

"Get your heroine up a tree and then throw stones at her. She must solve her problems herself—you can't have others intervene."
Patricia Matthews, romance author

The climax can be a stormy quarrel between the lovers, ending in a seemingly final parting. Maybe the heroine makes a discovery about the hero that throws her into uncertainty again, in spite of the happiness she so recently found in his arms.

The climax should evolve out of *the most important complication* between the lovers. For this reason, solve the smaller complications before you get to this scene, in ascending order of importance. Save the biggest for last.

A good example of a well-handled, carefully plotted climax scene occurs in *Her Decision* (Ballantine, Love & Life), by Irma Walker. The heroine, Alison Ward, Doctor of Veterinary Medicine, is a strongly motivated contemporary woman working in a field she loves. At age thirty, however, she feels a void in her life. She wants a child. The nesting instinct hits when she least expects it, a timely problem reflecting the feelings of many career women in real life.

Alison wants a child, but she isn't sure she wants a husband. She is disillusioned by her mother's many unhappy relationships and broken marriages.

Cole Hamilton, the hero, is equally wary of commitment because of an unhappy marriage. (Alison assumes Cole is divorced. Later, she learns he's a widower.) Alison realizes that Cole is:

> the obvious choice to be the father of the child she wanted so badly. He was intelligent, ambitious, obviously in perfect health, and she had no doubt he came from sturdy stock.

Eventually she invites Cole to dinner. After dinner, the two dance, and the sexual tension mounts between them until it explodes in passionate lovemaking, explicitly described. Because of the reservations each has regarding the lasting quality of love, they make no commitment, but Alison becomes pregnant. She is going to have the child she wants so desperately, alone, without Cole's help. Everything is as she wanted it to be. Or is it?

She delivers a healthy boy. The *climax scene* arrives when Cole comes to see the baby after he and Alison have been apart for some time. Alison has just nursed the baby, and the infant is now asleep.

> There was a sound at the door. She (Alison) looked up, into Cole's unsmiling face. For a long, long moment, they stared at each other, and then he came into the room, closing the door behind him.
>
> "I'm glad you came," she said, the words slipping out. "He—he looks like you."
>
> He didn't answer immediately; his eyes were guarded as he stared down at his sleeping son's face.
>
> "He's my son, all right," he said finally. "I've never doubted that part."
>
> Stung by his tone, by his coldness, her hands tightened around the baby. "Why did you come here?" she demanded.

> *"To see my son."* The purposefulness in his voice made her mouth suddenly go dry. *"I realize he should be with his mother these first few months, but I think it's only fair to warn you that eventually I intend to file suit for custody."*

What a climax! Alison realizes that Cole could very well win the custody suit. She is a single woman without the financial resources to give the child the kind of advantages that Cole Hamilton can provide. She stands to lose the baby she wanted so desperately.

This shocking and unexpected turn of events brings on the next element, which must always follow the climax scene:

The Romance Novel's Dark Moment

The dark moment following the climax scene is exactly what the words imply: a moment of great unhappiness for the heroine, when all she yearns to possess seems to be slipping away. Your plot will be stronger if you include such a scene.

In *Her Decision*, Alison tries to forget her disturbing encounter with Cole, but as the time comes for her to return to work, she is filled with anxiety. She must leave the baby with a neighbor, Mrs. Knowles, a dependable middle-aged woman who will give her son good care. But Alison has expenses she hadn't planned on, and she comes home at night, exhausted from her duties at the clinic, to a mountain of chores. The custody suit still is a threat. Irma Walker describes her heroine's *dark moment* in this way:

> *Like a small, dark presence, it (the custody suit), hung over her head, intruded upon her sleep, threaded through her days and nights. She couldn't even discuss it with Ginny (her friend), or her mother, because to say it aloud, to articulate Cole's threat to someone else, was to give it reality, something she couldn't bear to think about.*

The Romantic Resolution

After the climax scene has raised the level of sexual tension to its limit, and the dark moment has reduced the reader to despair, you bring the lovers together in a final lovely, loving, and, at last, harmonious scene of *resolution*. This scene demands your best writing. The reader has known all along that your heroine and hero were made for each other, and that eventually they would remove all obstacles in their path. Seeing how they work their way out of their difficulties provides the reader with exciting suspense. Now, in this final resolution of all complications, the reader needs to feel, of course, full satisfaction—as if the story could have ended in no other way.

"To become a successful writer of romance, consult your own emotions. Reach way down, below the surface, and find the core of the romantic woman you know you are. Project this into your characters, along with the tenderness, the confusion, the passion, and the glory of being in love." Helen Santori, a.k.a. Helen Erskine, author of contemporary and young adult romances

---

The resolution of a romance novel is like the last bars in a symphony, in which we hear the major themes repeated and everything brought together in one final harmonious chord.

Irma Walker is a consummate artist when it comes to plotting. She works everything out carefully in advance, and knows from the beginning of her novel where and how it will end. As we might expect, the resolution to *Her Decision* is well motivated and *believable.*

Cole does begin the custody suit, but later he drops it. Alison asks:

> *"Why did you drop the custody suit?" she (Alison) asked, just as if they had parted the day before instead of a month ago.*
>
> *"Because I finally had to admit the truth, that Jaimie wouldn't be better off without you. I could be a good father, yes, but I couldn't be the mother you are, Alison."*
>
> *"Then why did you put me through that hell, Cole?"*
>
> *"Because I was hurting. Because I thought I was doing the best for Jaimie. Because I didn't realize the truth until the hearing."*
>
> *"The truth?"*
>
> *"During the hearing, I finally understood that I was wrong about you—and about a lot of other things.*
>
> *"I realized that you could have won the custody suit simply by denying that I was Jaimie's father . . ."*

This exchange begins a string of explanations of all the misunderstandings that have stood between these two nice people, whose love for the child now overrides all personal considerations. Then, returning to the original problem, that Alison and Cole have both suffered disillusionment in love, the author shows us the breaking down of the last barrier. Alison and Cole have both admitted they were wrong in their first judgments of each other. They are honest at last.

> *"Will it always be the way it is now?" she said finally. "Can we keep on talking, listening to each other?"*
>
> *He shook his head. "No, not always. We're the walking wounded and we'll slip back sometimes. But maybe that isn't important as long as we don't lose sight of the important things."*
>
> *"Like what?"*
>
> *"Like loving each other. Like putting the two of us ahead of everything else. Like being loyal to one another."*
>
> *"Where do we go from here, Cole?"*
>
> *"We live together, stay together no matter what. Slug it out together. I'm willing to go for broke. How about you?"*

Of course, Alison is willing to take the big leap, now that she realizes that without Cole, without love, there's nothing.

Her Decision is 166 pages long. The reader has had to wait for this final, very tender, very believable resolution scene until pages 165 and 166.

In the historical romance, the elements of the plot—the central problem, complications, climax, dark moment, and resolution—are treated in the same way, but always within the context of the period and the setting of the book.

Of course, the manner in which women were raised and educated in the past, and the restrictions placed upon them, will color your choice of events in plotting an historical.

Again, plenty of sexual tension is necessary to keep the unresolved relationship between hero and heroine interesting and alive.

Pacing Your Novel

As you plan the scenes that will tell your story, whether you are writing a contemporary, historical, or young adult romance, you will want to plan them so that the action of the book is well balanced. Since you want the reader to be hooked in chapter one, you have started off either with dazzling action, an intriguing situation between the hero and heroine, or perhaps with your heroine's tumultuous inner thoughts.

In any case you need to plan your next scene or chapter with contrast in mind. A turbulent lovers' quarrel might be followed by a chapter full of the heroine's conflicting thoughts about the quarrel: her anger at the hero's despicable behavior versus her regret that she had been so touchy herself.

These quieter scenes allow the reader to reflect, along with the characters, on what is happening, and to have a rest before the next high point. Quieter scenes should balance scenes of action so that your novel is well paced—not too slow and not too fast, so that the reader can savor both.

How can you check the pace of your novel? You need an objective reader to give you an opinion on this, since you are so close to your material. But if you keep pace in mind now, as you plan your novel, you'll go a long way toward preventing pacing problems in the finished product.

Make a chart showing the number of scenes you plan for each chapter. Underline scenes of action in red. Underline scenes of reflection in green. Then note the balance. Pacing is subtle and important, and a skill you will develop with experience.

Questions to Help You Plan Your Plot

Good plotting is *planning ahead.* You may have devised a way of plotting that works well for you. If so, stick to it. However, if you're having trouble with your plot, ask yourself the following questions:

1. What is the primary or major problem that will push my heroine and hero apart?

Write the problem out on a large index card. You may have to write several versions of this conflict before it becomes clear in your mind.

Make sure your problem is suitable for the type of romance you plan to write. What would be suitable for a contemporary novel would certainly be out of place in an historical romance set against the background of the French Revolution. An idea suitable for fairly sensual adult romance, such as a Second Chance at Love novel, couldn't be used in a Silhouette First Love young adult romance.

2. What are my secondary problems?

Again, studying romance novels will help you understand the types of secondary problems used in each category. Make a separate index card for each secondary problem you plan to use in your story. For each of them, ask yourself, *how does this complicate the primary romantic problem?*

3. What event or events will bring on the climax or most intense crisis of my story, and the dark moment that follows?

4. What will happen in my last chapter to resolve all the complications that have kept my heroine and hero in conflict? What will release the sexual tension that has been building since chapter one?

It may take you some time to decide on these crucial events in your plot. Don't hurry. Don't fall into the trap of thinking, "Well, it really doesn't matter. I'm only writing a trifling romance."

The day when you could throw together a tired, much-used plot, or one that is so thin the light shines through, is gone. The market is growing more competitive all the time, and while there is always room for one more *good* romance writer, the careless, lazy writer will get only a rejection slip for his or her half-hearted attempt.

Your Working Outline

Now you are ready to put together all the ideas you have for your plot: it's time to make an outline of your novel. This is not the outline you will use to sell your book much later, as part of your proposal to an editor. (We'll discuss that in chapter thirteen.) This is your own *working outline.*

"First, I think about the plot a lot—it's all inside my head. I picture scenes and play around with the story and development, and then I start making notes longhand. If the book is historical, I do a lot of research, and I scatter research books all over the floor. Then I sit down at my word processor and put everything down, like seeds, and then go back and rework it. In most of my books, I rip out more pages than I leave in." Rosemary Rogers

---

The mere mention of the word *outline* makes many writers cringe and turn pale. Memories of structured outlines for high-school or college English classes haunt the mind, outlines in which alphabetical sequence and progression of Roman numerals were as important as content.

Cheer up! You can forget everything you ever knew about writing *that* kind of outline. The working outline that romance writers make are as different from that, and as different from one another's outlines, as their writing styles.

At this point, while you are still thinking through your idea, your working outline is your security blanket. It's not a straitjacket which will bind you irrevocably into your first ideas. It's a lifeline to which you can cling when the going gets rough, or if, as often happens, your writing is interrupted and your train of thought is broken.

The length and scope of your outline will depend on your market. The shorter category romances may only require an outline of six to ten double-spaced pages. A long (95,000- to 150,000-word) historical novel or family saga might demand an outline of thirty to fifty pages or more.

The purpose of your working outline is to help you take that exciting idea floating around in your imagination and flesh it out, so that you'll know whether or not it has enough substance to support the number of pages you must write.

The easiest way to write an outline is as follows:

1. Write in the present tense. Example: When Martha Davenport *meets* Kirk Weston for the first time, she *is* torn with conflicting emotions. Kirk *is* the man she once loved, but he *is* also the man who sent her father to prison.
2. Write your outline as you would tell a story, as a narration. Explain who the heroine and the hero are, where and how they meet, why they are attracted to one another, and what starts the conflict or primary problem between them. Describe the geographical setting briefly, not in detail.
3. What is your "plus," the "something different" that will set your novel apart from others of its kind? Include this in your outline so that you can plan events and scenes to show it off.
4. Explain the secondary problems—the complications—and how they affect the primary romantic problem.
5. List important scenes—crisis scenes, the dark moment, and the resolution scene. Where does each take place? What characters appear in each scene, and what specifically happens?
6. How will the story end? What will happen to bring the heroine and hero together for good?
7. Approximately how long will your novel be? How many chapters; how many words? Editorial guidelines will help you plan.

"I read a lot . . . newspapers, books. I never know when or where an idea will come to me. One time I wrote the entire plot for a romance novel during a sermon at church."   Helen Mittermeyer, a.k.a. Ann Cristy, romance writer

---

As I mentioned earlier, the manner in which you arrange this information is not important in this nuts-and-bolts outline, which is for your eyes only. But it will take time to write. It can't be done in an hour, an afternoon, or even in several days. You must live with your idea and think about it constantly as you go about your daily routine. If you have an idea about a certain element of your plot, jot it down on one of the index cards you carry with you at all times. If you don't, it will slip off into oblivion. Later, you can expand as you work with your outline on the typewriter.

Now let's look at another problem basic to planning your romance novel. You have your characters, setting, and plot, but what are you going to do about *viewpoint?*

LOVESWEPT • 1

Sandra Brown
Heaven's Price

21603-1 ★ $1.95 ★ A BANTAM BOOK

Chapter **8.**

FROM THE BOTTOM OF HER HEART...OR HIS?
The Question of Viewpoint

Skillful handling of viewpoint can be your most powerful tool in writing not only romance, but fiction generally. In real life, we seldom know what another person is really thinking until he is ready to reveal his thoughts to us. Only in fiction can we see into the hearts and minds of others, and in doing so, understand ourselves a little better.

But in working with creative writing students over the past twenty-plus years, I've found that the question of viewpoint causes more confusion than all other aspects of writing combined.

If viewpoint is clear to you, congratulations. Go to the head of the class. If you're still struggling with the meaning of viewpoint or with the problem of *staying in viewpoint*, be comforted. You are not alone.

If you are an aspiring romance writer, this chapter will shed light on this confusing subject. And even if you're an established pro, it doesn't hurt to review the basics every once in a while.

Viewpoint in Fiction

First, let's define the term *viewpoint* for any of you who haven't wrestled with this problem before.

Fiction is storytelling. *Once upon a time there lived a beautiful girl named Cinderella, who lived with her mean old stepmother and stepsisters.* So the story begins, and then unfolds as one event after another takes place.

But events of themselves do not a story make. In fact, the story isn't a story unless the events are happening *to someone.* That particular person is usually the *viewpoint character,* the one through whose perceptions the reader experiences the story.

In the tale of *Cinderella,* the reader identifies with Cinderella herself. When she is treated badly by her cruel stepmother and stepsisters, we feel sorry for her. We identify with her problems. When the fairy godmother comes along and makes it possible for Cinderella to have beautiful clothes and go to the ball, we rejoice. And when, finally, after losing the prince, she finds him again through the magic of the glass slipper, we're emotionally satisfied. We don't care what happens to the others in the story. They're only functional characters, symbolizing the darker side of life. Who cares what happens to mean people? But we sympathize with sweet Cinderella, trying to do her best, being knocked down continually. This is her story and she is our heroine.

Every story has a heroine or hero. If it is written in *single viewpoint,* that is, from one person's viewpoint only, it is most often the heroine or hero through whom the story flows. Everything that happens is told as that one character sees it, hears it, feels it, or thinks about it. Since the reader identifies with the viewpoint character, he or she cares about what is happening in the story to the same degree that the viewpoint character does.

It is only logical that the viewpoint character will usually be the hero or heroine, the one who stands to win or lose the most.

In *Cinderella*, the heroine couldn't possibly be the stepmother or either one of the stepsisters; the reader has no sympathy for them at all. Certainly the prince wouldn't go chasing over the land trying to find *them*, and he must have been considerably relieved when the glass slipper didn't fit their feet.

The character who stands to win or lose everything is Cinderella. If she wins, she'll have the prince and go to live in the castle. If she loses, it's back to the ashes for her.

In short, when a story is brewing in your head, ask yourself "Whose story is this, anyway?" and you'll have your viewpoint character, or principal viewpoint character.

In writing romance fiction, you'll usually choose your heroine as your viewpoint character. She should be the strongest, most memorable figure in your story. Why? Because most readers of romance fiction are women. They identify with the problems, the fantasies, the hopes, and the dreams of other women. That is why they are reading your book in the first place. You want your heroine to be as real and special to your reader as possible. The more vividly you can present her—heart, body, and mind—the better. Telling the story from her point of view usually accomplishes this most effectively.

"Readers are not interested in the mechanics of sex—they're interested in how the heroine feels when the hero looks at her or touches her."   **Karen Solem, romance editor**

But before you start writing, you need to decide whether you are going to write *strictly* from the heroine's viewpoint, or whether you'll opt to leave her eyes and ears occasionally, keeping her, though, as the principal focus of your story.

Single Viewpoint / If you are telling your story in *strictly single viewpoint*, at no time will you enter any other character's thoughts, or present any information that the heroine could not have seen, heard, or experienced herself. You will never describe her as someone would see her across a room, but always in terms of how she sees herself—in a mirror, thinking about her appearance, or in the hero's words as he tells her how she looks to him.

By and large, this has been the technique used in contemporary category romances until recently.

Brief Shifts of Viewpoint / In writing the contemporary category romance, I have said that you will want to use the viewpoint of your heroine to tell the story, and that you will stay within her thoughts and feelings at all times. There are two exceptions to this rule, however.

First, you will notice that some authors may open the story with a brief statement of *facts* about the heroine or the event of the opening scene.

This information is given *objectively;* that is, the author does not go into the *subjective* thoughts of any character. She merely reports—describes a place, an event, or an action, as a newspaper would—without reference to how anyone thinks or feels about what is taking place.

In category romances, objective narrative is usually used only at the beginning of the book, to help set the stage, and occasionally at the opening of a chapter. (In a long historical, however, the author may sprinkle such passages thoughout the book.)

The second exception to staying strictly within the heroine's viewpoint in the category romance occurs mostly in love scenes. More and more often, authors will shift briefly into the hero's viewpoint to give the reader a glimpse of how he feels in a tender or passionate moment. In general, guidelines will tell you whether or not the line you are aiming for encourages this shift in viewpoint.

If you do shift from the heroine's viewpoint in such a scene, you must make the transition as smooth as possible, and keep the shift fairly short. It is still the heroine's story. We'll look at examples soon.

Multiple Viewpoint / If you are writing an historical romance, a saga, an historical series, or a sprawling mainstream romance novel, the action might span several decades and involve a huge cast of characters. You would probably have to use *multiple viewpoint,* that is, the viewpoints of several characters, to tell your story. No one person could see and hear all the action, or be in several places at one time.

Multiple viewpoint allows you to enter the thoughts of more than one character. When you use this technique, however, *one character still predominates,* and is stronger and more central to the story than any other. It is still fundamentally this person's story. All the peripheral viewpoint characters exist to shed light on the character of the hero or heroine and on events in his or her life.

Viewpoint in the Contemporary Category Romances / If you are writing a category contemporary romance, the sooner you establish the heroine's viewpoint, the better. In that first paragraph or two, include if you can her name, her location, some indication of her physical appearance, and, most important, some of her inner thoughts and feelings. *The sooner the reader identifies with the viewpoint character, the better.*

Consider the opening of *Aphrodite's Legend* (Jove, Second Chance at Love), by Lynn Fairfax. Page one begins:

> *Jessica held her breath for one brief second as she looked down at the throng of society patrons filling the huge Central Gallery of the Manhattan Museum of Antiquities and Natural History. She smoothed her clinging togalike gown, in a lustrous shade of spring green, over her slim hips. Her tapering fingers traveled back up the length of her long, well-proportioned torso to check the drape of material covering her left shoulder. It was too daring a dress, she thought suddenly and with a self-consciousness she hadn't known in years. No, a foolish dress, she decided, designed too closely along the lines of the garments associated with that legendary goddess who'd brought Jessica her early fame and fortune as an archeologist.*
>
> *Aphros. She sighed at just the thought of that isolated Greek island where, nearly ten years before, while only in her teens, she'd made her most famous discovery. All because of Aphros—and Aphrodite, of course—was she, Jessica Lofting, the celebrity who would turn heads tonight as she moved through the crowd in the Gallery below.*

I think you'll agree that this is an effective beginning. Jessica is the heroine and the viewpoint character. In the first line we jump immediately into her thoughts, and in two short paragraphs we learn a great deal about her. We know where she is, what she is wearing, that she has slim hips and tapering fingers. We know that she is an archaeologist, and that she is in her mid to late twenties.

We have learned all this in her viewpoint, by being part of her own thoughts about herself. Most important, we know that she is feeling self-conscious and nervous. She holds her breath, and we learn why as we read on. A man, of course; her ex-husband, whom, we're told, she hasn't seen since their divorce, but for whom she still feels fascination. In the first four pages, the author hooks us into the plot and enables us to identify with the heroine, Jessica, and her problems.

Let's look at another example of an opening in which the reader is pulled quickly into the story through a strong introduction of the heroine, the viewpoint character. This second example comes from *Bitter Victory*

(Silhouette, Special Edition), a longer contemporary romance by Patti Beckman. Notice that the author uses one sentence written *objectively* (see boldface type) before entering the viewpoint of Veronica Huntington.

> **Veronica Huntington tossed the newspaper onto the top of her refinished desk.** *It was no concern of hers, she thought bitterly, that Slade was running for one of the highest offices in the state. He had always been ambitious. Too ambitious, Veronica remembered with a pang. Still, she thought, a man like Slade had no business being a senator. He was too morally corrupt.*
>
> *The photograph of the dashing silver-haired man Veronica had fought so hard to forget smiled confidently at her from the front page of the paper. For a moment Veronica couldn't tear her gaze from the rugged features, the broad forehead, the strong chin, and the depth of his intelligent brown eyes.*
>
> *"No, I won't fall into that trap again!" she muttered aloud. "He may be devilishly good-looking with that shock of silver hair, but I know what a rat he really is."*

The first sentence places Veronica at her desk. In the next sentence we jump immediately into her mind and into her central problem. Veronica is fighting her attraction to Senator Slade. We learn what he looks like and something about his character, and we can guess that he will cause her a lot of trouble before the story is finished.

In this book, the heroine herself is not described until page 16. Notice how skillfully the author handles this:

> *"Welcome home, my lusty little Aussie girl," he (Slade) murmured. His fingers buried themselves in her thick hair. "I've often, late at night, pictured you with that chestnut mane tumbling down around your bare shoulders, those bronze freckles across your stubborn chin. I've thought about the proud way you cock your head. I remember your exclamations of pleasure when we made love, and remember often seeing you in the shower, with water slick and glistening on your leggy, rangy body."*

Through Slade's words, we not only get a vivid picture of what Veronica looks like, but also a good idea of her character: stubborn, proud, lusty.

By having Slade describe Veronica, the author has not broken viewpoint. With the exception of dialogue—words spoken aloud by other characters—the reader experiences the story entirely in Veronica's viewpoint.

You can see that getting immediately into the mind of the viewpoint

> *"Even when you are writing strictly from the heroine's viewpoint, the hero has still got to be thinking. He's still got to be a character. He can't be just a wooden figure or a piece of paper. He still has to be real."* Georgette Livingston, a.k.a. Diane Crawford, romance author

character not only gives the reader a character with whom she can identify, but in the process hooks her on the problem of the story.

Brief Shifts into the Hero's Viewpoint in the Category Romance / As the heroine battles out her conflicting emotions in the heat of the hero's embrace, what does *he* feel? See how skillfully Janet Joyce has handled a brief transition into her hero Devlin Paige's thoughts (in boldface type), as he embraces heroine, Raine Morgan, in *Winter Lady* (Silhouette, Desire).

> *Raine felt cold. He (Devlin) was monumentally egocentric, thinking only of his own desires, with never a care of her own feelings. Her mouth thinned and she averted her face, denying him even the slightest softening of understanding. She had wanted him, still wanted him, but Devlin Paige desired her passion only on a physical level. She wanted far more from him and doubted that he was capable of giving it to her.*
> **Sitting close to her, Devlin realized several things at once. She was terribly hurt, she was as beautiful as he had remembered, and he was steadily losing ground. He shut his eyes momentarily to savor her sweet feminine scent . . . She was getting to him and his temper was near the boiling point. Most women let him handle everything with no questions, but this one, this one not only required explanations but made him feel like he had egotistically mishandled the entire episode. He was determined to crack through the defensive barrier she had erected against him and his lips quirked upwards. No understanding and welcoming smile for me, Raine? We shall see, Snow Maiden, we shall see, he said to himself. He allowed her to sulk for a few more minutes before he went on the attack again. He needed to see if she had shut down her reactions to him on all levels . . .**

Then notice the smooth transition back into Raine's viewpoint:

> *Raine sat mutely, trying to strengthen herself against the effect of his*

nearness with her internal sensors screaming alarms to her entire body. Her view was limited to the compelling liquid brandy of his eyes and the gold lights which ignited his pupils. "Don't," she whispered, but her breathlessness was more invitation than denial and he smiled, indulgently. The taste of his mouth was thrillingly familiar, sapping her resistance as he stroked her tongue with enticing probes meant to excite her response. All thought was centered on the overpowering touch of his lips . . .

Multiple Viewpoint in the Historical Romance / As I've said, the scope of a big historical romance demands that the story flow through the experience of several characters. This means that you must use multiple viewpoint.

Just as in a contemporary category romance, an historical romance usually opens with the focus on, or about to be on, the heroine. She might not actually be on stage in the opening scene. The reader might be introduced to her through the eyes of the hero who overhears a conversation about her before he meets her, or even through the thoughts of a minor character. But whether the heroine is introduced directly or indirectly in the first few pages, we know it is she who will dominate the story.

If you introduce the heroine through a secondary character's viewpoint, the shift into the major viewpoint should follow fairly quickly. A good example of this is seen in *The Marriage Contract* (Fawcett Gold Medal), Virginia Nielsen's historical romance.

Notice that the first sentence is objective narrative (see boldface), in no character's viewpoint. The second sentence brings us into the mind of Madame de l'Ouvrier. The last line in the third paragraph (in boldface type) leads into the shift of viewpoint, which occurs in the fourth paragraph; there we enter the mind of Amalie, her youngest daughter, and become aware that she will be the central figure in the story.

Had it not been marred by an unfortunate intrusion, the entertainment Monsieur and Madame de l'Ouvrier gave at their plantation, Les Chenes, to honor their guest, young Armand, le Comte de Valerun, would undoubtedly have been called incomparable by that little band of émigrés who had succeeded in transplanting a small remnant of Versailles, to this remote bayou wilderness of Louisiana. *Instead, as Madame de l'Ouvrier told herself in angry humiliation, it was to become one of the most memorable.*

Her friends, alas, were amused, and her enemies delighted. Her usually mild and somewhat vague husband was in a temper. The elder of her two daughters, Claudine, for whose benefit the elaborate affair had been staged, seemed to be in a daze. What Monsieur le Comte thought, no one knew.

Fuming, Madame de l'Ouvrier did not even wonder what her younger daughter thought. Amalie (the heroine), after all, was not yet of marriageable age. **But Amalie, dark eyes sparkling, was wickedly enjoying herself.**

The transition line is a small bridge, allowing the reader to shift painlessly from Madame de l'Ouvrier's viewpoint into Amalie's. The next paragraph is given in Amalie's viewpoint:

Maman had really outdone herself for Count de Valerun's visit. Anchored out in the bayou was a flatboat, transformed into a veritable fairyland by a profusion of flowers and colored paper lanterns whose glowing lights were reflected in the still dark water.

The description goes on with vivid details of the preparations and festive touches as seen through Amalie's eyes.

Throughout the book the author manages to weave skillfully in and out of the minds of several characters, always anchoring our interest in Amalie and keeping her central to the story.

It takes good control and expert technique to make such shifts of viewpoint from one character to another within a single scene. Ms. Nielsen, an established writer with many novels to her credit, intentionally structured her opening as she did to establish the historical background and the moods of the various family members, and then to throw the spotlight on the youngest daughter. *Amalie was wickedly enjoying herself* is a line sure to arouse reader interest and curiosity.

If you are new to romance writing, and you want to use multiple viewpoint in an historical or in a longer contemporary, it is probably wise to make your viewpoint shifts from chapter to chapter until you feel completely comfortable with multiple viewpoint. You'll save yourself many headaches.

Some authors are so proficient and so much at ease with multiple viewpoint that they can make a viewpoint shift within a paragraph. Unless the transition is made smoothly, however, the result is complete confusion for the reader, so I advise you to work up to this skill gradually.

Viewpoint in the Young Adult Romance / Young adult romances are written in single viewpoint because, again, this is the best way to establish immediate reader identification. The heroines here are fifteen to sixteen, the readers even younger—somewhere between twelve and fifteen. These young readers identify with the heroine, the girl in the story who is like the girl they dream of becoming.

One difference in the use of viewpoint in young adult romances is that some of these books are written in the *first person*, using the pronoun *I*. Although gothics are also told sometimes in the first person by the heroine, it is rare to find a category romance or an historical written in anything other than third person, that is, using the pronouns he and she.

In young adult romances, however, use of the first person is very effective. The heroine can tell about her problems in an intimate way which brings the young reader even more directly into her feelings.

Let's look at two examples of viewpoint in the young adult romance—one written in the third person, the other, in the first person.

Beth is the heroine and viewpoint character in *I've Got a Crush on You* (Scholastic, Wildfire), by Carol Stanley. The book opens with dialogue, which shows us right away that Beth is spunky and humorous. Then objective narrative (in boldface type) is used to locate the speakers, Beth and Matt, for the reader. More dialogue follows, and then we enter Beth's viewpoint, where we stay for the rest of the story.

> *"You think you can find another girlfriend for rainy nights?"* Beth asked Matt.
>
> *"What do you mean?"*
>
> *"I don't think the top on this thing (Matt's car) is real watertight. I'd be willing to let someone else get drizzled on."*
>
> **They were sitting in the ancient MG Matt had bought the week before, being pulled along—by a chain attached to the front bumper—through the Speedee Car Wash on the corner of Elm and Bryant. A steady trickle of water was running down the inside of the door on Beth's side.**
>
> *"I guess you'll have to snuggle up closer to me,"* Matt said.
>
> *"I think just sitting in a car this small qualifies as snuggling."*

The car comes out of the car-wash and the dialogue continues:

> *"Top down?"* he asked her.
>
> *"That's what you bought it for, isn't it, to feel the wind through your hair and the envious eyes of pedestrians upon you?"*
>
> *"Actually, I thought it might help me attract the right sort of girl, the kind who doesn't make fun of me so much."*
>
> *"I know a couple of nice, meek ones,"* Beth told him. *"I'd be glad to fix you up."*

She knew she was safe, that—teasing and all—Matt would rather be out with her than with any other girl at Hamilton High. Which was a nice secure feeling.

She could see him in fifteen years as the kind of guy who played the father in one of those family TV shows. The problem was that, more and more, she could not see her own future resembling anything she saw on TV.

You can see how effective it is to lead the reader straight into the heroine's viewpoint and right into her problems, and that there are many ways to do this. A blend of dialogue and objective narrative, leading into the inner thoughts of the viewpoint character, guide us nicely into the story. We now know that Matt has a crush on Beth, a crush she doesn't exactly reciprocate. What will she do about this? We are already involved in her dilemma.

Now let's look at a young adult romance written in single viewpoint, first person. *P.S. I Love You* (Bantam, Sweet Dreams), by Barbara Conklin, opens with a short foreword. After the first four paragraphs, the reader already feels that she knows the heroine, Mariah Johnson, and is intrigued to learn more about her romance with Paul Strobe. As you read this, ask yourself how the material is strenghtened by being written in the first person. You might want to try rewriting it in the third person to compare the effect.

In one corner of my room there stands a creamy white-topped vanity table, dressed in yellow and white ruffled organdy. I made the skirt a long time ago, all by hand, long before my mother bought our sewing machine that does everything.

Attached to the vanity are three mirrors, hinged together and when tipped a certain way, I can see three of myself from three different angles. For sixteen years, I've watched myself grow up in those mirrors and sometimes when I peer intently into them, I can not only see the outside of me, but the inside as well; the soul of me that no one can see—but me.

The most important part of this little table is not the creamy white-ness of the smooth top, not the cascade of carefully handmade ruffles, not even the three revealing mirrors. It is the shiny yellow bumper sticker I have pasted to the top of the middle mirror. It reads, P.S. I Love You.

The city of Palm Springs is proud of that bumper sticker. You can see it on so many cars all over California. I remember how hard I fought against our trip to that city the summer I turned sixteen, and now I know if I hadn't gone, I would have never met Paul. I would have never experienced the exhilarating joy of knowing him, of loving him, the agonizing frustration of knowing how it would all end.

In these examples, the viewpoint character is introduced immediately. The reader doesn't have to fumble through several pages wondering who the story is going to be about. In either third person or in first (as in the last example), the viewpoint of the heroine, once established, is rarely broken, except in the adult contemporary category romances. There the writer may change viewpoint very briefly if a shift into the hero's viewpoint during a love scene seems appropriate, or if brief passages of objective narrative are necessary.

Points to Remember

When you are thinking about your characters and plotting your romance novel, ask yourself the following questions about how you plan to handle viewpoint. If you can make most of these decisions ahead of time, before you start the actual writing, you will prevent many problems that might otherwise erupt.

1. Will you use single or multiple viewpoint?
2. Is your choice in keeping with the requirements stated in the editorial guidelines (if any) for the specific publisher you have in mind?
3. Select at least five romance novels that use viewpoint as you plan to, and study each one. Were there places where the author shifted viewpoint? If so, why? How long was the shift—a few sentences; a few paragraphs, a chapter? Did the author accomplish his or her purpose?
4. If you are writing in single viewpoint, will you need to shift into the hero's viewpoint—very briefly—in a love scene? How will you handle the transition?
5. If you are going to use *multiple viewpoint,* into how many characters' minds will you need to go? Name them, and be sure you have a *reason* to use each one as a viewpoint character. (Reminder: It is easier to shift viewpoint between chapters than to do it within a scene.)
6. If you will use single viewpoint, which is best, first or third person? Is your choice in keeping with the specific requirements stated in the guidelines of the publisher you have in mind?
7. The major portion of your romance novel will be told *subjectively* by the viewpoint character (and possibly other characters) through that person's or those persons' thoughts and feelings. Will you need to use an occasional passage of objective narrative? For what purpose? In which scenes? (Reminders:
   a. Short contemporary category romances use a minimum of objective

narrative. Longer historical romances, family sagas, and longer contemporary novels, such as Superromances, allow a little more. In young adult romances, the *less* objective writing, the better.

   b. If you must use short passages of objective narrative, use them sparingly. Remember that emotional impact comes from the subjective voice of your viewpoint character. Your reader will respond emotionally only to what is taking place *in viewpoint.*)

8. After writing two or three chapters of your novel, ask yourself if your viewpoint character—most likely your heroine—is coming through easily. Or does she seem stiff and lifeless? Are you continually putting words in her mouth, or is she giving you the words? She should be. If she isn't, take time out to get to know her better.

58

0-515-06411-4 1/A SECOND CHANCE AT LOVE BOOK

Second Chance at Love

THE
GOLDEN
TOUCH

ROBIN JAMES

Chapter 9.
THE HARSH AND TENDER WORDS OF LOVE: Creating Lively Dialogue

When your heroine and your hero gaze into each other's eyes and whisper words of love, or when they glare at one another and spar in verbal combat, their romance comes alive for the reader. Dialogue is the living, breathing part of your romance novel. Description and narrative set the stage and tell what's going on behind the scenes, but when your characters are talking to each other, they are "on stage," alive, and visible. They may pour their hearts out, or just say what they think they should. But in either case, when they speak for themselves, your characters *show* the reader who they are.

As we discussed in chapter three, one of the main purposes of dialogue is, indeed, to reveal character. Dialogue also allows two characters—in romance fiction, primarily the hero and heroine—to relate to each other. No amount of narrative can illustrate fully how these two interact. What he says to her and how she responds is the core of their relationship. And hearing these two argue or whisper words of love gives your story an immediacy that nothing else can.

"Dialogue is fun to write. You can quickly catch the reader up on what has happened in the past or jump right into what's happening in the present. You can make your story move at a rapid pace when your characters are talking." **Shannon Harper, one half of Anna James, romance author**

Thus dialogue will be your best vehicle for creating and sustaining sexual tension between your lovers. You will show them locking verbal horns. You will show them trading sweet nothings or passionate declarations. You will show her saying, "No!" when her heart is wildly beating and her inner voices are saying "Yes!"

And all along the way you will be using dialogue to accomplish its basic functions: to characterize, to give necessary information, to show action and move the plot forward, to foreshadow coming events, to allow a character to reflect on an event that has just taken place. You may also use it to inject humor, to give relief from longer passages that show a character's inner thoughts, or to pick up the pace and allow the reader to skip along enjoyably for a while, following short bits of banter.

All dialogue must serve a purpose. If any dialogue you have written does not accomplish one of these things, *take it out.*

Because dialogue accomplishes so much in fiction, writing it is a skill you will do well to develop. In fact, dialogue will constitute a major portion of your book.

In chapter three, you scanned a sampling of chapters in romance novels and estimated what percentage of each was dialogue. You might want to review them now. Do the percentages for those chapters hold true for the book as a whole? Is fifty percent of the book dialogue? Sixty? In a young adult romance, dialogue can make up as much as ninety percent of the book. As you can see, it is time to learn how to write it.

Hearing Your Dialogue

To be convincing, those words printed in quotation marks must seem to the reader to be coming straight from the mouths of your characters. Writing effective dialogue takes practice, and requires developing an ear for the words your characters would naturally say to one another.

One of the best ways to train yourself to catch the rhythm of dialogue is to read it aloud. Settle in again with several of your favorite romance novels and *speak* the dialogue as if you were reading roles in a play.

While you are at it, locate in each book the first words the hero and heroine say to each other. Read these passages aloud, too. Now find the last conversation they have together, at the end of the book. Ask yourself, what does that first conversation tell you about each of the lovers? What problems in their relationship are apparent right there at the start? On that final page, do you feel that at last they speak from their hearts and in their true voices?

Is some of the dialogue from your own book ready for scrutiny? Read that aloud, or, better still, have someone else read it to you. The rough spots, the stilted phrases, the unnecessary verbiage will all stand out like porcupine quills.

Playwrights know the need for testing their dialogue before they take their plays to Broadway. They play to small towns first, and if some lines don't draw the audience response they intended, they rewrite the scene.

Does your dialogue *flow?* That is, does it seem natural, easy, comfortable? When your characters talk, they should not sound like you. Nor should each character sound like every other character. Does each player on your stage seem to speak with a voice distinctly his or her own? Try to give each of them a few special phrases of his or her own to repeat from time to time.

Using Dialogue to Characterize

The more intimately you know your characters, the better your dialogue will be. The things they are thinking and feeling, or the situations they are in, will determine the words they say.

Dialogue, in fact, is an integral part of characterization. In what she says, your heroine will reveal her femininity, her attitude toward herself, her feelings for and against the hero. Your hero will reveal himself to be tantalizingly masculine, self-assured, humorous, or gentle at various points in your story, depending on the words he chooses.

"My characters start out as cardboard people. Then small things like pockmarks start showing up on cheeks, and speech patterns begin to emerge. Speech is very important—no two persons talk the same way, and you don't want your characters all sounding the same. I hear my characters speaking to me." **Parris Afton Bonds, romance author**

No two people speak alike in real life, and to forget this fact when writing dialogue is an unpardonable sin for a writer. No two characters will be in exactly the same situation, and each has a very different background, which you have worked out in his or her character biography.

Even in families, where ties are close and hereditary factors give a similarity to tone and timbre of voice, speech still varies widely. Age, health, mood, and, above all, personality color the tone, tempo, and spirit of speech.

Geographical background also affects speech: the soft drawl of the Southerner, the twang of the Midwesterner, and the down-East accent of some New Englanders are only a few of the wide variations. You will have to consider your setting and the individual backgrounds of your characters as you imagine how they would speak.

If your hero is a doctor, lawyer, or engineer, it is likely that his highly specialized profession has contributed a few words to his vocabulary. If your heroine is a writer with a new word processor, you may have to force her not to speak as if in a foreign tongue! But let her show off her new vocabulary a little.

If you are writing an historical romance, put words into the mouths of your characters that were actually in use during the period of your story. "You turn me on," would never do for a Revolutionary War hero. And teenagers in a young adult romance will speak in current slang, at least to some extent.

So the first rule for writing good dialogue is this: make sure the words fit the character's personality, general situation, mood of the moment, geographical and professional background, age, and sex.

Then, if you have done all that but still feel that you're stuffing words into your characters' mouths, take it as a warning that you haven't lived with them long enough to know how they would really speak and what they would really say. In other words, you don't yet know what is inside their heads and hearts.

When you flesh out all the facets of a character's personality and temperament, dialogue will flow naturally from that character's mouth. You're no longer programming words for a puppet. Instead, your character is actually speaking. You hear the words because the character has become real to you. It's all you can do to catch the conversation and put it down on paper fast enough.

If this moment hasn't come for you, go back to your character biographies and ask all the basic questions over again. Develop your characters fully, so they can come alive.

Dialogue is also the way to make full use of your minor characters. Even when these characters are simply functional, serving as foils for the heroine or hero, you can give them personality and reality. Is the Other Woman in your story cruel, scheming, or stupid? Show that in her speech. Focus on the one aspect of a minor character that serves the purpose of your story.

And don't forget to use your minor characters freely to bring in information that would make boring narrative. Let two minor characters exchange in dialogue the peripheral but necessary facts you need to tuck in along the way.

Building Sexual Tension with Dialogue

I have said that you should use dialogue between your heroine and hero to build up sexual tension between them. Their conversations must either bring out the love they really feel for each other—the *pull* between them—or show the conflicts that *push* them apart. Or both.

Since conflict and misunderstanding go on for most of the novel, you are likely to alternate between passionate words, spoken in sincere adoration, and words of rage and tantrums, as the two rail against each other. Most often, you will need to combine the push-pull in every scene in which the two are together. How do you show that although these two desire each other, they are fighting the fact tooth and nail?

Dialogue is made up of the *words spoken, speech tags*, and *bits of business*. We'll get to speech tags in a moment. Bits of business are gestures, movements, and facial expressions, as well as the short narrative interspersed between spoken words that show the reader the unexpressed emotions of the speakers.

To orchestrate a scene for high sexual tension, have the words of the dialogue run counter to the unspoken thoughts in your heroine's or hero's head.

For example, play the spirited independence in the heroine's words against her inner longing to be enveloped in the hero's arms. Show the hero's frustration with her attitude in a torrent of angry words. If you are also using his viewpoint, let us know that his unspoken desire to possess her is reaching explosive intensity. If you are staying strictly within the heroine's viewpoint, you can indicate the hero's hidden passion for her by putting a seemingly incongruous look of longing into his eyes as he speaks angrily, and let her wonder about it.

You can end the scene with one of them hurling a final verbal brickbat at the other and then stomping off. Or you can let the heroine reveal her vulnerability for a few brief moments as she melts into the hero's arms. As soon as the embrace has been savored by lovers and reader, however, get right back to the *push* with some new misunderstanding, further evidence of her irritating independence or a sign of possible insincerity on his part—all brought to light, of course, in lively dialogue.

Let's see the push-pull of sexual tension in some dialogue from a contemporary category romance. In *Bird of Paradise* (Jove, Second Chance at Love), by Winter Ames, the story takes place in Panama, where the heroine, Sara Mancini, and her hero, Eric Thoreson, have been separated by a bad storm. Watch the counterpoint of bits of business which reveal inner passion (in boldface), played against the melody of angry dialogue:

> *"You didn't have to come charging out into the storm. I managed perfectly well and would have made it back on my own."*
> **He came toward her, his eyes lit by an inner fire, which glowed brightly as the burning wood.** *"If you lived that long. Do you have any idea how many ways there are to get killed out here?"*
> *"I can take care of myself."*
> **He grabbed her shoulders and pulled her close.** *"Si. So you have reminded me on several occasions. Damn you and your independence, Señora Mancini. You've put me through hell tonight, Si . . . more than tonight. I have been on a rack since the day I first met you."*
> **She put her hands against his chest to push him away, but the warmth, combined with the heady scent of him, made her hesitate. On their own volition her fingers brushed against the thick mat of hair exposed where his shirt was unbuttoned at the neck.**
> *He swore softly. "Be warned. I have reached my limit, Sara. I will not permit you to destroy me in this way."*

"How could I possibly destroy you?"

"From the inside out, Sara. You've been eating away at me since you came here. All I can think of is you, needing you, wanting you. Each time I take you in my arms something happens to take you away."

"If that's true, Eric, then we must be plagued by twin devils." **She wound her arms around him, pulling his mouth down to hers.**

Although Sara speaks negative words, "on their own volition" her fingers reach for Eric's hair. Let your heroine's words reject the hero while her body does the opposite. Dialogue in romance fiction is an integral part of love-making. While arms enfold and fingertips brush intimate places, the murmurings and the whisperings of love are just as intimate, and add excitement to the scene both for the characters and for the reader.

And as they get to know each other, light banter between your hero and heroine can be arousing, flirtatious, and sexy. Notice in the following example how the author has brought out the underlying sexual tension, which is already present, in what is nearly the first conversation between the hero and the heroine.

The book is *Lover From the Sea* (Dell Candlelight Ecstasy), by Bonnie Drake. The heroine, April Wilde, has rescued the nameless hero from the sea and taken him into her isolated Nantucket cottage. He is speaking.

"Well, I can't just lie here. There must be something I can do to keep busy . . ."

"There is."

She should have felt it coming, yet despite the strong vibrations coursing through her own body, she was unprepared. When he lowered his head, she froze. Then his lips touched hers lightly, tasting and teasing in feather-faint brushes, moving across her closed mouth in gentle exploration. When he drew back, the light of desire shone bright from deep within his dark and mysterious depths.

"Can you kiss back?" he murmured softly.

Hers was a fast whisper in return. *"No."*

"You seem very sure. Why is that?"

"I don't even know you."

"To the contrary. I'd say"—a black eyebrow arched roguishly into his forehead—*"considering the fact that I was stark naked in your bed when I awoke this morning, that you can't consider me a total stranger."*

"That was different," she argued quickly, her cheeks flaming. *"Your clothes were drenched. If I hadn't taken them off, you might*

have caught pneumonia. I acted out of pure necessity. But . . . I don't even know your name . . . nor do you!"
    He grew more serious, his voice dropping in deep flow. "Does that really seem so important right now?"

Notice how Bonnie Drake has used bits of business to control timing and tone, as in this sentence: *"To the contrary. I'd say"*—a black eyebrow arched roguishly into his forehead—*"considering the fact . . ."* etc. Having that eyebrow arch in mid-sentence is somehow suggestive, even sensual. Go back and read the sentence without the arching eyebrow, and compare the effect.

Bits of business should always be used in this way, that is, interjected between or into lines of dialogue in short takes. Don't block the flow of conversation with long chunks of narration, except, as in the third paragraph above, to describe a kiss, or lovemaking in a passionate scene. In a sensual romance novel, you always make room for description of the physical side of love.

Whether your lovers are just breaking the ice or deep in passion, use dialogue to show them and their relationship as fully and as appealingly as you can.

Speech Tags and Punctuation

Speech tags are the "he saids-she saids" that tell the reader who is speaking. You have the choice of sticking to the simple "said" and risking monotony or of reaching for alternatives which can become ridiculous if allowed to get out of hand. It is easy to be carried away making one tag more elaborate than the last.

Personally, I consider the fancier speech tags excess baggage. Once the speakers are identified, as are Michelle and Dominic in my example below, it is not necessary to clutter the scene even with "said," much less with "cried," "shouted," "exclaimed," or "uttered," until a third person enters the scene. The scene might begin like this:

"I told you, I'm not going with you to the party," Michelle said. "I have no intention of allowing your wife to make a fool of me again."
    "Ex-wife," Dominic corrected.
    "What's the difference? You're still as good as married to her—the way she keeps you jumping."
    "That's a lie!"
    "Well, you go running every time she calls."
    "Only in emergencies. Never because I want to."

If Michelle and Dominic are the only two in the scene, the dialogue itself identifies the speakers. If another character joins them, then start the identification tags going again.

If you are unsure whether or not you should identify a character's dialogue with "he said," try reading the passage aloud. Bear in mind, however, that on the printed page, the use of quotation marks helps to set off the characters and reduces the confusion as to which one is speaking.

New fiction writers often have difficulty in determining the proper way to write dialogue into a scene. Here are a few guidelines that will make the task easier.

1. As you know, the words the character says are placed *within* the quotation marks. Example:
   "Sorry, Debbie. I didn't mean to hurt your feelings."
2. Punctuation—the comma and periods above—is part of the dialogue and is placed inside the last set of quotation marks.
3. A separate paragraph is required for each character who speaks—*even if that character says just one word.* Example:
   "May I see you again?" he asked.
   "No!" she cried.
   "Why?"
   "Because."
   "Tell me," he demanded. "I have a right to know."
   "If you must know, I'm married."

If, for some reason, dialogue runs on for several paragraphs, repeat the initial set of quotation marks but do not close the paragraph with the second set until the speech is ended. However, it is rare in a romance novel to have such a long stretch of unbroken dialogue. Most dialogue in this genre is short, continuing for one brief paragraph of six or eight lines at the most.

In fact, if your heroine is delivering a long tirade, you would do well to break up her utterances into two or three short paragraphs rather than to keep it in one long block. It is easier to read short paragraphs, and the reader's pace will not be slowed.

In general, though, you will not have this problem. Dialogue is brief in the romance novel for several good reasons. First, short, intense passages of dialogue build sexual tension. Long, windy passages destroy it. How long will the heroine maintain her state of arousal if her hero is making an hour-long speech about his business, or even, for that matter, about their relationship?

In real life, when we are emotionally moved, we tend to speak in short, jerky sentences or even in broken ones. We start to say something and break off, or we are interrupted before we get all the words out of our mouths. Only when a speaker has a captive audience—the minister at the pulpit, the teacher behind the desk, the politician at the podium—does he expound at great length, ignoring the yawns of boredom. The romance writer can't afford to run that risk. Once your reader yawns, you've lost your audience.

Television has played a tremendous part in conditioning our expectations. We've grown accustomed to tightly written dramas with short scenes of highly emotional dialogue. We now expect the same in our reading; our ears and eyes are set to the faster pace of contemporary drama.

Let's go back to the scene that follows our last example from Bonnie Drake's *Lover From the Sea,* and see how skilled this author is at capturing the rhythms of natural speech. In this sample of dialogue, again between April Wilde and her lover from the sea, the author never uses "he said" or "she said," but uses bits of business *as* speech tags.

> *"You rescued me from the storm and took me in, didn't you? . . . Then let me do something in return."*
>
> *Swallowing hard, she struggled to speak. "You could build a fire . . ."*
>
> *"I could."*
>
> *"Or"—she moistened her lips with inadvertent allure—"Make us some lunch . . ."*
>
> *"I could."*
>
> *"Or. . ." Her mind drew a blank, all power diverted to her budding senses.*
>
> *He drew her to her feet with a gentle hand, threading his long fingers through the thickness of her chestnut hair. "Why not kiss me, then we'll decide what to do . . ."*
>
> *"No . . ." Her whisper was feeble, her entire being mesmerized by the aura of masculinity that had enveloped her and seized control.*

The half-sentences and the single word "or" show us April's confusion in her attraction to this handsome stranger. Certainly this dialogue sounds like a conversation that might actually take place between two people in this situation. The author has inserted bits of business, breaking off talk at just the right places to create the illusion of natural speech.

This passage also shows how bits of business can be used in counterpoint to dialogue to show the reader the heroine's true feelings. April swallowed hard, she moistened her lips with inadvertent allure, we know her senses are budding, her whisper is feeble, and her entire being is mesmerized, while out loud she is saying "No . . ."

Now let's look at a sample of dialogue that uses as few speech tags and bits of business as possible, so as not to interrupt the pace of the exchange and the flow of the argument. This excerpt is taken from *Call It Love* (Dell Candlelight Ecstasy), by Ginger Chambers.

Joanna Davis, the heroine, is walking along the edge of the Gulf of Mexico; the hot Texas sun blazes down upon her. A voice calls her name, the voice of Philip Cole, the man from whom she's trying to break away. We're told that Joanna was warned against trusting a man like Philip, but her infatuation with him was so great that she didn't listen.

Now Philip catches up with her and blocks her path. The following dialogue takes place on the second page of chapter one. Philip is speaking:

"It's not like you think, Joanna! Not at all! You've got to let me explain! I'm getting a divorce. As soon as it's humanly possible, I'm getting a divorce!"

"Now that is an interesting bit of news," she jeered. "And since I know, why don't you try telling your wife! Oh, but remember to do it carefully. It may come as quite a shock . . . her being pregnant and all."

"She told you that?" Philip looked like a man who had been hit, hard, in the stomach.

"Along with a few other things," Joanna confirmed coldly. In a gesture of mingled contempt and dismissal, she turned her back and started to walk away.

Philip lunged forward, once again impeding her progress. *"I won't let you do this, Joanna!"*

"You don't have a choice, Philip. All along you've lied to me. You told me you were already divorced—that you had been for the past year. I believed you!"

"I lied because I knew you wouldn't have anything to do with me if I didn't! Alice and I were as good as divorced. There was nothing left of our marriage. We were like two strangers!"

"Two strangers don't have babies, Philip! Or are you trying to tell me that the child isn't yours?"

Philip's dark eyes could not leave the smoldering anger of her own. Finally he choked out, *"No, it's mine—but Alice tricked me. She knew I was seeing someone else and she's spiteful enough not to want to let me be happy."*

Several long seconds passed before Joanna questioned softly, *"What happened? Did she rape you?"*

The man winced visibly under her taunting. Then a look of desperation settled on his chiseled features, and his hands shot out to pull her tightly against his body.

"I don't want to lose you, Joanna—and I can't lose you! I love you!"

"You don't know what love is, Philip!"

"I know that I don't want to live without you!" he rasped.

If your characters call each other by name, you can eliminate the need for repeated speech tags. Try writing a two-page conversation between your hero and heroine, using no more than three tags for each of them.

Try to vary the tempo of dialogue in your novel. If you use many speech tags and bits of business in a slower scene, speed things up and have several pages of rapid-fire dialogue with few interruptions in the next. Use the rhythm of your dialogue to establish the pace of a scene.

The Plunge Opening

If you use dialogue to begin your novel, this is called a "plunge opening." The reader jumps right in on a scene without narrative explanation. It takes skill to write dialogue that will make clear to the reader who is speaking and what is going on, so that she is not hopelessly confused. Also, the words spoken must be powerful, so that the reader is involved immediately.

Consider the opening of Dorothy Garlock's *A Love for All Time* (Bantam, Loveswept). Although the first two sentences are not actually dialogue, this can be called a plunge opening because we are thrown immediately into scene one without any introduction, and hear the heroine speak almost at once.

> *Someone was crying.*
>
> *The sounds were so soft that at first Casey wasn't sure what she was hearing. They were coming at quick intervals with intermittent panicky little gasps.*
>
> *"Is someone there?"* Was that her voice? *It was muffled and strange . . . Why couldn't she see?*
>
> *"Are my eyes open?" she asked aloud, forcing her tongue to make the necessary movements.*
>
> *"I can't see!" The words were anguished. Panic, then terror seized her.*
>
> *"Shh . . . Lie still." The voice was deep, masculine and muffled. "Don't be frightened. You can't see because there's a bandage over your eyes."*
>
> *The calm words drew her well back from the edge of hysteria. "You're in the hospital, but you'll be all right."*

We are plunged into Casey's panic as she awakes in a hospital bed after a car accident, her eyes bandaged. We hear her fright. We hear the kind words of "the voice," who will be the hero. We are into the story, all on page one.

If you find it too difficult to plan an opening scene in dialogue for your novel, try opening a chapter in this way. After the story is under way, the reader knows the characters. It is less confusing to drop her into the middle of a conversation between people she already knows, though you must still make sure you clearly tag all characters present.

Humorous Dialogue

Dialogue is an excellent tool for bringing humor into your romance novel. As you saw in the example from *Lover From the Sea*, by Bonnie Drake, light banter and clever repartee, can be teasing, flirtatious, sexy, and fun to read.

Your heroine might use humor to cover up her real feelings, tossing off the hero's painful remarks with a forced smile and seemingly lighthearted responses.

Even an argument over basically serious misunderstandings can be written in amusing quips tossed back and forth between these two devoted opponents. And humorous dialogue can be intimate. Even in the act of making love, one of the lovers can say something funny and private.

Lighthearted and humorous dialogue is particularly appropriate in historical romances, in which conversation is not so direct and open as in a contemporary romance. Social intrigue and romantic scheming are part of the period historicals, such as Victorian, Regency, and Edwardian romances. The people who lived in those times prided themselves on their conversational abilities, and light, teasing humor was part of their social life.

Humor in romance fiction should never be vulgar and lewd or cutting and destructive, unless, of course, it comes from the mouth of the wicked villain in an historical. And humor, like spice in a recipe, requires a light hand. Don't try to sustain witty repartee beyond its natural life.

Of course, as with all dialogue in your novel, humorous exchanges must serve a larger purpose than just to amuse. Remember that humorous dialogue too must characterize, set the scene, advance the plot, or give information.

Robin James' *The Golden Touch* (Jove, Second Chance at Love) is on its way to becoming a classic, in part because of the author's deft use of humorous dialogue. In the excerpt that follows, instrument repair technician and piano teacher Kathy Carter faints when Neil Stratton, songwriter, musician, and celebrity of international repute, walks into her shop. He picks her up and puts her on a couch, and these are the first words he says to her when she revives:

> *"You know, I could see it if I were Elvis," he said. Kathy could hear the smile in his voice. "I don't get many swoons these days. It was charm-*

ing though, if a little old-fashioned . . ."

"I know how it must have looked, but it wasn't anything to do with you. I was hungry."

"You saw a hamburger on the floor and made a nose dive for it," he said, his tone too cheerfully agreeable.

Kathy tried again. "The only thing I've eaten all day was one cup of blueberry yogurt for breakfast."

He shook his head in mock condemnation. "When I saw you I thought—that looks like a girl who eats blueberry yogurt for breakfast." His finger traveled to her forehead and smoothed back the straying tendrils that had gathered there. "Hang on, all right? Don't try to stand up. I'll be right back."

When he reappears, he offers her a sandwich wrapped in aluminum foil.

"Wheat bread!" she exclaimed with involuntary dismay, and regretted the words instantly.

"Good for you," he said . . .

"I suppose," she said, "that I ought to be grateful it's not a vegetarian sandwich. Shredded seaweed, pate of aloe vera . . ."

Good naturedly, he picked up Kathy's wrist and carried her hand and his supper to her lips. "Never look a gift sandwich in the mouth, darlin'," he said. . . .

"Well," she said, after finishing, "I'm sorry now that I ate it. I ought to have saved it for posterity, it being your sandwich and everything."

"Don't worry," he said pointedly. "I'll autograph the crust."

Rude of him to mention how she hadn't eaten it.

This conversation reveals Neil as fast-talking, witty, and charming, and Kathy as self-assured and spirited enough to be a good match for him. It introduces them in an unusual way—most heroes don't have to pick their heroines up off the floor—sets the tone of their relationship, and lets the reader know that the story will be lively and fun as well as romantic.

"One of the best parts of being a romance writer is that you can think up clever, witty things for your characters to say, even though you yourself can never come up with such gems on the spur of the moment in your own life."   Debbie Gordon, a.k.a. Brooke Hastings, author of contemporary romances

---

Warning: unless humorous dialogue comes naturally to you, don't try it. Nothing is less successful than unfunny funny dialogue. If lighthearted quips fall off your own tongue, go ahead and plant them on your hero's or heroine's. Otherwise, you'd better play it straight.

Accents and Dialects

What do you do if the hero of your contemporary romance is a Frenchman, or a Bostonian with a Kennedy accent? A European or regional accent is part of the man and cannot be totally ignored. What if your book is a historical, set on a cotton plantation in the deep South, one hundred and fifty years ago?

First, in a contemporary category romance, avoid extended use of dialect, repeated foreign phrases, or words spelled to reflect regional accents. Select one or two phrases that give the flavor of the hero's speech, or words that suggest his exotic or special accent. Occasionally you can have the heroine refer to his "smooth and sophisticated French accent" to remind the reader, if he's rattled on too long without sounding one French "r."

If your hero is a Texan, as is interior designer Julia D'Amati's suitor, Brad, in *A World of Her Own* (Gallen Contemporary Romance) by Anna James, you can handle it as this author does. Often, in his pursuit of Julia, Brad speaks along without dropping a "g." Only a word is needed to suggest his Texas drawl and vocabulary, as in this example:

> *"I'll take you any way I can get you (Julia). There's nothing you can say that would change my feelings for you, and once you're mine— you're going to be mine, too, gal—you won't regret it for a minute. There's nothing I wouldn't do for you . . ."*

Only the word "gal" reminds us of his accent in this passage.

At other times, as when Brad is heatedly trying to convince Julia to marry him, the author emphasizes his accent and peppers his speech with more of the folksy phrases a casual country Texan might use:

> *"When we've all been together this past week, I've watched you with Carla (her daughter), wishin' that you were my family . . ."*
> *"Brad, don't. Don't rush this."*
> But he would not be stopped. *"I keep thinkin' of the children we could have together."*
> *"Brad . . ."*

"I'm as healthy as a jackrabbit, *but I'm forty-eight, and I don't want to wait a heck of a lot longer."*

"But I want to wait, Brad; I need to wait. Don't back me into a corner."

"Maybe I've put too much pressure on you, but this week has told me so much about you—about us—that I can't help wonderin' what we're waitin' for." *When he received no response, Brad added, "I can be patient awhile longer, I guess."*

The dropped "g's" and expressions like "healthy as a jack rabbit" and "heck of a lot longer" serve to remind us of Brad's Texas roots and his rural background.

If you are creating characters who speak with accents in your contemporary romance, handle them subtly. Don't show off your own knowledge of linguistics by having every Southerner or Frenchman speak with a thick accent. Be selective; just suggest regional speech differences.

Historicals are another matter. First of all, careful research is needed to make dialogue convincing in an historical romance. The vocabulary must be right for the period. A woman raised as a proper Victorian in England or as the aristocratic daughter of a Southern cotton grower would use a very different vocabulary from your own. Background, setting, social values, and roles of the time are all important in determining the tone of conversations and the words you will choose for your characters to say.

In a way, you have more freedom in an historical romance, since readers expect the characters to speak differently and are interested in the era of your story. You can choose to stress accents to bring out the flavor of the period and locale.

One way of doing this is to let minor characters speak in thick accents and reserve standard speech for the hero and heroine, only suggesting their accents. Too many words spelled to sound like Southern pronunciation can clutter up and slow down your story.

In *The Black Swan,* by Day Taylor (Dell), the author chose to make Carrie Pickett's Southern accent dramatically strong. Carrie is a minor character and a type, and her speech brands her as such:

"Tom! I was beginnin' to think you were goin' to insult me, not comin' to my pahty!" The Widow Pickett wore a low-cut dress of magenta silk . . .

He looked deep into her eyes. "Miss Carrie, if I insulted you, may I pick the weapons?"

She laughed, a happy gushing sound, "What might youah weapons be, Tom?"

"Would you accept sweet nothin's at two paces?"
She blushed clear down to the top of her gown. "Tom, youah
awful! Merton better fetch you a drink, so's you'll have somethin' to
hol' beside mah hand!"

The hero, Adam, and the heroine, Dulcie, are also Southerners, but do not
speak with exaggerated accents. Thus the atmosphere feels authentic, but
the pace of the story is rapid, not slowed by phonetically spelled dialogue,
when the hero and heroine themselves are on stage.

Now see how Dorothy Dowdell handles dialogue in her historical romance, *Glory Land*, already mentioned in chapter seven. This lusty tale of
love and adventure is set against the colorful nineteenth-century background of the railroad that linked East and West.

Garnett, the heroine, daughter of a Rhode Island minister, has just
arrived at the home of her fiance, Roy Edward, in Sacramento. As you read,
decide what words and what in the tone of this dialogue succeed in taking
you back in time.

As she (Garnett) entered the room, the Governor rose from a loveseat
and smiled, looking splendid in a white dinner jacket. "You're as beau-
tiful as always, Garnett. What a pretty red velvet gown."
"Thank you." She touched her skirt. "It's a lovely dress but not at
all appropriate for a warm summer evening like this. Tomorrow I'm
going to the dry goods store and buy materials to make myself some
cooler clothes."
"The best place is Wellington's. You can easily walk over there—it's
five or six blocks. Charge anything you want and have the store send
the bill to my accountant as Nelda does."
"Oh, Governor, I couldn't do that—"
"Of course you can." He poured a glass of sherry and handed it to
her. "I've been meaning to speak to you. Nelda has grown very fond
of you, and I have too, of course. We've never had a daughter—just
our four sons who've all left home with families of their own, as you
know. What I want to say is—we hope you will stay with us indefinitely.
It's so good to have someone young and lively around this big house
again.
"Thank you. Of course it's a dream come true for me to be here in
California." She raised her glass in a toast.
He touched her glass with his and went on. "I mean it, Garnett.
You are to feel free to buy whatever clothes you need or have Nelda's
dressmaker make them and charge them to me. We entertain a great
deal, and I want you to look your best. As you know, Nelda is not very

strong, so you can help her with her hostess duties as a daughter would."

The formality of this conversation and such words as *parlor, coming to dine, dressmaker, dry goods store* give us the flavor of the period. But beyond that, the author has woven into this conversation attitudes and assumptions common to the period. Rather than explain in narrative passages that women in those days were financially dependent on men—a father, lover, or benefactor—she shows it in dialogue.

The Governor is paternal and protective toward Garnett, and she is grateful for his kindness and generosity, as becomes a young lady without means of her own. She welcomes the opportunity to help Nelda *with her hostess duties as a daughter would.*

You can display the period you are writing about not only in characters' vocabularly, but also in the tone of their conversations and in *what* they say to each other. Make their social relationships and behavior reflect the attitudes and customs of their period.

Dialogue in Young Adult Romances

This chapter would not be complete without some mention of dialogue in young adult romances. I have said these books are apt to be dominated by dialogue. Conversations are informal, fast-paced, direct. Teenagers come right to the point.

Though colloquial expressions, such as "hi" and "whew" in the following example are fine, be careful not to use such up-to-the-minute expressions as "right on, man" or others that will date your book. "In" words go "out" quickly. Use slang, use contractions, but try to keep the speakers' vocabularies broad enough so that if your book should remain in print for several years, it will still seem current.

The following is typical of dialogue in romances for young readers, an excerpt taken from *Love at First Sight,* by Elaine Harper (Silhouette, First Love).

Notice here that just as in the examples from adult romances given earlier in this chapter, bits of business serve to establish the young adult equivalent of sexual tension.

This scene takes place early in the first chapter. Janine, the heroine, is baby-sitting for five lively youngsters. She's having a hard time controlling the children as she tends to the laundry, when the hero, Craig Matthews, arrives to mow the lawn. Craig speaks first:

"Haven't I seen you at Blossom High?"

Janine nervously swept the unruly strand of hair away from her face again. His eyes roved questioningly over her fair skin and blond hair. . . . Their hands brushed as he helped her with the laundry. . . .

"Yes, I go to Blossom Valley," she answered after a short interval. His presence seemed to paralyze her into slowing down her accustomed reactions.

"I thought I'd seen you around." His eyes swept the disarray in the kitchen and family room. "Whew, you've got your work cut out for you. I'll take the little guys out in the yard with me. That should help."

They discuss where the broom and tools are kept; Janine is very much aware of Craig's charms. Then, in a few simple lines of dialogue, they sweep away the rest of the formality with:

"What did you say your name is?" he smiled into her awestruck round blue eyes.

"I'm sorry, I don't think I said." She felt again the trancelike bewitchment of his presence, and her voice sounded strange to her. "I'm Janine Anderson."

"Hi, Janine." He extended his massive hand and enclosed her small one in it. She felt an unbearable thrill at his touch.

The dialogue is straightforward, casual, unsophisticated, and youthful, as it should be. Otherwise, though, techniques here are the same used in adult romances: casual, controlled words spoken between the hero and heroine, while interspersed narrative reveals their true, intense emotions to the reader.

Points to Remember:

1. When writing dialogue, establish right away where the conversation is taking place. For example:

A tall, lean-faced man, dressed in a Bill Blass three-piece gray suit, rose from his desk, walked slowly to the window, and gazed through narrowed lids at the stream of traffic on Fifth Avenue. It was several minutes before he spoke. "There's never been another woman in my life, darling; only you."

Then remind the reader frequently what that location is like through character action, reaction to the place, or brief bits of narration.

2. Dialogue should reflect the background, temperament, and present feelings of the speaker. Use dialogue to characterize the speaker.

3. In general, enrich your dialogue with bits of action, reaction, thoughts, and description. But keep these bits of business *short*. Don't break the flow of a conversation with long chunks of narration.

Occasionally, for example, when an argument is taking place, let fast-paced dialogue snap along with no narrative interruption and very few speech tags. Your handling of dialogue can speed up or slow down the pace of a scene.

4. Avoid slang or clichés that will date your novel, unless, of course, yours is an historical that reflects intentionally the flavor of a certain period. Since long passages of dialect can slow down your story, select phrases that give the flavor of the region or the roots of the speaker, and sprinkle them lightly through that character's speech.

5. Avoid using academic or pedantic dialogue. Use simple words, as people do when they speak, including contractions such as *I'll* for *I will*.

"Have a love affair with words. Words are a writer's hammer and nails, so learn to manipulate them to evoke the unique qualities of whatever genre you are writing for. 'Cease this henwitted gibberish!' 'Stop being a damn fool.' The thought is the same, yet these two sets of words instantly draw the reader into different moods, different genres, even different centuries. Work at your profession and remember, eclectic reading and a passion for words will help make you a writer who can create for more than one category of romance." **Betty Henrichs, a.k.a Amanda Kent, Emily Doyle, romance author**

---

6. All dialogue should serve a purpose, either to give information, further the plot, characterize, foreshadow events to come, allow a character to reflect on past events, or increase sexual tension between hero and heroine. Don't decorate your book with unnecessary chatter. For example, you do not need this sort of thing:

"How are you?"

"I'm fine. How about you?"

"Can't complain."

"Glad to hear it. Say hello to the wife and kids."

"Will do."

This exchange may be true to life, but it serves no purpose and makes pretty dull reading.

7. Give each character's speech in a paragraph of its own. Insert actions and reactions between lines of dialogue in the same paragraph, unless it runs too long. In that case, break the passage into two paragraphs.

8. Make sure that dialogue reflects the professional, economic, and cultural background of your characters. If yours is an historical romance, research carefully the vocabulary of the period.

9. By reading their "lines" out loud, check to be sure each of your characters has his or her own way of speaking. Give each a few characteristic phrases or expressions, a special speech pattern or way of talking, so that the reader recognizes that character the minute he or she starts to speak.

10. Be careful in your use of adverbs as modifiers after passages of dialogue. For example, if your heroine has just attacked the hero, hurling angry words at him, do not follow her diatribe with, "she said angrily." You have just shown *angrily*.

On the other hand, you can use adverbs effectively to clarify the tone of voice if it is not evident. "I love you, you know. I always have," he said huskily, or softly, or slowly. In this way you can add the touch that makes the words more romantic.

11. To improve your dialogue, listen to people around you. Eavesdrop when you are riding a bus, train, or plane, or at a cocktail party. How do a couple of teenagers sound when they are chattering together? What does a handsome young man say to his date as the evening begins? How does a man introduce himself to an attractive woman he has never met?

12. Above all, make your dialogue *romantic*. Your hero's voice is a deep baritone that sends a tingling thrill up the heroine's spine. The words he chooses reflect his self-confidence and his way with women. Her words tell him of her essential femininity and her special charms. Harsh or tender, make the words between these two a lively melody running above a throbbing base of sexual attraction.

JANET
JOYCE
*Winter
Lady*

Chapter **10.**
WILL THEY
OR WON'T THEY?
Writing Sensual
Sex Scenes

Romance without sex is like the Fourth of July without fireworks: disappointing.

"We want good sex scenes," romance editors advise writers in editorial guidelines and at writers' conferences.

Good has different definitions, depending on the type of romance and particular line. What constitutes a hot love scene in one type of romance novel would be cold potatoes in another.

To give you an idea of the range of sexual explicitness in the category romances, here are the guidelines for a few of the lines on the treatment of sex.

First, the editors of sweet and fairly unsteamy Silhouette romances state their requirements this way:

> *It is all right for the hero and heroine to go to bed together, although they should not make love before they are married. Bringing them to the brink of consummation and then forcing them to retreat, either because of an interruption or because one or both of the lovers suffer from doubt or shame, is an appropriate Silhouette device. Descriptions of lovemaking should be sensuous with some details. They cannot be limited to "he kissed her passionately."*
>
> *However, there are some limits to what can be described and how. Nudity is permissible, depending upon context, but it should not be too graphic . . . Above all, Silhouette love scenes should be romantic. Our readers should be as in love with the hero as the heroine.*

Since the hero and heroine will probably not marry until the end of the book, actual intercourse may not take place at all in a sweet romance, though there is embracing, kissing, even passion. Generally, these stories are more romantic than erotic.

For me, writing love scenes is like a reward for muddling through description, which I hate. I don't have to go to any great lengths to put myself in the mood to write them. I just need an uninterrupted block of time—at least three or four hours.   **Debbie Gordon, a.k.a. Brooke Hastings, author of contemporary romances**

Compare guidelines for the Rapture Romances, published by New American Library:

> *The heroine and hero will become intimately and intensely involved early in the plot and will make love several times in the course of the*

romance. Each passionate kiss, each tender caress, each earth-shattering climax will be described in length, in lavish, specific (though not clinical) detail.

. . . The relationship must proceed logically from first encounter to first kiss to love-making; we do not expect the hero and heroine to jump into bed the minute they meet, and careful thought should be devoted to setting up a situation in which rapid intimacy is possible.

Since the emphasis will be placed heavily on the physical expression of love, it is important that each love scene . . . be an integral part of the plot development and contribute something new to the relationship, that it have its own mood.

Foreplay and afterplay, with descriptions of what the heroine thinks and feels, what the hero says and does, before, during and after making love, can provide this, as can a change in setting (i.e. outside in the afternoon, rather than in the bedroom at night); a switch in the seducer/seducee roles; a change in the level of experience or attitude of one of the participants. And the love scenes should be described in full and lavish, moment-by-moment detail.

For most historical romances, there are no specific rules to guide you. You will learn from reading erotic historicals how authors of these books handle sex.

Jove does include in its guidelines, however, a word on handling sex in the Regencies they publish:

In Regencies, the sex can stop before intercourse, since the lack of birth control devices creates an element of worry that isn't present in the contemporary romances. Plot situations that circumvent this problem will be welcome.

If you are struggling with this "element of worry," with the moral values of the times, or with the appropriateness of the sex scenes you have in mind for the type of historical you want to write, address your specific problems to the editor you hope to submit your manuscript to. Write or telephone her. Romance editors are generally eager to help writers with such problems, and will reply.

How is sex handled in the young adult romances? Guidelines from Scholastic's Wildfire line are typical of requirements for these books:

The heroines are 15 or 16, and the heroes are 17 and 18. The girls are high school students. There can be no explicit sex and, in fact, no sexual involvement between the couple except kissing and feelings of attraction.

Planning Sex Scenes in Your Romance Novel

Let's assume that you are writing a category romance—contemporary heroine, contemporary hero, and, of course, contemporary sex. Though the sweet romances continue to hold their audience, the trend is definitely toward the more sensual books, so let's say this is the type you are writing. Since guidelines specify so clearly how sex scenes should be handled in these books, we can talk concretely about how you should plan this aspect of your novel.

Building sexual tension is probably the most difficult challenge facing the romance writer and unfortunately, there is no simple recipe to make it happen. I strive to focus on the action and more importantly, the reaction of the lovers, emphasizing the depth of feelings between them. It's this emotional impact that ignites passion on the pages— and what separates the highly sensual from the merely explicit."
Prudence Lichte, a.k.a. Prudence Martin, Henrietta Houston, romance author

---

Whatever line of sensual romances you might be aiming for, some of the points in Harlequin's guidelines for their Superromances can serve as general principles:

> *Sexual awareness should always be present between the hero and heroine.*

This you know. We have called it "sexual tension." In all category romances, that magnetic attraction between the lovers begins with their first glimpse of each other. It is sustained, heightened, and finally brought to the point of explosion—emotionally and physically.

> *The sex can be fairly explicit without being too graphic. It should be in good taste and should focus on the sensuous rather than the sexual; the love bond should be stronger than the physical.*

The importance of good taste can't be overemphasized. Many hopeful new romance writers think that by throwing in paragraphs of borderline pornography, they'll make a sale. They're wrong. All sexual detail must be shaped by the emotional atmosphere of the story. Sex included just to embellish your manuscript will not impress an editor.

Harlequin guidelines continue:

Sensuous scenes may be frequent, but not overwhelming and should never be gratuitously included. They should be part of the plot and fit naturally into its sequence.

Neither will an editor of category romances be charmed by violent sex or rape:

In the sex scenes, the emphasis should be on a shared feeling *rather than on pure male domination.*

Here again, it is the sincere, mutually enjoyed sexual moments which will enhance your story. Love between your hero and heroine must seem genuine to make their lovemaking effective.

Above all, sexual experience for your heroine should be romantic and pleasurable, with emphasis on the caring and loving emotions she feels as she finds herself responding to the equally caring and loving hero. Sexual attraction, of course, should be powerful, sweeping the two lovers up in a tidal wave of desire, but beneath this boiling vortex is the even more powerful force of love, which gives *meaning* to the physical side of sex.

Now for some more general principles, which I emphasize in my classes:

1. Give your sex scenes definite crescendos. A well-written sex scene has a pattern to it. As your hero and heroine approach each other, dramatize the physical attraction they feel for each other through thoughts, actions, and dialogue. There may be a good deal of conversation, even argument, before one or the other reaches out and makes physical contact.

This overture, when it comes, is either accepted or rebuffed. In the latter case, it must be made again and accepted. Then the two begin to touch and respond to each other's physical closeness. The tempo increases with their ardor, and then comes the crescendo—either consummation in the physical act of intercourse or a break in their passon; someone's ardor cools or someone withdraws from the embrace.

2. A new complication must arise during or immediately after the love scene, to pull the lovers apart again. When the heat of the moment subsides, one or both might feel they had acted unwisely. Although this was a passionate, sincere, and thoroughly enjoyable sexual encounter, the heroine is more confused than ever. Perhaps an earlier misunderstanding between them comes back to haunt her. All her doubts about him come rushing back. Or something has happened during their embrace to make her doubt her

own emotions. Only if this is the last scene in the book can the lovers be totally at peace with themselves and with each other.

"Because I work from a detailed plot outline, I know well in advance when I'll be reaching a serious love scene, and long before I get there I begin thinking of how I'm going to (pardon the expression) handle it. Although naturally the sensual scenes, like the rest of the book, are basically works of imagination, probably I draw on my personal experiences and preferences more for such scenes than for any other part of the stories."   Lynda Ward, romance author

---

At the conclusion of the scene, we usually return to the heroine's thoughts (if we have been temporarily in the hero's) and learn how this encounter has affected her—that is, how this scene has moved the plot. For move the plot it should.

3. Whatever takes place in the boudoir should motivate the next thing that happens in the plot. From the push-pull of emotions in the sex scene spring the confrontations, the chaos, or the contemplations in the next scene. When you plan the heroine's feelings and thoughts as she lies in the hero's arms, think ahead. Lay the groundwork for the next thing to come.

4. You are probably wondering how many sex scenes to include, and how often. How many should be tame and controlled before you allow your heroine and hero to go "all the way"?

There are no absolute answers to any of these questions. Obviously, a Rapture romance will require more consummated sex scenes than a tamer line. But then, one romance in Jove's Second Chance at Love line might have several full-blown sex scenes, while another has only one.

Whichever type you are writing, be sure to use your initial sex scenes to pave the way for more explicit ones, which might begin halfway through the book or later. Remember that the triumphant embrace, in which both partners are totally satisfied in every way and ready to make their final commitment to each other, cannot happen until the very last pages.

5. How long should a sex scene be? Certainly long enough to allow the reader the full satisfaction of a sensual read; several pages if possible. Dramatize as much as possible of what the heroine feels—and the hero, if that is acceptable in the line you are aiming for.

6. Show the reader the physical, emotional, and rational sides of the hero-

ine's experience while making love. If the hero's hand travels up and down her spine, physically she feels his strong fingers on her skin. Emotionally, she is swept to a new level of passion. Rationally, she may be thinking, "I must not give in to temptation." Make your sex scenes multidimensional by keeping your reader aware of your heroine's total experience all along the way.

7. Make your sexual description imaginative and poetic—*never clinical.* While biological terms are used in describing parts of the body above the waist—words such as "breasts" and "nipples"—anatomical references below the waist are given in euphemisms, such as "her intimate places," or "she felt the surge of his masculinity."

These words from Jove's Second Chance at Love guidelines may be helpful here:

> *The hero and heroine do make love even when unmarried, and with plenty of sensuous detail. But the explicit details will be used only in foreplay, and the fadeout will occur before actual intercourse.*

Though the lovers may be aware of their bodies as they first approach each other, their passion takes on a soaring, poetic quality once excitement has increased. So should your description.

Use of symbolism is the key to success here, and a technique that will enable you to create romantic word pictures for your reader.

When you write *symbolically,* you use a concrete object, such as the ocean, the wind, the pine trees, the burning logs in the fireplace, to represent and dramatize an idea or an emotion. I'm particularly drawn to the ocean, since I spent my childhood and adolescent years in a house built on a cliff overlooking the Pacific Ocean. In a sex scene, I might use the ocean symbolically as follows:

> *As Lisa's passion mounted to match Eric's, she heard the eager voice of the sea as the waves rushed shoreward, and it seemed that she was now a part of the sea's cycle, rising on the crest of a wave that had its beginning in some fathomless depth.*
>
> *The wave rose to a towering crest, carrying her to its peak, held her captive for a breathless moment, and then set her free in a paroxysm of sensual pleasure such as she'd never known before.*

In my practice scene, notice that there is no physical, clinical description of the act of love. But when I use the symbol of the sea and its cycle, I can dramatize Lisa's mounting sexual frenzy and her final orgasmic climax.

Nature can furnish you with an inexhaustible supply of symbols to use in creating sensual sex scenes, beautiful physical phenomena that suggest emotion. I have found, though, that for a symbol to work, you must be emotionally moved by that symbol. It must have a very personal meaning to you. So list the aspects of nature that are close to your heart.

"All you need to be able to write a good love scene is to enjoy making love yourself. Any good romance writer is a romantic and knows that's one of the best things in life. It should come pretty automatically."
Joyce Thies, one half of Janet Joyce, romance author

Of course, the symbols you choose must also fit the setting and the story line. If your characters are desert rats, it would be wrong, of course, to use the ocean as a metaphor.

It takes great imagination and creativity to come up with fresh and original phrases, phrases that haven't been used a thousand times before, to describe sexual arousal. If you're a new romance writer, you may need a little time to develop a flair for orchestrating your sex scenes. But the more you work at it, and the more you study techniques used to create good sex scenes, the easier it will become. Before you know it, you will be enjoying the challenge of seeing just how sensually you can write.

The Whole Spectrum: Sweet To Sensual Sex Scenes

Now let's scan the spectrum of sexuality in romance fiction. In the sweet romances, as a rule, sexual tension is expressed much more as emotional push-pull than as confrontation on the physical battlefield.

The heroine is filled with concern as to whether or not the hero really cares about her. She longs for some sign that he finds her attractive and desirable, and attaches great importance to the expressions on his face and his tone of voice. Sometimes she's ecstatic because he has said something to imply that he does care. At other times she's in the depths of despair because she has misinterpreted some remark of his, a misunderstanding that can darken her life for many days and nights.

In the sweet romances, reader suspense comes from wondering how the two bickering lovers will ever clear the air between them. The final satisfaction comes when the lovers finally make a commitment to one another, usually on the last page.

In contrast, readers of the more sensual category romances enjoy each level of physical contact between the lovers, as the sexual tension between them mounts.

"I look for quality writing—immediacy, intensity, sincerity, good dialogue and action, and a rapid plot development that keeps me turning the pages. Where sex is concerned, emotion and sensuality are important, not clinical details. Whatever turns the writer on will come off the page." Jacqui Bianchi, romance editor

---

In the erotic historicals, readers thrill again and again to the hero's sometimes rough-and-ready pursuit of the heroine, to her intense sexual arousal, and to his ravishing conquest of her. Lusty passion, mixed with intrigue and sweeping views of times gone by, holds the reader's attention until, at the end of the book, the hero commits himself seriously at last to our (often) long-suffering heroine.

The Sweet Romances / Now for some examples from this spectrum, starting with the sweet and simple and proceeding to the hot and steamy.

First, the final love scene in a sweet romance, *Windward Crest* (Harlequin Presents), by Anne Hampson:

> *"My precious girl," he [Jake] whispered in the tenderest tone she had ever heard him use to her, "my adorable angel. . ." He took her face between his hands and looked into her eyes; she caught her breath in wonderment, for never in the most intimate moments they had spent together had she seen so softened an expression on those stern and haughty features. "I shall never let you out of my sight again, Dominie, I need you so . . ." His strong deep voice actually broke and . . . she flung both her arms round his neck, went up on tiptoe, and pressed her lips to his.*
>
> *"I love you," she whispered simply, and tenderly gave him her lips again.*

The physical contact is limited; the expression of sexual feelings, restrained.

The Category Romances / Now for a look at how two authors of the more sensual category romances handle sex scenes.

In Janet Joyce's *Winter Lady*, mentioned earlier in this book, let's watch the progression toward sexual intimacy for magazine writer Raine Morgan and popular singer-composer Devlin Paige, who meet in the Minnesota woods when Raine loses her way skiing.

After a snowball fight in the second chapter, they enjoy their first kiss:

> *They were lying in a fir-fanned bed of soft white powder, an outdoor boudoir as intimate as any bedroom. Icicle flames burst and melted inside her as his tongue licked the flakes of snow from her lips and his dark eyes turned the intoxicating color of brandy. He kissed her again and again, his mouth running over her face, tasting the snowflakes on her lashes and numbed cheeks. She no longer felt shivers of cold race down her spine, but hot waves of pleasure welling up from deep inside. Helplessly, her hands ran up his arms and across his broad shoulders, then locked behind his neck, drawing him closer. . . . When her tongue slipped into his mouth, he immediately pressed her back upon the snow. With a deep groan of male satisfaction, his body covered hers. His powerful thighs straddled her legs, making her aware of the urgent hardness of his desire. Their tongues met, his encircling hers enticingly until she was frantic for more. She was unprepared when he suddenly pulled away from her and sat up.*
>
> *"We had better get inside before we both die of pneumonia," he stated matter-of-factly.*

Several points deserve notice here. First, the author has developed the scene fully. You can feel the cold and taste the snowflakes. You feel you know exactly how Raine felt when Devlin Paige kissed her. Notice how sensual and intimate their contact seems, even though they are dressed in thick winter coats. The phrase "the urgent hardness of his desire" conveys basic information to the reader without being clinical.

This scene is also a good example of the pleasure the modern heroine takes in sexual contact with the man she loves. If she resists, it is not because she *wants* to, but usually because, for some reason, she feels she should. Here, in the heat of their intimacy, it is Devlin who pulls away. The author knows it is too soon to deepen the physical relationship.

In chapter six, after several false starts, the lovers are finally allowed to possess each other:

> *She (Raine) surrendered to the glorious feel of his body pressed against hers, the rough crisp hairs of his chest brushing her throbbing breasts and heightening her response. She wanted to touch him, could not wait to feel the entire length of his naked body with her hands . . .*
>
> *"Devlin," she moaned, as his hands began a tantalizing journey*

down her silken skin, caressing the smooth flesh over her hips and across her buttocks. His lips were at her breasts, licking the fevered curves until she trembled with need . . .

It is not until five pages later, though, that consummation finally takes place. Arguments and disagreement, doubt and suspicion on Raine's part intervened. (Did he love her? What about all the other nights after this one?) Finally—

Tenderness was replaced by a voracious hunger that consumed them both. They feasted on the manna of shared passion, stroking, caressing and drinking of each other as if they had both been starving. They were together at the zenith of their desire and together when they plunged over the edge and flamed into one fire of exquisite sensation; they rose and fell from one level of feeling to the next, until they had mounted and savored them all. As the climactic shudders shook them, Raine grasped Devlin tighter, overcome by his power and drowning in the wonder of being his.

Notice the tasteful use of figurative language in describing the sexual act. "They feasted on the manna of shared passion as if they had both been starving." Such phrases as "the zenith of their desire," "plunged over the edge," "flamed into one fire," "rose and fell," "mounted and savored climactic shudders" convey dramatically what is happening without a single anatomical reference.

"We don't want to know that the moonlit night was romantic; we want to know that the sky was a dark velvet canopy over their heads. We don't want to know that his touch aroused her; we want to know that the rough feel of his calloused fingertips, as he wonderingly explored the outline of her face with featherlike caresses, set her trembling as no arrogant and inescapable embrace could have."   Guidelines, a contemporary category romance line

---

Learning to substitute symbolic or metaphorical words for clinical terms is not easy. Start your own list of words and phrases to use in describing the physical manifestations of sexual arousal. The hallmark of a good romance writer is the freshness and originality of her style, which shows up particularly in sex scenes. You must avoid phrases that have become clichés through overuse, but don't copy your favorite author's approach, either. The world doesn't need a carbon copy of her.

The key to writing your sex scenes in original and powerful figurative language is this: if you are emotionally involved in the scene, the words will begin to flow. On the other hand, if you write like a biology professor drawing diagrams on the blackboard, you will be in trouble. Your sex scenes will

---

"How do I write my sensual scenes? I write through my senses. I see colors, I hear music, I think of how things feel and smell. Usually by the time I reach a love scene in a book, my characters take over and handle the scene for me. I fall in love with my heroes, cry a lot as I create tender, emotional scenes, and always try to say whatever has to be said in as few words as possible." Georgette Livingston, a.k.a. *Diane Crawford, romance author*

---

be stiff and cold and very much of this world.

You should transport your lovers to another world altogether and make their physical contact heavenly, describable only as stars bursting, planets spinning, suns on fire.

Let's see how another master of the craft, Donna Kimel Vitek, handles sex in another contemporary category romance.

Laine Winthrop, daughter of a college president, is the heroine, and Nick Brannon, representative of a foundation which may withdraw its annual million-dollar grant to the school, is her hero in *Passion's Price* (Dell Candlelight Ecstasy). In the following excerpts, notice the progression from one level of physical awareness and contact to the next.

In chapter two, Laine, making a salad in the kitchen, looks out the window to notice:

> *The sleeves of his white shirt were rolled up to just above his elbows, exposing cleanly muscled forearms bronzed by the sun.*

She is aware of his body and his sexuality from the very beginning. By chapter three, Nick and Laine enjoy their first kiss:

> *"Don't talk," he commanded, and when she started to anyway, he lowered his head to brush her lips with his.*
>
> *Whatever words she managed to utter were captured, then totally forgotten. His kiss slowly, seductively, deepened in intensity until his hard mouth took complete possession of hers. Spreading warmth weakened her legs . . . Startled by her own intense desire to respond*

with total abandon, she tried to resist. She meant to push away from him, but instead her hands lingered on his shoulders. Fascinated by the contours of taut rippling muscles, she traced them tentatively, then cupped his neck in trembling hands. Her fingers tangled compulsively in the crisp clean hair brushing his nape and she pressed closer to him . . .

Laine's passion didn't rise to equal his until his lips sought the curve of her slender neck. Before, his kiss, his embrace had only been thrillingly electric, but when the tip of his tongue tasted the hollow at the base of her throat, he awakened her primitive desire. Her breath caught when a shattering emptiness bloomed centrally within and clamored to be filled.

Resisting the dangerous lethargy that dragged at her, she turned her face into the warm hollow of his shoulder when he lifted his head, meaning to take possession of her mouth again. "No," she breathed and pushed lightly against his broad chest.

Nick's hands slipped slowly from her waist as he reluctantly released her. A faint smile of indulgence gentled his hard mouth.

Notice in this scene, that kisses are the only physical contact between the lovers. It is made clear, however, that Laine's passion comes from deep inside her. Such phrases as "her primitive desire" and "a shattering emptiness bloomed centrally within her and clamored to be filled" let us know that she has the feelings and impulses of a mature woman, and there is no question as to the strength of her attraction to Nick.

But Laine can hardly give into such feelings in chapter three. Caution and her better judgment intervene to slow her passion, and she forces herself to say, "No."

Later in chapter three, however, physical contact progresses to a more intimate level:

His mouth enclosed the rose-colored tumescent peak of one breast then the other, again and again, until both were throbbing with exquisite sensation and she was warm and weak and all yielding femininity. Entangling her fingers in his hair, she urged his mouth up to hers again, and she only fully realized exactly what she was inciting, when she felt the weight of one of his legs entangling with her own, and she felt his passion surge against her.

As she trembled violently, Nick tensed, then pushed himself up, away from her. "This has to stop now or it won't stop at all."

Laine was unwilling to let him go completely. One hand feathered down his back when he sat up beside her as she whispered en-

treatingly, "Couldn't you just kiss me once more?"
"For God's sake, you surely know I need a lot more than a kiss
from you now," he muttered with some impatience. "But it's too soon
for you to give me what I want."

This time it is Nick who withdraws from their passion, knowing that it is still too soon to ask for full surrender from Laine. Notice, though, that their bodies have become more intimately involved. He has kissed her breasts; his "passion has surged against her." Study carefully the words the author has chosen here to convey the lovers' deepening passion. The way has been paved for the ultimate intimacy, when it comes in chapter six:

In Nick's room, he threw back the coverlet on his bed and lowered
Laine gently onto the mattress. She lay very still on the cool percale
sheet, watching spellbound as he quickly stripped . . . As a woman,
she found him intriguingly magnificent; as an inexperienced bedmate,
she was apprehensive, somewhat intimidated by such obvious virility
. . .

  Responsive to every caressing touch and kiss, her own hands and
lips were eagerly exploring him. She delighted in his passionate sigh of
pleasure, eager to give back in full measure the tender, exquisite de-
light he gave her. When finally he moved above her, arching her to
him, her small cry soon altered to a long shuddering sigh of ecstasy.
  ". . . Oh Nick, I . . ." She never said the words, but she gave her
love without hesitation. And with each slow rousing movement of his
hard body, that love deepened as she was swept up in a whirlwind of
passion. In his quest to give her pleasure, he conquered all her inhibi-
tions and carried her upward in a tide of ecstasy so devastating that she
cried out his name when piercing fulfillment cascaded in hot pulsating
waves inside her. The throbbing ripples receded but the warmth re-
mained, and she clung to him as he took his own satisfaction with a
compelling urgency, no longer capable of gentleness.

Again, notice such phrases as: "such obvious virility," "moved above her," "slow rousing movement of his hard body," "whirlwind of passion," "tide of ecstasy," "piercing fulfillment," "hot pulsating waves cascaded," "throbbing ripples receded," "took his own satisfaction."

  In your reading of romance, read sex scenes carefully. Watch to see how the author builds the intensity of the lovers' passion. Notice the point at which physical description of foreplay becomes metaphorical.

  Chart for each book the number of sex scenes in the story; how long was each? In what chapters do they fall? Which are broken off short of sexual fulfillment, and how is this done? How many scenes of sexual consummation are there?

Take a sheet of paper and draw a line down the middle. For as many scenes as possible, write on one side what *she* is thinking and feeling; on the other, what *he* is thinking or feeling. If the scene is written entirely in the heroine's viewpoint, extrapolate as much as you can about the hero's response to her from details given about the expression on his face, the touch of his hands, and whatever words he does say.

Study afterplay. Does the author create warm feelings of tenderness between the lovers? Is it obvious that they really care for each other? How does the author reintroduce conflict after or during an intimate love scene?

This may seem a very calculating approach to the subject of sexual passion, but it will give you a way to study the techniques used by skilled and experienced writers, as well as a way to compare the roles of sex scenes in sweet, sensual, and more sensual romances.

Historical Romances / Sex scenes in the erotic historicals can be violent, with the heroine succumbing to what could only be described as near rape. Sometimes, in fact, out-and-out rape carries the day. But the trend seems to be away from these "bodice rippers," toward gentler treatment of heroines and softer presentation of sex.

Sex scenes in historicals, though, can be more graphic than in contemporary category romances. The heroes are a bit rougher and the author's language somewhat more explicit.

These scenes can be done perfectly tastefully, however, as in the following examples from *This Calder Sky* (Pocket Books), by Janet Dailey. (Although this book is set in present times, we'll consider it historical in tone and approach, since it is part of the four-volume Calder family saga which spans many decades.) The passionate sexual encounters between heroine and hero are suited to an epic romance that revolves around the struggle for possession of land and power in a time when "old codes die hard and even the greatest love must fight to live beneath this Calder Sky."

These excerpts also illustrate the shift into the hero's viewpoint, which is common in historicals and is being used more and more often in category romances as well. Do you find that knowing how *both* lovers feel as they become sexually aroused gives the reader a more intimate vicarious experience?

In chapter four the hero, Chase Calder, kisses young Maggie O'Rourke and tells her not to be frightened as she gives him her virginity.

> *Frightened. Was that what she was feeling? She was nervous, but there wasn't any fear involved . . .*

> *. . . Her hands glided over the bulging muscles of his arms to the back of his shoulders, silently assuring him that she wasn't afraid. A slender hand curved itself to thickly corded muscles of his neck, fingers sliding into shaggy dark hair to apply a downward pressure when his mouth opened on her breast and he took the nipple inside it. His erotic suckling caused a peculiar tightening of the muscles low in her stomach, creating a raw ache that begged to be assuaged. She writhed slightly in an attempt to ease the building pressure, tightly clenching her inner thighs together.*

Now comes the transition line that moves us into Chase's viewpoint. The transition words are in boldface:

> **Aware of her signaling movement,** *Chase let his hand roam downward from her breast while his tongue and lips continued to give it their attention. On the slow descent, his hand caressed the curve of her waist . . . then paused on the quivering flatness of her stomach. At the slight arching of her hips against its weight, his finger slid into the silky patch of hair and rubbed the area with gentle firmness . . .*
>
> *Instinctively her hips began to move in slow, rhythmic gyrations. Sidetracking her attention, he dragged his mouth from the peak of one breast to let it climb to the peak of the other. While he teethed the pointed crown, his massaging fingers made a more intimate search until he could feel the warm moistness of her . . .*
>
> *With a groan, Chase ripped his mouth from her breast to bruise her lips, separating them with the hard thrust of his tongue. His own fevered throbbing was driving him; need was screaming through his system. While one hand continued to work her until she was loose and ready, the other unbuckled his belt and unfastened his Levi's. She moaned in protest when he took his hand away to hunch out of his pants.*
>
> *Wedging her legs apart with his knee, he slid himself between them, priming her again with his hand before attempting entry. Hot eagerness boiled inside him, but he beat it down, probing into her by slow degrees.*

It is worth including here the moments after Chase and Maggie make love, which show him to be not only a virile lover, but also a tender and caring person:

> *Holding her close against him, Chase lay on his back and stared at the dazzling blue sky overhead. Both of them were quivering in a kind of*

stunned aftershock. His hand was burrowed into the slight dampness of her hair, while she rested her cheek on the hard pillow of his chest. Thoroughly content, he angled his head to see the way she curled against him.

"I was right, wasn't I? I did give you pleasure." He wanted to hear her say it, to know beyond any doubt that it has been a shared experience.

She tipped her head way back to meet his eyes, boldly proud, exhibiting no shyness. "Yes." The simple affirmative answer told him all he needed to know and more.

Young Adult Romances / If, after reading these sensual and downright explicit sex scenes, you feel that you can't bring yourself to write one, do not despair. You don't have to write books in which the hero and heroine actually make love, if you are not comfortable in doing so. Sweet romances are still being published today, and, as you have seen, they demand more discreet, less passionate expressions of physical desire.

Also, there are the young adult romances. Perhaps you will be reassured by this scene from *The Voices of Julie,* by Joan L. Oppenheimer (Scholastic). As in most young adult romances, the sweet and tender scene in which the heroine, Julie Enright, and her hero, Tony Martone, recognize and admit their feelings for one another comes near the ending, in the next-to-last chapter. This is only Julie's second kiss. The scene takes place at a hoedown.

She (Julie) knew he was going to kiss her. She had known the moment he detoured her into the alcove what he had in mind. On one level, she didn't want it to happen. Yet at the same time, she must have wanted it because she lifted her face to meet him halfway.

The same magical response as she had the first time he kissed her that night in his living room in front of the fire. She was not aware of the door opening behind them until she heard a familiar voice exclaim, "Excuse it, please. Don't let me interrupt anything."

Julie backed away, her face burning, in time to see a wide-eyed K.C. staring at her, then giggling as she scooted past the phones and around the corner. The motormouth of Mesa Verde High, Julie thought wearily. Of all the people to catch her kissing Tony Martone, it would have to be the one girl totally incapable of keeping the incident to herself.

Is this more your style? Then perhaps you have found your goal—a well-written young adult romance.

Whatever the level of passion in your romance novel, bear this in mind: boudoir acrobatics alone won't do it. In fact, no sex scene will really move your reader unless you *keep the emotions of your characters central* at all times.

In the beginning of this chapter, I pointed out that love without sex is pretty disappointing. So is sex without love. The love your heroine and hero feel for each other must come through in your sex scenes. What they feel for each other must absorb the reader.

I repeat—physical passion must always be secondary to the emotional climate of your story, whether you are writing a sweet romance, a sensual category, a steamy historical, or an innocent young adult romance.

Setting Your Sex Scenes

Give as much attention to *where* your love/sex scenes take place as you give to the action and dialogue. The setting can help to intensify the sexual chemistry flowing between the heroine and hero and to arouse the romantic in the reader. What is more sensual than the wind sighing through the pines, or the murmur of the waves as they break upon the beach below the bedroom window?

One excellent device for increasing excitement in your sex scenes, particularly if your book has several, is to find unconventional settings for these tender moments.

The out-of-doors offers the chance to use the elements of nature to embellish and enrich the scene. Janet Joyce places her hero and heroine in *Winter Lady* in the deep, cold snow, where their warm kisses contrast with their cold skin.

The scene from *This Calder Sky,* which you have just read, takes place on the bank of a river where Maggie has been swimming nude. Chase builds a roaring fire to warm her shivering body before he makes love to her.

Naturally, I like to use the ocean and warm golden sand as my romantic setting. The ocean can be stormy and thundering against a rocky shore when my heroine and hero are quarreling and unhappy. When things are going well, it can be lapping as softly and gently as a love song. Of course, I used it in the first romantic young adult novel I wrote, *Song of the Ocean* (Arcadia).

All through the book, the ocean has been fluctuating between storm-tossed rage and the tranquility of a lake on a summer day. Robbin, the heroine, and Steve, the hero, are both interested in oceanographic research, and are both professionally and emotionally bound to the sea. Therefore it was believable that the ocean would have emotional significance for them, a natural symbol with which to end the story:

> *They (Robbin and Steve) left the car and walked arm in arm toward the laboratory building, now silent and dark. The December night was crisp and clear, with a half-moon riding high over the dark table of the sea. Before Robbin and Steve entered the laboratory, they embraced again, while the waves breaking ceaselessly against the shore filled the night with their own special love song.*

Be sure to tap the romantic elements of your setting, whether they be salt breezes or snowy winds, and weave them into the intensity of the feelings your hero and heroine have for each other.

Creating romantic love scenes and sensual sex scenes is what romance writing is all about, no matter what particular line you choose as your market. The love scenes, more than any other, draw the reader into the story and then give her the payoff of emotional satisfaction. The reader wants to identify with the heroine and the hero. She wants to feel as they do in their quest for love and in their ecstasy when the moment of physical and emotional commitment arrives.

If you feel inhibited or embarrassed at the thought of writing sex scenes for your romance novel, or worried over what your family and friends might think, you must purge yourself of this feeling if you have decided to write this type of book.

"I'm always in the mood to write sensual love scenes, undoubtedly influenced by my office being in one corner of a very sexy (to me) bedroom. If this isn't enough, I need only walk down the stairs and seek my husband. After thirty-three years of marriage, his love is still inspiration enough to have fueled several novels." **Alice Morgan, author of contemporary romances**

First overcome your own inhibitions by realizing that you are not describing your own romance, your own erotic thoughts, or your own sexual experience. You are bringing to life characters who have sprung from your imagination. Your reader does not identify with you, but with your heroine.

If you do a sound job of characterization, your sex scenes will come through as satisfying reading—exciting, sensually thrilling, absolutely inevitable, and *right,* in the context of your story.

If you truly bring your characters to life, you will find that as you write, you are inside your heroine, listening to *her* telling *her story.* In some sense, it is she who is tapping the typewriter keys, not you. She is doing in her story what she was destined to do, in the boudoir and out of it. You are merely transmitting it to your reader.

If you still feel squeamish, attend a professional writers' conference. Listen to the pros. You'll soon discover that as they talk about their stories, it is not of themselves they speak. They talk about their heroines and heroes as if they were separate, living people. You'll have to remind yourself that the subjects of the conversation are fictional. Professional writers have no difficulty in putting themselves aside, and you won't either, with a little practice.

Points to Remember:

1. It takes practice to write a sex scene that will give your reader a sensual, satisfying read. If you are having trouble getting started with this, try copying out, by hand or on the typewriter, some sensual scenes you have admired. Let your mind fall into that writer's way of thinking. Experience the way in which the words came together in her head. The idea isn't to plagiarize, but to get the feeling of being able to produce these scenes. As you read, underline words that arouse you. Keep adding to your list of romantic, sensual phrases.

2. Whenever possible, use figurative speech and sensual metaphors as substitutes for clinical anatomical terms designating parts of the human body, especially those below the waist.

3. If you're a bit rusty on the subject of erotic sexuality, start reading sex manuals, such as *The Sensuous Couple* by Robert Chartham (Ballantine). At the end of this book you'll find a list of books which will help you increase your sensual and sexual awareness. Romance writers must have a basic understanding of the erogenous zones of the body, as well as a knowledge of the differences, physical and psychological, between men and women.

4. In planning sex scenes for a category romance, be sure to consult guidelines and gear the level of physical intimacy to what is expected for that line.

5. Whether you are writing a contemporary or an historical romance, be sure your heroine is shown enjoying and participating in—and sometimes even initiating—sex. She should thrill to the final climax of consummated love right along with the hero. The day when a woman *pleasured* her man out of duty is long gone. If yours is a young adult novel, your heroine should thrill to that first timid kiss just as the more mature heroine thrills to the ardent lovemaking of her hero.

6. Be sure your sex scenes are fully developed. In fact, after you write each sex scene, let it cool for a day or two. Then go back and write it again—and make it twice as long. There are two reasons for this advice:

   a. If you are a new romance writer, you will probably find it difficult to write these scenes. Therefore, you will try to get them over with as quickly as possible and move on to the easier scenes. For this reason, it's more than likely that you will have shortchanged the reader. You will probably need more sensual words and phrases, more emotion, more action, and more dialogue between your lovers.

b. Editors of romance fiction want sex scenes to be long enough for the reader to become emotionally involved. This can't happen in a brief paragraph or two. It may take three, four, or more pages to build sexual tension to the point that the reader can vicariously become a part of what is taking place.

When your novel is published and you hear a reader say, "That was such a beautiful love scene! I had tears in my eyes as I read it," you'll be glad of the difficult hours in which you struggled to write it.

SCHOLASTIC
1.95
SCHOLASTIC
WILDFIRE
LISA
0-590-32001-7
ARLENE HALE

Chapter **11.**
HAPPILY EVER AFTER:
Planning Carefully for a Satisfying Ending

We thrill to the happy ending of a romance, whether in real life or in the last pages of a novel. When love conquers all, our faith in the ultimate goodness of life is reaffirmed.

We all need happy endings; sometimes they move us to tears. (Don't we go to weddings and sit misty-eyed, listening to the lovers whisper their vows?) The need for happy endings also moves more than twenty million women in America to read romance fiction avidly.

But achieving happy endings, whether in life or in fiction, requires adjustments, concessions, and planning.

In a romance novel, the beginning and the ending are wedded together in a perfect circle; the beginning paves the way for the ending, and the ending justifies the beginning.

Planning Ahead

A believable ending is a *planned* ending. If you throw your final scenes together like a hurry-up stew, or tack them on with no planning, they will come through to the reader as contrived. On the other hand, if you know where your story is going from the start, your ending will feel right.

"The trick on endings is not to inject too much description and narrative. An ending should be mostly dialogue and emotions." Tom Curtis, one half of Robin James (with his wife, Sharon Curtis)

The following suggestions will help you plan a convincing "and-they-lived-happily-ever-after" ending for your romance novel, whatever type you are writing:

1. If you haven't already done so, go back over your outline and write out each of the problems you've created to keep the heroine and hero from admitting their love for one another. Then, on a separate sheet of paper, write out all the possible solutions your ending could hold for each problem. Give yourself several choices, in case the solution you think is best doesn't work when you come to that last chapter.

   Knowing how your characters will solve each problem also allows you to *foreshadow* the endings; that is, to plant clues along the way that the reader will remember in retrospect.

2. Remember, when the time comes to resolve your problems, just before the final scene, solve the smallest one first. Then take the next largest, and so on. *Save the most important for last.* The reader's suspense is in direct proportion to the intensity of the problem. Save solutions to the

largest problems for last and your reader will want to stay with your story to the very end.

3. Review your scenes of sexual tension, your push-pull scenes, to make sure you haven't erected *impossible* barriers between the heroine and the hero. By impossible, I mean, for example, unforgivable action on the hero's part, acts of meanness, or evil intentions; these would make him so unsympathetic that no reader would believe the heroine could forgive and forget. Check your heroine's actions as well to make sure she is sympathetic at all times.

Sympathetic characters err because of human frailty. Because the reader is human too, with the same frailties, she understands. Understanding is the essence of reader identification and sympathy. Unsympathetic characters have no place here and do not deserve that happy ending.

4. Before writing your final scenes, go over your scenes of sexual tension and emotional conflict to make sure you've dramatized the sexual attraction between the heroine and hero in generous descriptions of physical interaction.

Have you managed to show plenty of touching, caressing, kisses taken with or without consent? How about physical contact in abundance, to heighten the mutual sexual attraction that will triumph over all problems in the final scene?

Without a strong and consistent buildup of sexual desire, felt by both lovers, the final surrender will seem contrived. If the heroine doesn't care deeply for the hero, *in spite of their differences,* why would she put up with all the trouble he causes her?

5. Just before their final embrace, when the lovers melt into each other's arms and declare their love, summarize all the problems that have kept them apart. Make this summary in the dialogue and through realizations in the mind of your heroine (and of your hero, too, if he is also a viewpoint character).

Let's take time here for an example of this kind of summarizing from a contemporary romance—*Amber Wine* by Fran Wilson (Silhouette):

Several barriers have stood between Gayle Eberly, the American heroine, and Ramon Albariza, the Mexican hero. In seeming contempt for women, he has taken over her winery, all but her inherited share. As a Mexican, he has an old-fashioned attitude toward women who take an active part in a male-dominated business. There is also Carmelita, the beautiful Mexican girl who Gayle assumes is a contender for Ramon's heart.

Gayle's self-erected barriers to her love for Ramon are her pride, which is threatened by a financial setback to the winery; her recent broken engagement, which has made her wary of emotional involvement with any man; and a natural jealousy of the pretty Mexican girl who seems to have captured Ramon's love.

Just before the final love scene, Ramon explains that his scorn for women, particularly American women, has been the result of his part-American mother's infidelity to his father. And then:

> In one swift movement, Ramon swept her up into his arms and carried her back across the room to the window seat.
> "Querida—querida mia [my beloved] you are stubborn and foolish and beautiful." His arms were beneath her, cradling her against the warmth of his body. The way he was looking at her released a storm of emotion within her.
> "What strange notions have filled that lovely amber head of yours . . . **Darling, Carmelita is my sister, my half-sister, that is.**"

Furthermore, he points out, although they come from different backgrounds, they do share the same love of growing grapes and making fine wine.

With these obstacles out of the way, Ramon sweeps Gayle into his arms, kisses her passionately and tenderly, and continues:

> "It is this hand of yours which I wish to hold in mine for a lifetime. I'm asking you to stay in my country, in my vineyard, in my casa, in every part of my life, Gayle, because we belong together. Will you stay?"

What woman in her right mind could refuse such a proposal? The differences that caused doubt in Gayle's mind have been removed. She replies in the words Ramon has taught her:

> "Si (yes) querido mio, si."

She returns his kiss passionately and we, the readers, feel that Gayle and Ramon will indeed live happily ever after.

6. Think of your ending as a *reversal* of your beginning.

> Beginning: problems presented
> Ending: problems solved

> With the obstacles removed one at a time by convincing explanations or action, the true love shared by the heroine and the hero can now be recognized by both.

7. Avoid being anticlimactic. The story is over when the lovers have resolved their differences and have admitted their love for one another. Any necessary information about their future should be woven tightly into the dialogue that accompanies their last embrace. Then your book should end.

8. Avoid rushing your ending, but at the same time, be careful not to over-write so that you lose tension. One passionate declaration of love from each lover is sufficient. More than one kills the effect.

For the same reason, limit this rehashing of explanations for imagined transgressions by the heroine or the hero. Make them long enough to clear up the misunderstanding, short enough to hold the reader's interest at its peak.

An emotion felt either by reader or characters can be sustained for only a short time. Capture it at the moment of greatest intensity, and then move on.

9. Show through dialogue and the character's thoughts how your heroine and hero have changed. Each has gained new insight and better under-standing of self and lover.

10. KEEP YOUR ENDING ROMANTIC. The time is past for heavy accusa-tions and chilling hostility. Even before the passionate words are whis-pered, the heroine knows in her heart and admits to herself that she is hopelessly in love with the hero. He, too, knows that he loves her. Now only the final barrier between them has to melt away so that the lovers can be free to declare their true feelings.

That Final Scene of Passion

How your lovers express their ultimate commitment to each other will de-pend on the particular market you are writing for. In the sweet romances, physical contact in the last pages is intensely romantic and full of controlled passion. As in *Amber Wine*, which we have just looked at, the final love scene, and the book, usually end *on the verge of* consummation.

In the more sensual category contemporaries, the final scene often contains fully consummated sexual passion, with plenty of erotic description to help the reader share vicariously in the ecstasy of the lovers.

Here is an example of such an ending from *Renaissance Man*, by Stephanie James (Silhouette, Desire):

When rare-book dealer Alina Corey finally succumbs to the charms of Jared Troy, a Renaissance scholar with whom she has had a fiery and com-petitive professional correspondence, the encounter takes place in the swimming pool:

> *(Jared) settled her (Alina's) eager body along the length of his, taking possession of it as he took possession of her mouth. They made love with a grace induced by the watery environment, slowly, lingeringly, lovingly . . .*
> *Alina arched thrilling, her ecstatic cry caught in her throat. . . . His*

own muffled shout soon followed as he surged powerfully upward, holding her so tightly she had to gulp for breath.

Down, down they came, literally, figuratively, each lost in their very private world, clinging to each other until they finally found themselves trying to tread water . . .

"This particular technique may take a little practice," Jared admitted with a grin, catching his breath. "We'll work on it after we get the (marriage) license."

In writing endings for the longer category romances, such as Harlequin Superromances, Silhouette Special Editions, or for historical romances, family sagas, and series, much more preparation and advance planning are needed to resolve plot complexities. Not only the primary conflict but also the subplots and secondary problems must be resolved.

While the final embrace and avowal of mutual love may fill only the last few pages of a novel of 500 pages or more, you must begin early, probably by the last third of the novel, to resolve the many secondary problems. You must account for a large cast of characters and explain what happened to each one.

Death by fair means or foul usually disposes of more than a few characters in a lengthy historical. Treat these deaths with sensitivity but without heavy crepe-hanging or breast-beating, which would spoil the romantic tone of the novel.

Secondary characters can move away or fall in love and get married which removes them as threats—if that has been their role in relation to the heroine.

In a family saga, the natural process of aging diminishes the cast of characters as the next generation rises in importance. The focus shifts and roles change; perhaps the once young and beautiful first generation heroine becomes the matriarch of the family. Into her place steps the equally beautiful and interesting daughter, followed possibly by an intriguing young granddaughter.

All of these events take time and words. You, of course, have kept track of the events and changes in each character's life on a carefully thought-out chart, showing where each one is at each given time. Your careful planning has shown you just where to begin solving the problems that stand in the way of the happy ending.

In these longer romances and big historicals, plenty of physical contact takes place between hero and heroine throughout the book, so that they may or may not actually make love in the last pages. But in either case, when the reader has stayed with your novel for hundreds of pages, she deserves the full satisfaction of a well-written, solidly plotted, and highly romantic ending. She doesn't want to be left hanging, wondering whatever happended to that ravishing Other Woman who seemed to be stealing the show back in the beginning.

In Laurie McBain's *Tears of Gold*, mentioned in chapter six, the reader is left with no doubts about the fate of each character:

Don Andres believes for many pages that the heroine, the actress, Mara, is the girl he was betrothed to in childhood and the woman he will marry. Just before the end of the book, he is left sadder for the moment, but wiser, when he finds out she is not. It is suggested that he will wed the Spanish señorita, a girl more like himself than the fiery Irish Mara.

Big Swede, a good-hearted man who befriends Mara and falls in love with her, realizes and accepts that she is not for him, and turns his attention to a more likely prospect.

Nicholas Chantale, the hero, realizes three or four pages from the end that he doesn't really love Amaryllis, the Other Woman who really only wants to marry his *name*. He loves Mara, our heroine. He has always loved her, but only now can he admit it to himself and to her.

In the final scene, Mara playfully matches Nicholas' Irish brogue, as—at last—she accepts his love and admits her own love for him:

> *A smile curved Nicholas' mouth and a devilish light twinkled in his eyes. "Since you've assumed so many identities in your short but colorful life, Mara, me love* [i.e. as an actress] *I think there might be room for one more. And the final one will be," he added in deadly seriousness, "Mara Chantale. It sounds right," he whispered, as he enclosed her in his arms, holding her as if he would never free her, "as if it belongs to you, and only you."*
>
> *Mara's arms encircled his strong neck and she gazed up at him with all her love revealed. Never had she looked more beautiful, Nicholas thought humbly. He knew all too well the great effort it had taken for her to declare her love to him.* [It took her 568 pages.]
>
> *" 'Tis a fine name. And to be sure, there's none other I'd care to be takin'," Mara answered as she reached up and met his seeking lips half way.*
>
> *The long voyage ahead of them was temporarily forgotten as they lost themselves in each other's love.*

Again, here is a satisfying "they-lived-happily-ever-after" ending with the lovers in each other's arms, their differences resolved in a credible manner, and other characters accounted for in a realistic way.

In the young adult romance, you must not only resolve all romantic complications but also highlight the heroine's character growth, probably the hero's, and possibly that of other young characters as well. As in all other types of romantic fiction, the ending is a reversal of the beginning. The story circles back to whatever critical situation opened the novel. Those doubts are now balanced with certainties; new insight and maturity have been gained.

Again, lingering glances, tender kisses, and handholding are sufficient for the concluding scene. The young lovers are, after all, just on the threshold of adulthood, with other goals to achieve before full commitment to a mate. Usually the story ends with bright hope for the heroine's career or personal future, as well as the promise of an eventual happily-ever-after, perhaps with the hero, or possibly with someone else far down the road.

Helen Erskine's *Kate Herself*, mentioned in chapter seven, opens with Kate very unsure of her identity and of her ability to gain the attention of Ross, the most popular boy in school and a senior.

The book ends with each of these problems reversed. That is, they are solved, all summed up in four short, tightly written paragraphs.

> *"See you, Kate!" Ross called after her.*
>
> *She laughed, thinking of how that parting had worried her in the past. Not anymore. "I love you," he'd said. And I love you.*
>
> *They might love each other for the next six months, or the next year. Maybe they'd love each other forever. They were too young to be sure. She might decide to go on to college and study child psychology. Ross had no idea of what he wanted to do.*
>
> *He'd told her she'd confused him. I was confused too, Ross, she thought. I wasn't sure of what I was. But now I know myself, at least a little bit better. And she knew as time passed, she would find out even more.*

Points to Remember:

Whatever type of romance novel you are writing, think out your ending carefully. As soon as you know your story well enough, try to carefully see and hear it happening. . . the place, the circumstances, the romantic words of love your heroine will whisper.

If that last scene, or a piece of it, jells in your mind while you're at work on chapter three, quickly jot it down. Don't let it slip away. You may have to rewrite it many times before it feels perfect, but at least you'll have a starting point.

Your endings should be a showcase for your best writing, writing that is sensuously descriptive and glowingly romantic.

Like the graceful figure eights that iceskaters seem to perform effortlessly, satisfying, credible, and romantic endings take practice and a full understanding of what is expected by the reader.

In addition to practicing, that is, rethinking and rewriting your endings many times if necessary, continually study those written by writers you admire.

When at last you've written an ending you like, put it aside and let it cool for several days. Then read it one more time and make a final check:

- Have you accounted for all the characters?
- Have you given sufficient summary of past action to remind the reader of the problems that had to be resolved?
- Is there poetic beauty in the hero's declaration of love and in the heroine's revelation of her true feelings?
- Do the heroine and hero have sufficient intimate physical contact to form a counterpoint to their verbal expression of love?
- Will your ending give the reader an emotional experience, a feeling that love truly does conquer all?

If you can answer "yes" to all these questions, you have a believable and satisfying ending for the heroine and the hero, who have waited so long for this moment; for the reader who felt all along that the lovers were meant for each other, but wasn't sure *how* they'd ever resolve their differences; and last, but not least, for the writer, who, with a sigh of relief and confidence, can write those magic words—THE END.

2.95
70065

SUPERROMANCE

A PERSISTENT FLAME LINDA TURNER

THEIR MEETING WAS FATE,
THEIR UNION UNDREAMED-OF ECSTASY

Chapter **12.**
FINAL TOUCHES:
A Last Check for
Perfection

At last your romance novel is finished! You can't wait to put it in a box, wrap it, label it, and take it to the post office. By this time, you're (understandably) weary of the long and concentrated effort now behind you. And you're eager to get on with your next book.

Wanting to move to a new idea is healthy in a writer, and it should be nurtured by all means. But leaving the old idea too soon can be dangerous. You need to take the time for one last check to be sure your book is all it can be. But before you do this, take a break. The effort of writing that happy ending, and all the chapters before it, has left you emotionally drained and physically exhausted. You need time in which to revive and to put emotional distance between you and your work.

So no matter how much you are tempted to run to the post office—*wait.* Put the manuscript away some place where you can't see it. Forget it! No, don't even reread that last beautiful chapter.

"You have to be ruthless. I've cut out many scenes that I've really loved, and whole chapters, because they didn't fit. Before a book gets mailed out, I rewrite and cut out and edit, very, very ruthlessly."
Rosemary Rogers

How long must you wait? Several days at least; a week to ten days would be better. You'll know when your emotional involvement with your story has cooled enough to allow you to look at your writing calmly and objectively. Only then can you determine whether what you thought you wrote is really there on paper.

This final check you'll give your romance novel—front, back, and sideways—will increase your chances of catching any flaws that may have gone unnoticed in the heat of creativity. Paint a room. Plant your garden. When you have had a real vacation and can come back to your manuscript with a clear head and renewed energy, turn to the checklist below.

Now, you are going to read your book through for the last time, not to make drastic changes, but to polish and refine. Here are suggestions for checking your story from every angle:

1. Check Your Overall Organization

a. Does your novel read well? That is, does it go along at a good pace, never too slow, but never galloping? Are exciting, fast-paced scenes followed by quieter, slower-paced scenes of reflection on what has happened or anticipation of things that might happen? Your slower scenes allow your reader to savor and enjoy the exciting ones. Think of them as resting places between the high points of dramatic action in your novel.

b. Is your primary plot—the interaction between the hero and heroine— always at the forefront of the story? Think of their relationship as a red string running through the book. Everything else must connect with it.

c. If you have subplots, do they help to complicate and delay the resolution of the main plot? They should.

d. Does each chapter contain a plot step that paves the way for the next chapter, an event that forces the heroine or the hero to make a new decision or take a new action?

"One of the most frequent mistakes beginners make is putting too much background in the first three chapters. A lot of the background should be spread throughout the story."   **Carolyn Nichols, romance editor**

---

e. Do you need to tighten some scenes? Are some bogged down with too much narration? If so, you can put narration into action and dialogue.

f. If you used flashbacks, have you kept them short and woven them into your story as short scenes of recall? Are they always relevant to the main story problem? If you must have longer flashback scenes, remember that you can dramatize them in action and dialogue so that they seem to be happening in the present.

2. Check Your Characterization

a. Have you described your heroine, hero, and other characters sensuously with word pictures that appeal to all five senses? Will the reader see the golden shine of your heroine's hair, hear the rustle of her silk skirt, feel the softness of her skin, and taste the salt air on the hero's skin, as she does?

b. Did you weave descriptions of your characters into the action and dialogue within your scenes? If so, check to make sure you haven't stopped or slowed down your story or your plot action with description.

c. Are the heroine's feelings toward the hero well motivated? Do you show the physical attractiveness of the hero, which *pulls* her toward him, and do you also show actions, words or reactions on his part that *push* her away?

d. Is your characterization consistent with the time period of your novel, the ages of your characters, and their professional or educational backgrounds?

e. Are your heroine and hero sympathetic to the reader? Are they realistically motivated, so that the reader can identify with them and see them as romantic at the same time?

3. Check Your Setting

a. Is your setting consistent with the requirements set forth in editorial guidelines for the type of romance you've chosen to write?

b. If your romance is contemporary, have you done adequate research to make your setting seem authentic?

c. If your setting is historical, is your authority established in accurate descriptions of such things as climate, geography, plant life native to the area, types of houses, means of transportation, food eaten, manners, and social customs?

d. Have you given all descriptions of the setting in sensuous words and phrases that create romantic pictures in the reader's mind?

e. Have you given descriptions between the scenes of dialogue and action, or else combined them with the dialogue and action, so that the story unfolds without interruption?

f. Does your setting seem to be a natural extension of the characterization and the plot? Will the reader feel that your story could have taken place only in this setting?

g. Is your setting exciting and romantic, a place the reader would want to visit?

4. Check Your Plot

a. Did you heroine meet the hero directly or indirectly in chapter one? By "indirectly," I mean that the heroine knows about the hero. He is already disturbingly in her thoughts. By "directly," I mean that he is actively on stage.

b. Did the first meeting with the hero cause sexual arousal within the heroine? Did you show the sexual chemistry beginning to flow between them? Make a list of all the feeling words you used in this important scene.

c. Have you established in this scene, and in every other scene between your hero and heroine, the crucial push-pull element—the attraction vs. the complications?

d. Have you given motivation for all character actions, reactions, feelings, and thoughts?

e. Do you have several crisis scenes, in which you place the heroine and the hero in explosive situations?

f. Did you bring your story to a suspense-filled climax, in which the heroine and the hero appear to be lost to each other just before the ending?

g. Is your resolution of this climax believable? Is it soundly motivated by character growth, new insight, and credible solutions to the many problems that have kept the heroine and the hero on a seesaw?
h. Did you remember to pick up all clues, plants, and foreshadowings, and make them pay off at the conclusion of your novel?
i. Are you sure your ending is not anticlimactic? That is, does your book end at the moment of resolution with the final embrace or consummation of love between the heroine and the hero?
j. Is your ending romantic? Can you add one more final touch to make it even more romantic?

5. Check Your Handling of Viewpoint

a. Have you chosen the right viewpoint for your romance as set forth in the editorial guidelines for the line, if any?
b. Have you stayed in viewpoint in every scene—that is, in the thoughts of the character holding center stage at the time? If you switched viewpoint within a scene, did you have a valid reason for doing so? Was there no other way for you to handle the scene? What did you gain by shifting viewpoint within the scene?
c. If the kind of romance you've written allows for multiple viewpoint—entering more than one character's thoughts—did you prepare the reader by means of careful transitions? In other words, when you made the shift from one viewpoint to another, did you point to the next speaker through a reference or through some action?

6. Check Your Dialogue

a. Is dialogue consistent with the time period, the age of your characters, and their professional and educational backgrounds?
b. Do any of your characters talk or sound alike? If so, rewrite the dialogue.
c. Does your dialogue reflect *your* voice rather than that of the characters? If so, rewrite.
d. Does each passage of dialogue between your hero and heroine advance the plot either by pulling the heroine toward the hero or by creating further obstacles to push her away?
e. Does the dialogue help to characterize the speaker?
f. If the dialogue doesn't advance the plot or characterize, does it give information that another character doesn't have access to or already have? Dialogue must serve a purpose—to advance the plot, characterize, give information, or all three.
g. Does your dialogue add to the romantic atmosphere of the story? Does your heroine speak with the voice of somebody in love? Does the hero?

(Even when the lovers are quarreling, the reader should be able to hear the whisper of love beneath the words of conflict.)

7. Check Your Sex Scenes

a. Are your sex scenes written in keeping with the editorial guidelines for your kind of romance novel?
b. Do your sex scenes build reader interest and suspense through dramatic push-pull?
c. When describing the physical action of lovemaking, have you also given the reader access to your characters' emotions through what they say, do, and think?
d. Have you dramatized fully the action of lovemaking through plenty of description, physical and emotional, so that the reader can experience vicariously the same ecstasy felt by the heroine and the hero?
e. Are your sex scenes a sensual *and* a sensuous experience for the reader, written to appeal to all five senses?
f. Do you show your hero to be tender as well as passionate, and always sensitive to a woman's erotic and emotional needs? If not, does he grow toward this in the course of the story?
g. Does your heroine take an active part in sex, showing her pleasure and actively participating in the act of love?
   If you have written an historical romance set in a period when women were restricted and inhibited in their attitudes toward sex, is your heroine a woman ahead of her time, able to respond passionately to the right man?
h. Have you used original, fresh phrases to describe parts of the human body and the way they respond to arousal? Are your descriptions in good taste?
i. Compare what you consider your best sex scene with a passionate but tastefully written scene of lovemaking in a romance novel you admire. Is that scene better? Why? What can you do to improve yours?

8. Check Your Ending

a. Is your ending the logical outcome of all that has happened throughout your novel?
b. Did you remind the reader of past obstacles, now overcome, just before the final scene?
c. Have you resolved all of the problems that kept the heroine and the hero uncommitted until the final scene?
e. Does your final scene reflect the best writing of which you are capable at the moment? Is it romantic? Is it believable? Does it show character growth and change?

f. What emotional response do you think the reader will feel as she reads the last lines of your romance novel? If possible, test your ending on at least three potential readers. Ask them what they felt as they read it.

9. Check Your Style

a. Is your style appropriate to the type of romance novel you selected to write? If your novel is contemporary, does your style reflect the way men and women think and talk in today's world?

   If your novel is an historical romance, have you checked to make sure you used words that would have been used in that period?

   If yours is a young adult romance, have you caught the essence of today's young people in the characters' thought, action, and dialogue?

b. Is your style sensuous and romantic, appealing to all five senses? Check your descriptive paragraphs to make sure you've used the most sensuous words possible in describing people, places, and particularly the sexual responses of the heroine to the hero, and vice versa.

c. Does your style reflect a concern for the tools of your profession—proper spelling, grammar, punctuation, and sentence structure?

d. Have you used clichés, words and phrases used too many times by other writers, so that they have lost their freshness and originality? Watch for such phrases as *pale as a ghost, violet or emerald green eyes, well-defined features, deep baritone voice, well-rounded breasts.*

   Substitute your own fresh, original descriptive tags for those that have been overworked.

All this may seem like a great deal of work at this point, but the time you spend in final polishing will pay off when the editor opens your manuscript and starts to read.

   Editors are becoming more selective as the marketplace fills up with more and more romance writers seeking publication. Your words on paper are all that you will have to speak for you as you compete with hundreds of other writers. Make them the very best you can write.

   Like your heroine, who drifts out the door to meet the love of her life knowing she looks her very best, you'll feel confident in the knowledge that your romance novel is beautifully groomed for its debut on the editor's desk.

   With the final touches completed, you're ready at last to put together *the editorial package,* the supplementary material that will accompany your manuscript and your passport to possible publication.

Irma Walker

Author of SURRENDER
and A NEW TOMORROW

LOVE
& LIFE

WOMEN'S
STORIES
FOR TODAY

The Next Step

This honeymoon
must end—something for
a marriage to grow...

Ballantine/Fiction/31083/$1.75

Chapter 13.
YOUR PASSPORT TO PUBLICATION: The Editorial Package

Unlike your heroine, who only has a moment for that last pat to the coiffure and that dab of perfume to the wrists, you have all the time you need to see that your manuscript and the materials that will go with it to the editor's desk are well put together, seams straight and no stray threads. Eye appeal is one of the most important aids in selling any product, and your romance novel is no exception.

Put yourself in the editor's place. There you sit on a busy morning, with a stack of fifty or sixty manuscripts to be read. You pick one out of the pile. The writer didn't care enough to put a fresh ribbon in the typewriter. You can hardly read it. The next one has nice, clean, well-defined type. Which one are you going to read first? The one that is easier to read, of course.

When you type that final draft of your manuscript, spend the time and the money to buy a new typewriter ribbon and a good grade of paper so that when you have it copied, you'll get a clear, easy-on-the-eyes copy.

Typing Your Manuscript

Editors and agents may differ in their preferences for the way manuscripts are typed. But the following suggestions will guide you toward a fairly standard professional layout for yours.

If you're unsure how your manuscript should look in its final form, here are a few pointers.

1. It is nice to have a cover sheet, a page that helps protect your manuscript. Type the title of your novel in caps, centered, about halfway down the page. Then, four spaces below the title, center the word "by." Drop down another four spaces and center your name as you wish it to appear on the cover of your novel. This is the only place your pen name, if you are using one, will appear on your manuscript.

2. On page one, type your real name and address, single-spaced, in the upper left-hand corner. If you have an agent, his or her name and address go under yours.

3. In the upper right-hand corner of page one, type the title, and under that, the kind of novel it is—contemporary, young adult, historical. Then give the approximate word count.

4. Drop down a good fourth of the page, and center, in caps, CHAPTER ONE. Go down another four spaces, indent from 5 to 10 spaces, and begin your first paragraph. Keep indentation uniform throughout.

5. On each *subsequent* page, type your (actual) last name only in the upper left-hand corner and the page number in the right-hand corner.

SAMPLE

Annabelle Lee
1200 Rosewood Drive
Any Town, State 22222

ANOTHER LOVE
Contemporary Romance
70,000 words

CHAPTER ONE

Across the crowded room, her gaze met that of the tall,
lean-faced man standing in the doorway, and for a moment,
it seemed her heart had stopped beating. It couldn't be! But
it was—the one man she'd sworn to forget. She *had* forgotten him, hadn't she? Then why this melting sensation in her
bones, and the dryness in her throat?

After all these years, at least six, he could do this to her.
And now, as he moved slowly toward her, his dark eyes
moving over her in the old intimate way, penetrating her
fragile facade of composure, she knew she hadn't forgotten
him at all.

Keep plenty of white space throughout your manuscript: a good inch and
one-half at top and bottom and a generous margin on right and left sides.
Your editor may need to make some changes, and instructions to the printer
will go here, too.

As you type, check each page before you take it out of your machine.

Eliminate all typographical errors and misspelled words. When you have what you believe to be a perfectly typed, completed manuscript, proof it again. Then, if you can, have someone else read through once more for errors, just to be sure you haven't let some glaring mistake slip past you. You are so close to your work that a typo or misspelled word may be lurking on the very first page and you may have read right over it.

The Editorial Package

If this is your third or fifth or seventh romance novel, you probably already have a working relationship with an editor, an agent, or both. By now, you may not need to submit the full editorial package I am describing here. Perhaps your editor has asked you to send only a brief synopsis of your proposed next novel. But if this is your first book, check the preferences of the first publisher you have decided to send it to.

If the romance fiction editor at that publishing house will look only at a completed manuscript by a first-time author, you will need first to send a query letter, which contains a one-page synopsis describing in an interesting manner the hero, heroine, plot, and setting of your novel. The same applies if you are submitting to an agent. Your beautifully typed manuscript is all ready to go as soon as the editor or agent reads your query letter, decides your work is worth seeing, and writes or calls to say, "Send it!"

Most often, however, busy editors and agents prefer to see a partial manuscript, known affectionately as "a partial." Even though your book is completed, if you are submitting a partial, you will send only part of it at this point, along with an *editorial package* consisting of:

1. A brief synopsis of the plot
2. Biographical sketches of your heroine, hero, and other major characters, if any
3. Three sample chapters—the first three—and a chapter-by-chapter outline of the remainder of the novel.
4. Two well-developed, sensually written sex scenes taken from later chapters
5. Author credit page
6. Cover letter

This package will give that overworked and weary-eyed editor a chance to decide at a glance whether or not you have written a saleable romance novel. She can see whether the story fits her needs at the moment or whether a few changes in your book would make it acceptable.

Before we discuss each part of the editorial package in detail, it's important to review the differences between the working synopsis, character bio-

---

"What I usually look at is an outline and several sample chapters rather than a completed manuscript. Editors work differently—I put a lot of faith in the outline. It should clearly show your plot idea, the conflict, and suggestions for how it's going to be resolved. That tells me whether or not you can plot a book."   Robin Grunder, romance editor

---

graphies, and outline we suggested you make in the planning stages of your novel and those you'll make now for an editor's eye.

The character bios and working outline you wrote in the planning stages of your book were for your eyes alone, and therefore they could be written in any manner useful to you. You used them to plan and flesh out your ideas and to help you develop your plot line and good characterization.

Unlike your preliminary outline and character biographies, those that accompany your manuscript to market are intended for the editor and his or her staff. Their purpose is to display the virtues of your novel and to sell it.

The editorial package is your sales kit. Each of the six parts performs a vital function in selling your romance novel.

1. *Synopsis.* Keep it brief, one or two pages at most. Identify the heroine, the hero, and any other *major* characters. In a short paragraph describe the *critical* situation facing the heroine in chapter one. In addition to the plot line and the characterization of heroine and hero, your synopsis should give the specific professional and geographical background of the story.

The purpose of your synopsis is to sell the editor on the freshness and originality of your idea and on your abilities as a romance writer. Write dramatically with strong verbs. Make the idea sound exciting and romantic.

Imagine your synopsis appearing as a blurb on the back cover of your book. *Would it sell the novel?*

The following blurb from the back cover of Megan Alexander's *Contract for Marriage* (Harlequin Superromance, Worldwide), which I mentioned in chapter two, will show you the *tone* of an appealing synopsis. See how much can be packed into a few sentences and how interest and curiosity can be aroused:

> *I can't do it, Christy thought. I just can't. All week long she'd tried to convince herself that, she, Christy Steele, Aunt Martha's properly brought-up niece, could do such a thing—confront a man she'd barely met with a personal and deeply intimate request. . . .*

> *Yet an hour later in his executive office, she faced the urbane, unsus-*

pecting Mark Brandon. And with an almost physical shock Christy
heard herself say, "I want to have a child, Mark. Will you be the father?"

These two paragraphs would have been an effective opening for the author's synopsis of the book when she first submitted it.

The reader is interested immediately in Christy. We know that she is
Aunt Martha's properly brought-up niece. This kind of girl doesn't ordinarily
go around making such shocking requests, and we wonder why she is driv-
en to do this.

Your synopsis might begin in this way, with a terse and tantalizing
glimpse into the heroine's character and situation. Then continue in this vein
and summarize the story in short, power-packed paragraphs.

2. *Biographies of heroine, hero, and other important characters.* Changes
in characterization may have taken place since you wrote those first rough
character sketches. By this time you know your characters in depth. They're
no longer one-dimensional. Again, keep these biographies brief. Limit them
to one page each, if possible, for the heroine and the hero, and to a short
paragraph or two for each of the other major characters.

Go back to the guidelines. Be sure the biography of your heroine fulfills
these basic requirements. At the same time, though, you must also convey
that your heroine is different from all the others the editor has encountered.
You have given her an unusual career or some totally unexpected personal
background and problems. Possibly she must make an exciting or dangerous decision to solve her critical problem, as was the situation in *Contract for
Marriage.*

Highlight whatever is special about your characters and, as with the
synopsis, write their biographies romantically, with style, and as briefly as
you can. Every word counts.

3. *Three sample chapters and outline of the remainder of the book.* The
first three chapters of your novel are enough to display your writing talent
and to indicate your ability to plot, pace, and charm. The outline picks up the
story after the end of chapter three and indicates how the rest of the book
will go. You may want to use one-half to one page to describe each of the
remaining chapters. The length of the outline will depend on the type of
romance you're writing. Six to eight pages double-spaced is usually sufficient for a short (60,000-word) romance, while fifty pages might be required
for a 95,000- to 150,000-word historical romance or family saga.

In either case, your outline should lay out your story, chapter by chapter.
It should be detailed enough to show the major problems between the hero
and the heroine and how you resolved them. It should indicate how you
handled your crisis and climax scenes, and spell out the happily-ever-after

ending—*how* and *where* it takes place.

This outline is a real indication of your ability to plot a romance novel. Write it carefully.

4. *Two well-developed sex scenes* from a later portion of the book. You include these two additional scenes to show the editor you can handle a sex scene appropriately and satisfactorily. Well-written sex scenes illustrate your ability to write with emotion and sensuality. You can have the best plot in the world, but if you can't project strong emotion and sensuality in scenes of sexual encounter, you'll never sell your romance novel.

As you know, the sexual tension between the hero and the heroine is what keeps the reader turning the pages of a romance novel. Prove to the editor that you understand this vital ingredient and that you've put it into operation in your novel, and your chances of selling your novel will be increased tenfold.

5. *Author credit page.* Now it's time to toot your own horn. List any and all previous sales, whether or not they were romance fiction. If you haven't published previously, don't despair. Give a brief account of any special professional or technical knowledge that might have helped you in writing this book.

If you've visited or lived in the exotic place about which you wrote, or if you have a special interest in a certain period of history which inspired you to write your romance novel, include that information. Be professional. Do not refer to the praise given you by your writing teacher, or mention that your family considers you another Belva Plain. (What others think of your talent counts only if it brings you *publication.)*

6. *The cover letter.* The purpose of the cover letter is to package *you* as well as your novel. In the cover letter, you are selling yourself as a professional writer. Write it concisely. A cover letter should never exceed one page, and it's better if it's shorter.

Simply describe your romance novel—*"Another Love,* a contemporary romance of 70,000 words," for example—and sum up in a few titillating sentences the plot, the hero, the heroine, their situation, and the location.

Include a few sentences to tell why you think this book might interest this particular editor, and indicate that the complete manuscript is ready to be sent on request.

At Long Last—The Post Office

Check requirements for the publisher you have chosen, but it is unlikely that they will require the original of your manuscript. At one time, editors stipulated that they wanted originals only, but the hazards of today's mail are well known. Things do get lost. Editors agree that a good clear copy is acceptable. By good copy, I mean a manuscript that has been run off on a good copying machine. Don't use the one in your supermarket or drugstore. Go to a print shop and invest in their highest-quality reproduction.

"It's important to make a professional presentation of your material. A lot of readers don't realize they are sandbagging themselves with their scented stationery and little pussycats drawn over their i's."
Page Cuddy, Editorial Director for Avon Books

Before you rush off to the post office, be sure to record on your business calendar, in your notebook, or wherever you choose, the title of your manuscript, the number of pages, the date you are mailing it, and to whom. Also list all expenses connected with sending it out, such as copying cost and postage.

When your editorial package is finally ready to go, be as careful in choosing the conveyance as was Cinderella's Fairy Godmother in selecting the pumpkin coach. You'll need a presentable box, slightly larger than the 8$1/2$-by-11-inch size of your manuscript pages, and sturdy enough to withstand the stress of travel. Type an address label and tape it securely to the inside cover of your box. Wrap the box in good strong paper; address it clearly with the editor's name, the line (if any), and the address of the publishing house, and then put your own name and address in the top left-hand corner of the package.

The way you choose to post your package will depend on your pocketbook, of course. Personally, I think your manuscript deserves first-class postage, which will get it to the editor faster and protect it from the battering it is likely to receive if you send it fourth class, book rate. I also think it is worth an extra few cents to send it certified mail and ask for a return receipt, so that you will get a signed card from the editor's office and know your manuscript has safely arrived.

You've worked hard on your romance novel, and you want it to have a good chance in a highly competitive market. A little extra time, as well as some added concern for how your editorial package looks, will announce you to the editor as a *professional.*

Do You Need An Agent?

If this is your first book, you may be wondering whether it is best to mail your manuscript directly to a romance fiction editor at a publishing house or to try to find an agent to represent you in making this sale and negotiating your contract.

"I sold my first three young adult romances without an agent. My first advance against royalties was $2,000 then $3,000. Then, I did get an agent and my advances improved. In fact, they doubled."
Helen Cavanagh, author of young adult romances

There is no clear-cut answer to this question. Many of the writers you'll meet in chapter seventeen did not have an agent when they sold their first romance novel. More than a few still prefer to go it alone, now that they have established good rapport with an editor, or perhaps with several editors in different publishing companies, who like their work. Others sought out an agent after their first or second sale, and are enthusiastic in their praise of what their agents have done for them.

If you think, "If only I could get an agent, I would sell this novel," that is wishful thinking. An agent can't sell a bad manuscript to any market.

Will agents accept new and unpublished writers? Of course—*IF* perusal of that well-polished manuscript or partial proves it to be promising and professional. That's why agents are happy to attend writer's conferences and to go out on the lecture circuit. It gives them an opportunity to meet new talent.

Now that your novel is finished—or even if you are still in the last stages of writing—make an effort to attend such conferences. If you hear an agent speak, and he or she seems to be someone you could work with, step right up. Explain briefly the type of romance you've written and ask if you could send it to his or her office.

Don't expect anyone to read your material at the conference. Agents are much too busy, and that request would brand you an amateur. (There may be exceptions to this rule, but only if your idea is so intriguing to the agent that he simply can't wait to take a look.)

Another way to make contact with an agent is through the kindness of a friend who is a publishing writer and has a good one. But here, again, there are good and bad ways to make such a request.

If you come right out and ask your friend to recommend you as a future client for her agent, you put your friendship on the line. Your friend may have to say no. Her agent may not be taking on new clients; or your friend may love you dearly, but feel that your work isn't quite ready for her agent's eyes. Either way, you may feel offended.

It's better to let it be known that you are scouting for an agent, and then let your friend make the offer to write her agent in your behalf.

All this diplomacy may seem unnecessary, but too often new writers, in their enthusiasm, impatience, or desperation, kill a possible contact by thrusting a bulky package into some captive agent's hands at a writers' conference, or put their friends in embarrassing positions.

However, one nice thing about marketing a romance novel today is that you really *can* sell it without an agent, even the first time around. If you don't find an agent for your first book, send it out yourself. Then, after it is published and your second proposal is ready, you can approach an agent with confidence. Perhaps you can find one that specializes in romance fiction. You can ask your editor to recommend someone, or consult the section of *Writer's Market* labeled "Services and Opportunities," where you'll find an in-depth discussion and a good list of author's agents.

It is my opinion that once you are a published professional, you should have an agent to represent you in the editorial world. An agent can negotiate a better contract for you than you could on your own—larger advances and better terms generally—and will be your buffer if any difficulties arise in your relationship with the editor.

An agent can critique your work constructively and help you direct your talent in profitable directions. In fact, a good agent is the best friend you'll ever have in your writing life: a shoulder to cry upon when the going gets tough, a lifeline to cling to through the dry spells, and a friend to share your triumph when you succeed.

The writer-agent relationship is like a marriage, depending upon mutual trust and respect to survive and flourish.

In the same way that you learn about agents, you can also learn about editors, meeting them at various writers' conferences and wherever they appear on lecture platforms. Editors are just as eager to meet talented new writers as are agents. Competition for good, productive romance writers is keen.

Should I Use a Pen Name?

Here again, opinions differ. If your name is already known, and readers recognize you as, say, a mystery writer, you will probably want to establish a different identity in the romance field under a new name.

If you have published several books with one line of romances or one publisher, and you sell your next romance to a different publishing house, the first company may have legal possession, by contract, of the name they helped you develop. In that case you will have to find another name.

Or, if your own name is completely unromantic, your editor may suggest a glamorous pen name. Some names are hard to pronounce and difficult to remember; in that case, a simpler name is probably a wise choice for your byline.

But some publishers have begun to encourage romance authors to use their real names. After all, if you keep changing your name, how are your fans going to *find* your books?

Establishing your identity and building up a reputation as a writer is complex and obviously very important. This decision requires careful thought. Discuss it with your editor or your agent, if you have one.

What Do You Do If Your Novel is Turned Down?

You have waited for the mailman for six weeks (it might take that long), your heart full of hope, only to be crushed by a letter from the editor which says:

> *We've enjoyed reading your novel, but unfortunately it doesn't fit our present requirements.*

What exactly does that mean? Did she really enjoy your story? Probably. Any compliment you receive in a personal letter from an editor is likely to be sincere. A printed rejection, simply stating that your book does not fit present requirements, could be interpreted as flat rejection, although even then you should not be too discouraged.

Your story may be similar to one recently bought by this house. Or perhaps the editors have decided on the basis of new market research to change drastically the direction or tone of the line. Or they may simply have bought too many books in the last few months. A book can be turned down for a great many reasons.

So, what do you do? You might ask the editor whether revision of your story would open the door again. It is probable, though, that if the editor had thought changes would make your book suitable for her line, she would have suggested this. You might ask whether the person who read your manuscript would be willing to tell you specifically where you missed the boat. Sometimes an editor who turns down a good but unsuitable novel will suggest other houses to try.

If you know a romance writer who would be willing to read the first few chapters of your book and give you some pointers, her advice could be very helpful. (Don't ask her to read your entire manuscript, though. Her time is precious.)

Aside from all these options, however, the best course of action is probably to send your manuscript out again, to the next publisher on your own list of possible markets. Your novel could very well fit another line just as it is, without major revision. It may be just the kind of story the second company needs the week you send it in. Realize that Lady Luck has something to do with these things.

What if the letter reads,

> *We're sorry, but our present inventory is filled. If you'd care to try us in six months or a year, we'd be happy to reconsider your novel.*

This means the publishing house is overstocked at the moment. Later the situation may be different. Should you put your novel in a drawer and wait before resubmitting? No. Send it out and get the benefit of other editorial responses. Who knows? You could place it with the next market to which you send it. If you haven't placed it after six months, by all means resubmit it to the first publisher with a cover letter referring to your original submission.

No matter what kind of response you get from the editor—a telephone call, a brief note, a few words written on the margin of your manuscript— *always* write a letter of thanks for the attention given.

If Your First Few Tries Result in Rejections, Do You Throw in the Sponge? / No! As soon as that first proposal is in the mail, head back to your typewriter. It is time to start over again—a new heroine, hero, plot, and setting. Back to the working outline and character biographies. A professional doesn't wait around, placing her future on the fate of one manuscript. And once your second book is done, even if you haven't sold the first one yet, you guessed it—start number three. A professional writer always has proposals circulating, is always writing, and is also filing away ideas for the next book.

"Try to avoid the slush pile. Do you have any contacts in the business? Try to ascertain the name of an associate editor, sleuth shamelessly—go through an up-to-date **Literary Market Place** *at the library, or browbeat the switchboard operator—until you discover the name of an associate editor. Then, direct your manuscript to her. Addressing a book to the editor-in-chief is like sending a letter to 'occupant.' "*
Deirdre Mardon, author of contemporary romance

And If Your Novel Sells?

The day this happens, you will be propelled into a new existence, a time of intense excitement, and a period in which you will learn firsthand what writing professionally is really all about. With the letter or phone call telling you that your manuscript is about to become a real romance novel come new demands on your talent and your patience.

If the editor has based her decision on a partial submission, she'll now ask to see the entire novel. Then, after a careful reading and evaluation, she will make suggestions for improving it. The suggestions may be minor or they may be extensive.

Working with an editor to bring your novel up to its full potential is a real challenge to you as a writer. A successful, happy author-editor relationship can make the difference between a so-so novel and a very good book. So enter the author-editor relationship with enthusiasm.

HISTORICAL
ROMANCE
45035-2
$2.50
Tapestry
#15
Only $2.50
Sweetbriar
Jude Deveraux
Love is nothing without trust.

Chapter 14.
THE KNOT IS TIED —
Between You and Your Editor

"We've read your romance. We like it, and we want to buy it." No words could be sweeter to your ears! Whether it's your first sale or your tenth, acceptance of your work brings a thrill unlike any other.

If it is the first time you've heard these words, your life will be different from this moment on. You did it! You are about to make the transition from amateur to professional.

If this is a repeat success, you feel that much more self-confident. Your horizons expand even more. There's no limit to what you can accomplish now.

"No matter how tough things are, people with good stories will always get published. There's always a need for new writers. In a tight market, it may take you longer to find an editor who clicks with you, but persevere." Page Cuddy, Editorial Director for Avon Books

---

This novel has ended as happily for you as it did for your heroine. She is walking into the moonlight at her lover's side. Their arms are entwined. They have nothing on their minds but each other.

But for you, the situation is quite different. The euphoria that comes with the sale of your book doesn't last long. If an agent has made the sale for you, he or she will soon turn you over to the editor in charge of your book at the publishing company.

You come back to earth with a thud when you hear the follow-up request from your editor: "Your novel is good and we are buying it," the editor begins. "However, we feel there is a need for certain changes . . ."

The ugly specter of revision looms before you once again. If you've made previous sales, you're familiar with the hard truth that selling your novel doesn't necessarily mean you can sit back and forget about it until you see it in published form. But if this is your first sale, a request for further revision at this point can throw you into panic.

"How can I possibly tear into my novel again?" you want to wail. Your mind is filled with ideas for your next book and you can't wait to start it.

But now is the time to stifle your cries of anguish and listen carefully to your editor's suggestions for your book. Believe it or not, you *can* and *will* make even further revisions on your manuscript.

I say this with assurance because after all the hard work you put into writing your romance in the first place, you want it to succeed—not only with the editor at the publishing house, but with your readers. If they like your book, they'll want to buy other novels you write.

It's the editor's responsibility to bring your romance novel up to its full potential so that it can compete with other established authors and other publishing houses.

Your editor knows what the readers of a particular line of romance novel like. You don't—not completely. You have conceived the idea, given it birth, and brought it to life to the best of your ability. Your editor recognizes your talent and the quality of your craftsmanship, but he or she also knows from reading and working with countless manuscripts that certain places still need fixing—that some paragraphs should be polished and that sentences could be improved by changing only a word or two.

"Love Once in Passing took me a year of evenings to write; Hold Fast to Love slightly less, but in both cases I revised extensively after what I thought was my final manuscript. . . . I see both the line-edited and copyedited manuscript and in both cases am often asked to make clarifications and additional revisions. However, it's all worth it in the end." Jo Ann Simon, romance author

---

From my own experience as a writer and from watching many of my students work with their editors, I can say without hesitation that in most cases, editorial suggestions improve the chances for success of a romance novel or any other piece of writing. It is both professional and sensible to take your editor's advice seriously.

The following suggestions will make this phase of your career easier.

Don't Push the Panic Button

More than likely, after the initial telephone call or letter, your editor will send you a detailed memo with specific suggestions for revision. Read this carefully. Then let it sit for a day or two while you rid yourself of the emotional steam it stirred up. Then read it again as many times as necessary, until you can begin to see your work through your editor's eyes.

At that point, when your viewpoint is more objective, make a numerical list of all the editorial suggestions, writing each one as clearly and as simply as you can. By lifting the suggestions out of the text, you'll realize that the requests are not so overwhelming as you thought at first.

In some cases, suggestions will be very specific. "You must change the name of one of your characters, so they *all* don't start with the letter "K." Or "Move the sex scene in chapter three to chapter seven."

But some comments may be vague and general. Your editor may simply have the feeling that something is wrong with the scene on the sailboat without being able to pinpoint the trouble. Perhaps he or she has written, "Let's talk about this," or asked, "Don't you feel that sexual tension is lacking in this scene?"

This is an invitation for you to pick up the telephone or write back to discuss the trouble spot. You're free to disagree if you feel strongly about a certain suggestion and can't see your way to making the change. An editor will usually keep an open mind. The goal is to improve your novel, not to nit-pick. From two open minds, working together for a common purpose, come compromises that make everyone happy.

Before you refuse adamantly to make a change, play around with the idea. You might see suddenly that the suggestion isn't so bad after all. If you do not understand some of the comments or suggestions, by all means say so. Ask the editor as many questions as necessary to find out exactly where your novel is too thin, too contrived, or unexciting.

Keep in mind that the editor is not criticizing *you.* You're not a bad writer because your novel needs further revision. Your novel has sold because you've delivered a basically well-written manuscript. Your editor is simply doing everything possible to bring the novel up to its full potential.

"The most satisfying thing for an editor is to watch a writer grow." **Karen Solem, romance editor**

The editor-writer relationship is a partnership. Each half gives to the other. The editor offers a critical, sensitive eye, developed from reading hundreds of manuscripts. He or she is also familiar with feedback obtained from the readers through questionnaires, marketing surveys, and face-to-face meetings.

The writer brings creative talent, originality of plot, freshness of style, and a willingness to make needed changes that will improve the product.

Once you and your editor have talked about your novel on the telephone or by mail, and you have agreed to make the necessary changes, then you'll be sent a contract. One of the terms of the contract will specify the time allotted for you to make revisions.

Your Deadline

You must take seriously the date specified in the contract, on which you'll be expected to deliver the revised manuscript. Think carefully through your work schedule for the weeks ahead. Calculate how long it took you, on the average, to write each chapter. Then estimate how much time you'll need to make the necessary changes in each one.

If the revisions are minimal, you'll probably have no problems. If a major overhaul looms ahead, be sure the deadline gives you enough time to do the work. If it is obvious that you will need a few more weeks, speak up now. *This is the time to discuss this clause in the contract.*

The contract is a legal document, and once you've signed it, you've made a commitment that your editor and publisher will expect you to honor.

After you have signed the contract in good faith, you begin work on the revision. Everything sails along smoothly until a crisis occurs; illness, a domestic problem, or possibly the revision itself bogs down with its own unexpected problems. Again, you feel panic. What can you do to buy more time?

If an agent represented you in negotiating the contract, by all means discuss the situation with her or him. Your agent can talk with your editor, explain the situation, and ask for an extension.

"I've learned more about writing in the two years since I've started being published, than I did in ten years of writing on my own. I'm finally on the inside, being told what is required, how it really works, what you have to do to get published. My editors have taught me a great deal, but I've probably learned the most from my agent."
Joyce Thies, one half of Janet Joyce, romance writer

If you dealt directly with your editor, you'll have to talk over the situation with the editor yourself.

Editors are reasonable human beings, after all, and flexible to a certain point. If you have a legitimate reason for missing the deadline, you will probably get an extension.

On the other hand, if you ask for an extension because you procrastinated in getting down to work or took too much time off to go camping or sailing, then you're in trouble. You've not only let down your editor, but have delayed production of your book. The design for your romance novel, the illustration for the cover, and some of the details of marketing and promotion will have to wait until you've fulfilled your contract. *You must give top priority to delivering the product on time.*

If you are waiting for your contract, or are curious to know what a contract looks like, you can consult several books and magazines. In the current edition of *Writer's Market,* you'll find a reprint of an actual book contract.

A Writer's Guide to Book Publishing, by Richard Balkin (Hawthorn Books, Inc.) will give you a complete picture of the complex business of book publication.

How To Be Your Own Literary Agent, by Richard Curtis (Houghton Mifflin) is another helpful book.

Publishers Weekly, the trade journal for writers and booksellers, is also a fine source of information on the *business* end of the writing profession. And nearly every issue of *Writer's Digest* magazine carries at least one article on such business subjects as tax write-offs, how to read a book contract, and understanding subsidiary and foreign rights.

Apart from the business aspect of your relationship with your editor, you will probably feel that you are becoming good friends. In all probability, you haven't met face to face. You are only voices to each other, or shadowy figures behind the words in your letters. Of course, the warmth and enthusiasm of your voice on the telephone has done a great deal to create a flesh-and-blood image of you in your editor's mind, but you may want to send along an informal snapshot of yourself.

For me, it has always been important to break through the barrier of geographical distance and get to know my editor in person whenever possible. And your editor will want to meet you.

If you plan (or can arrange) to visit the city where your editor is established, by all means write ahead and express your desire to meet him or her and others on the editorial staff. You'll find that you'll be warmly received. There is no substitute for an enjoyable talk across a desk, over a cup of coffee, or at lunch, where editor and writer can really get to know one another.

There are a few male editors in the field of romance publishing, but most of the top editors are young, dynamic women. They are constantly in touch with their readership, and eager to pass on to you everything they can.

Male or female, romance editors are a special breed—astute business people, not only able to keep up with ever-changing trends, but also nearly psychic in predicting the future direction of the market.

Editors read their mail with care. If readers' letters flow with praise for a certain type of romance, they work to develop more of those books. If the mail brings letters reflecting disappointment in or distaste for another type of romance, they soon change or drop that category. Editors quickly pass readers' reactions on to the writer in the form of new editorial guidelines.

Your editor is an important link with your readers, and a well-informed advisor. Once you have established rapport with him or her, nurture the relationship as if it were marriage with a loving spouse.

Just as your hero and heroine waltz to three-quarter time on the dance floor, so will you and your editor work smoothly together—I hope—to the ever-busy beat of the typewriter. The relationship can and should be a pleasure for you and profitable for everyone—you, your editor, your publisher and his staff, and finally the reader, who feels that she has received her money's worth when she buys a copy of *your romance novel.*

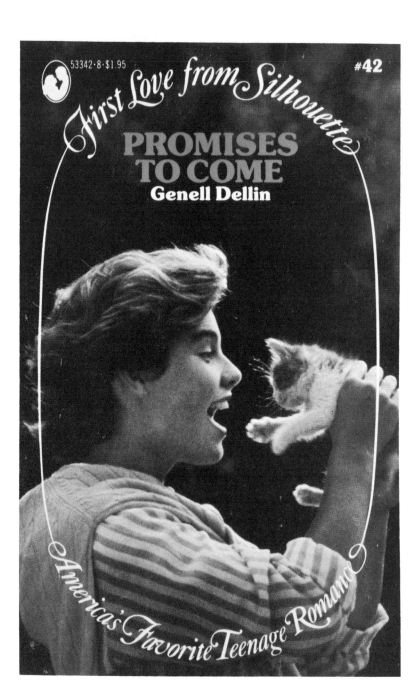

53342-8 · $1.95

#42

First Love from Silhouette

PROMISES
TO COME
Genell Dellin

America's Favorite Teenage Romance

Chapter 15.
SUSTAINING ROMANCE:
Next Steps
in Your Career

Magic Image Studio. Used by permission of Silhouette Books.

Your revisions are finished and accepted by your editor. Your romance novel will be on the racks of your local bookstore in a few months. You've done your part. You heave a big sigh of relief. What now?

It's true, you have finished the *writing* of this book, but your role in its success is not over. It is time to think about the *promotion* of your novel.

You thought the publishers did all that?

Wrong.

The publishers will do a great deal to publicize your romance novel. They will send advance copies or information about it to romance newsletters. They will write it up in their own mailing, which they send to romance subscribers, if they have this service. If this is your second or third novel, they may run ads in newspapers and magazines and arrange to have you appear on television talk shows.

Having invested money in your book, the publisher wants it to succeed as much as you do. But in many ways, *you* are still the best advertisement for your novel, and now, a few months before publication, is the time for you to blow your own horn and promote your book in the area where you live. Opportunities are limited only by your supply of energy, and, of course, by your eagerness to get busy on your next book.

1. Start with your librarian. Tell her about your book and ask her to put you in touch with the person on the staff who does the ordering. Go to other libraries in your town and neighboring towns. Wherever you travel, take along advertising flyers, which your publisher will have furnished.

   Most libraries offer programs of general interest to the public, such as talks on all the arts, writing included. Offer to give a talk when your book is out. Say that you'll be happy to autograph copies of your novel, and arrange with your publisher to be well supplied with copies hot off the press.

   Volunteer to help the library staff design and make appealing posters to advertise your talk. These will be posted at the library and, if you have the time, all over town. The posters are good publicity for the library and for you, and should help boost your local sales.

2. Your local radio station is always looking for talent, and will be happy to have you on a local talk show. This is another excellent way to tell a large number of people about your romance novel.

3. Your newspaper probably has a book-review section. Select a reviewer whose work you like, and send him or her a complimentary copy of your book. In a cover letter, say that you would appreciate an opinion of it. Keep your fingers crossed that the review will be favorable, but even a lukewarm mention is better than none. There's a good chance that your local reviewer will be happy to know a real writer, and will speak kindly of your effort.

4. Your supermarket, drugstore, and local bookstores all carry romance novels by the hundreds. Find out when the supplier or "jobber" is due—the

publisher's representative from whom the bookstore orders titles—and get to know him or her. Suggest that your book be among those ordered, and say that you would be glad to autograph copies of your novel between the cheeses and the paperback racks in the supermarket, or for several hours on the day the book arrives at the bookstore.

5. Interest your husband's business associates. Your husband may tease you a lot about writing all that passionate romance, but deep down, he's proud of you, and will probably be happy to play a part in your promotion.

My husband is a salesman who travels continually among a string of small and not-so-small dealerships all over northern California. Long before this book was published, he was busy setting up autograph parties for me at various stores. He had no trouble at all convincing the dealers to hold these parties, because he pointed out that a writer's autograph party would bring in customers they'd never seen before.

Perhaps you have friends who run stores or who work in places appropriate for this kind of event. Business people are always looking for fresh ways to bring the spotlight to their doors.

6. Writers' groups, women's clubs, schools, and other organizations are always looking for speakers. Now that your romance novel is set for publication, you'll be swamped with requests to speak. *Never turn down such a request.*

You're not an after-dinner speaker? No one is—at first. If you think you'll be paralyzed with stage fright when you reach the podium, take a quick course in public speaking. You can't waste time shaking in your boots just from the *thought* of getting up in front of an audience.

The first time out may be traumatic, but each time you stand up and speak, you gain confidence, and before you know it, you'll be *enjoying* the experience.

No matter how you feel inside, try to look self-assured. You're the authority. You have the published novel before you to prove it. Since you love to write, you may find that you love to talk about writing. What fun it is to answer questions about your setting, your characters, and, best of all, your next novel.

Do everything you can to bring your book to public attention and to keep it there. Your efforts will be reflected in your sales. If your first book sells well, editors will beat a path to your typewriter to buy the next one, and the next one after that.

Investing in Your Business

Now that you are a professional romance writer, it's more important than ever that you produce efficiently and keep up easily with the fickle, ever-changing romance market. To help you do this, plan to invest a part of your advance money in your *business. Writing is a business, after all.* There's an old axiom that says, "To make money you've got to spend some." Here are a few suggestions about where you can spend your hard-earned writing money wisely.

1. Join a local writers' club and national organizations such as the National League of American Pen Women, The Romance Writers of America, and Authors Guild. Contact with other writers, agents, and editors is well worth the dues. In addition, most writers' organizations put out newsletters packed with market tips and interesting profiles on other writers.
   You'll find a list of addresses of these organizations at the back of this book.
2. When you can afford a word processor, by all means buy one and learn to use it. Most romance writers I know work on a word processor, and are delighted with the time and energy it saves. You can nearly double your output when you know how to use one.
3. If you can't afford a word processor right now, perhaps you should invest in a better typewriter. Editors expect *good* copy. Also, if you are a hunt-and-peck typist, consider taking a quick typing course.
4. If you're just not a typist, think about paying someone else to do your final typing.
5. If you can't bring yourself to let any eyes but yours see your manuscript or any fingers but yours type that final draft, then spend some money to have someone relieve you of time-consuming household chores.
6. Invest in adult education or college lectures and workshops, not just on writing, but on any subject that broadens your knowledge. In writing classes, of course, you'll have the benefit of valuable feedback when you read your chapters to your classmates.
7. Add to your own personal library. As a romance writer, you should have on your shelves a cross section of romance fiction, novels representing all the major lines, as well as mainstream successes. You'll find a list of the established romance lines of the major publishers on page 259 of this book.
8. Invest in additional typewriter ribbons, file folders, and, of course, lots of typing paper. Stock your shelves with good office supplies so that you won't have to tear yourself away from the typewriter in the midst of a creative moment because you've run out of something essential.
9. This may be the time to buy a large four-drawer metal file cabinet. As you write book after book, you will need space for the manuscripts, not to mention the voluminous correspondence connected with each one.
10. Add to your magazine and newspaper subscriptions. Do you get *Affaire de Coeur, Boy Meets Girl, Romantic Times, Romance Writers' Report, Publishers Weekly,* and *Writer's Digest?* (See addresses on page 253.)
11. Set money aside in a special fund marked *"Conferences"* and plan to attend the next writers' conference in your area.

These are only a few of the ways in which you can invest in your business and your profession, and be assured of good returns.

Writing, Proposing, Publicizing—Your Three-Ring Circus

Yesterday you were an aspiring author, sitting alone behind your typewriter. Today you are suddenly the ringmaster in a three-ring circus. As a professional writer, there are three areas in which you will have to be active at all times. Writing, of course, is your top priority. How well you do it and how promptly you can produce are keys to your career. But if you are going to keep yourself always under contract and bring in a steady income, you must also constantly generate new ideas.

Every few weeks or so, you may have to lay aside your current book to put a new proposal in shape. Set up a schedule for yourself. Is one new proposal a month best for you? One every six weeks? Have you enough well-developed ideas to launch two or three proposals simultaneously? Now that you have published one romance, partials should certainly be sufficient to sell your next books.

You may find it difficult to break out of the story you are writing and step into a new idea. In that case, plan to put out several proposals *between* books. It can take several weeks, sometimes a few months, to hear back on a proposal. Think ahead to be sure you will be working on another contracted book a few months down the road.

The third ring in your act is publicizing your published book(s). You will have to strike a balance here between too few public appearances and too many. If you run off two days a week to talk about your books, you will have trouble producing any others. You will learn to judge which talks and which panels are most beneficial to say "yes" to. Soon you will see how much time you can afford to spend in this way. You must become skillful at arranging your calendar, with "writing times" always written in the biggest letters.

Writer's Block

I don't want to cast a shadow on things, but let's face it, there are bound to be days—sometimes more than a few—in which you just can't produce. You may simply be stuck in the middle of a book and in need of additional complications for your plot, or you may have a genuine case of "writer's block."

"I don't believe in writer's block. If you can't write, you are doing something that isn't you. Don't be someone else. You'll know when you hit it; your fingers will be flying. 'I know this is good,' you say to yourself, and you'll probably be right." Irene Goodman, literary agent

---

In the first case, the best cure may be a day or two away from your story and a rereading of the chapter on plotting in this book.

Or perhaps you are in a real unproductive spell, brought on by a rejection or two or by the frustration of too many interruptions, which have confused the direction of your writing. Your editor suddenly retires or goes into some other type of publishing, leaving you with the terrifying prospect of finding another editor who likes your work. Personal crises, illness, all of these things can cause the creative juices to stop flowing—temporarily.

Many things can cause you to sit there, hands poised over the typewriter keys, unable to press them. Fortunately, there are cures.

1. Don't Panic

When a crisis keeps you from your writing, comfort yourself with the thought that nothing stays the same for long; bad days as well as good come to an end.

Out of the crisis facing you will come personal growth, new understanding of what life is all about, and fresh ideas for your writing. Your forced separation from your typewriter is not wasted time.

2. A Change of Pace

Sometimes writer's block comes because the well has simply run dry. The writing stint you've just finished may have used you up completely. You need a complete change of pace.

If you can't run off to Bermuda for a few days with the love of your life, look over the movies playing in your town and make a list of all those which promise romantic stories.

If you can't go with someone, go by yourself to one movie each afternoon, all week. You will accomplish two things. First, you will break your routine; you will be a bit adventuresome. Take your lunch in a bag to feel even more as if you are doing something out of the ordinary. And then, of course, the lovers on the screen will be grist for your mill when you get back to work. Who knows? You may emerge with two or three new heroines in mind.

Perhaps you need to be physically active. Writing is very sedentary. Some daily exercise is always a good idea. To help you out of your slump, go to a spa or a pool and give yourself a workout.

Or do housework. (You probably haven't done *that* in a while.) Organize your attic. Sort out the basement. Maybe your windows haven't been washed in three years. Do something physical, concrete, so much in the real world that you are taken totally out of the other world in your head. *Turn off writing completely.*

If a day or two is all you need, well and good. If you need a week or two, take it. Relax. Don't feel guilty. Refuel at your own pace, until one day your feet carry you, of their own accord, back to your desk.

If you find that you are still absolutely stuck on the idea or story you were working on, put it away and try a different type of romance. Was yours an historical? Try a contemporary setting. Why not a young adult romance? Was yours a long, complicated superromance? Try a short, sweet one.

One advantage of being a romance writer is that you're not locked into a single format. The same idea can be developed into several different kinds of romance novel. Play with it. Get a fresh start.

3. Mail Something

Put something, anything related to your writing, into the mail. It could be a proposal, but if you aren't up to that, send off requests for new or updated guidelines from romance publishers. Write for a subscription to a new romance newsletter or writer's magazine or write to a friend who is also a writer, telling about your problem. It might do you good just to get it down on paper. These peripheral exercises might help you feel professional again.

4. Join the Crowd

Writing is a lonely, isolating occupation—just you and a stack of empty pages that must be filled. You need occasional socializing with other writers to make you feel human again. When you hear of someone else's ups and downs, you don't feel alone anymore. Exchanging shop talk about new markets ignites the spark of enthusiasm, and suddenly you *want* to get back to your typewriter.

Make sure, however, that the group you join is interested in your type of writing—romance fiction. It's always interesting to learn about other areas of

---

"Writer-friends are a necessity, not only to share in the frustrations, but to share in the joys of writing. Their successes encourage me. Pooling information on changing or new markets helps everyone. Dry spells are temporary when someone cares." Margaret Scariano, author of young adult romances

---

writing, but when you run into writer's block, you need the companionship of other writers who are interested in the same thing you are.

You might think of taking a writing class, but again, make sure the class is a productive one, taught by a *publishing* teacher-writer who understands and respects your genre. The teacher should be knowledgeable about marketing and able to pass on current information.

5. Revise an Old Proposal or Submission

Start retyping a musty, dusty manuscript that's been languishing in your bottom drawer, and before you know it, you'll be creating again. Take any page, any chapter, and just start typing. I guarantee the writing blahs will evaporate.

6. Read, Read, Read

You simply *can't* write? Catch up on your reading. It goes without saying that you, as a writer, love to read. If there were nothing to read but the label on a soup can, you'd devour that. As a writer, you never seem to have enough time for all the reading you want to do, but now may be that time.

"I am a very solitary person and now I can stay home and do what I want to do. The truth is, I love, love, love to write. It is an absolute joy to me. I feel almost sinful about it, I like it so much. I like to read about social history, research things, study costumes of different periods and make up stories. I have plots enough now to keep me busy for many years to come." **Jude Deveraux**

No matter what caused your writer's block, reading will both relax you and stimulate your creative mind. When you return to your typewriter, your head will be swimming with new and exciting ideas.

Read a line of romances with which you're not familiar. To your surprise, it may turn you on so much that you want to try one. *Your writer's block will be over.*

Writer's block isn't a terminal disease. Like the mumps, it runs its course. A well-deserved period of lying fallow, a change of pace, the stimulation of associating with other writers can do wonders in getting you past that frightening time when you think you'll never be able to write again. What you did once you can do again—and again. You are a professional writer.

Harlequin Romance

2552
1.75

Call Up
the Storm
Jane Donnelly

Chapter 16.

ANY MORE QUESTIONS?
What Beginning Romance Writers Most Frequently Ask

Used by permission of Harlequin Books

The most popular and lively part of any writers' class or conference is the time allotted for questions, and so I want to transport you for a moment into what might be a typical question period at a gathering of romance writers.

Perhaps some of these questions are still spinning unanswered in your head. Others I may have touched on briefly in the preceding chapters, but they may be worth further elaboration. I hope the answers will clear away the last vestiges of confusion and give you that final nudge toward your own success as a romance writer.

Q: What chance has a beginner to break into the romance market?

A: An excellent chance, if you read and study this book carefully, follow the suggestions, and constantly analyze the market by keeping in close touch with an agent, editors, or other writers. Keep in mind that a large number of novels on the bookshelves today are written by writers whose names were unknown less than two years ago. They were all *beginners* a very short time ago.

Q: Do I need an agent to submit my romance novel to a publisher?

A: No. Most of my students and many of my colleagues made their first sale to the romance market without the help of an agent. Their timing was right. They had page turners that fit the needs of the publishers they chose.

There is no question in my mind, however, that an agent is valuable to your career, once you've proved your professionalism with a sale or two.

Q: What exactly does an agent do for a writer?

A: Good question. A competent, caring agent can negotiate a better contract than you could. Most writers are poor business people, and need all the help they can get when it comes to negotiating a contract.

An agent is in a position to evaluate your manuscript according to market requirements, and will speed it on its way to the right place, while you might have difficulty knowing just where your book would fit best.

A diplomatic agent can act as an arbitrator when differences arise between you and your editor, smoothing the way so that you will remain agreeable in your editor's eyes. In editorial offices, troublesome authors are avoided like ants at a Fourth-of-July picnic.

Finally, once an agent agrees to represent you, he or she will do everything possible to assure your success. Over the long haul, it's nice to know you have someone in your corner.

Q: How do I get an agent if I'm not well-known? Are agents interested in first-time authors?

A: Check lists of agents for those who specialize in romance fiction. Then write or phone until you find an agent willing to take a look at your proposal or manuscript. If you have an editor already, ask her to recommend an agent for you.'

Yes, an agent will take on an unpublished writer, if he or she feels that the talent and persistence are really there. No agent worth his jelly beans is going to waste time on a writer whose work he feels is not salable. You'll get an honest appraisal of your work.

Q: How much will an agent cost me?

A: Usually an agent's fee will be ten or fifteen percent of all earnings from your book, including advance and royalties.

If you come across an agent who requires a large reading fee, go somewhere else. Agents who charge reading fees are more interested in quick cash than in riding out a sale. There are exceptions, of course. A few agents feel it is only fair to charge a nominal amount for reading a new writer's manuscript. This fee is usually returned upon sale, however.

Q: What kind of money can I expect to make from writing for the romance market?

A: *Good* money. Better than most other markets. Advances vary from publisher to publisher, but it is safe to say that you could receive an advance of anywhere from $1,500 to $5,000 on the sale of your romance novel if it is short, and up to $10,000 if it is a long historical. This, of course, will depend on the policies of the publishing house to which you submit. We're talking about advances now, the money a publisher offers you upon the signing of the contract. Royalty payments, anywhere from four to ten percent of the cover price, come dribbling in later—much later. It could be up to a year before you see any royalties at all. After that, if your book continues to sell, you will receive earnings twice a year, supposedly in March and September; but in fact delays are very common.

In other words, enjoy your advance, but don't buy a new house counting on royalties. Your book could sell a half million copies and go into foreign-language and other English-language editions, bringing you additional contracts and royalties. On the other hand, it could die a quick death after a month on the bookseller's shelf.

Q: How do I know which type of romance novel I am best suited to write?

A: This question has been covered in preceding chapters, but I think the answer bears repeating. You won't write well if you have to hold your nose while you're writing. If you read widely among current romance novels, you'll know soon which type you like, and which type you would probably enjoy writing. You will have to write a story that appeals to your reader. You want to give her what she's paid for, which in the case of the romance novel is good entertainment and a chance to escape the problems of the day; what editors call "a good read." You can't do any of this if you don't enjoy and respect what you're trying to write.

Q: I have trouble writing descriptions of places in my romance novel. Also, my characters seem a bit wooden. Why?

A: Most likely, you haven't spent enough time getting to know your setting and your characters. Stop writing and start thinking. Can you identify with the background, or is it something you pulled out of a hat because you thought it would make your novel more salable? If it's the latter, back up. You must have a *feeling* for your background. This doesn't mean necessarily that you must have been there. As I said earlier, many romance writers can describe places they've seen only in their vivid imaginations, with the help of exhaustive research.

Ask yourself the same question about your characters. Do you *see* them? Do you *hear* their voices when they speak? Do you know how they would react in all kinds of situations?

One romance writer I know sets up situations outside the story for her characters to face, such as meeting a strange man in an unexpected way, or a family crisis, a quarrel, a parting, or a wedding, and then she asks herself, "How would my character *feel* in this situation, and what would she do about it?"

You may see your characters physically, but you may not know them inside. Merely describing your heroine's auburn hair and green eyes won't work in romantic fiction. Your readers want to know the expression in her eyes in each scene. Is she wistful, apprehensive, filled with desire? And most important, the readers—and therefore you—need to know all the feelings behind that expression.

Remember, as you write, that you are creating an imaginary world for your readers. In order to make it seem, sound, and feel real, *you* have to live in that world while you are writing and know intimately the characters who live there. You must identify emotionally with what your characters are feeling to make your characters come alive.

Q: Is it all right to use real people as characters in my romance novel? For example, can I make the beautiful redhead who lives next door my heroine, and the good-looking man who works with me her hero?

A: Yes and no. If you use real people as your models, don't take them whole. If your heroine is that redhead in your mind, you will soon find yourself limited by reality. Take certain aspects of a real person's appearance and character, if you like. Then let your imagination soar. Build on reality and create a bigger-than-life character.

The redhead next door may have a terrible temper, be hard to live with in real life and hard to handle when you are trying to create a romantic character. Take her violent temper and soften it into quick anger, which she immediately regrets showing, and you have the makings of a sympathetic heroine.

Use real people to inspire your characters, if you want. But remember that you're writing fantasy, creating the kinds of heroines and heroes we'd all like to be. You need to exaggerate. Make a nice head of healthy dark hair into a cascade of shimmering velvet. Take a pair of friendly brown eyes, perhaps the eyes of the good-looking man who smiled at you on the bus this morning, and turn them into a strange shade of amber with gold flecks in them, mysterious above your hero's smile.

Develop the players on your stage according to the needs of the director—you.

Q: What is the best way to present facts about my heroine's past and background in chapter one? The reader needs to have certain essential information right away. If I use a flashback, I'll interrupt the flow of my story.

A: This can be a tricky problem. You want to plunge your reader into action immediately on page one, or as soon as possible, but it is often necessary for the reader to know something about the heroine and hero so that the action makes sense.

You are right—a long flashback at this point, or at any point in most romance novels for that matter, is not a good idea.

First, realize that you needn't give all the facts about that lovely girl and her handsome hero at one time, or even right at the beginning. Decide which facts are urgent, which can wait. Then sprinkle them throughout the first several chapters. If your reader must wait to know how and why the heroine's former marriage ended, it will add suspense to your story.

If it is absolutely necessary to use a flashback, keep it short. Brief flashbacks work if what is pulled from the past has direct bearing on what is happening in the present. The flashback should provide the motivation for the action, reaction, or decision taking place in the present. Then, slipping a few sentences of memories into the action will seem only appropriate.

If you feel you need to show a scene from your heroine's past, do just that. Dramatize your flashback—that is, give it as a scene, complete with dialogue. But again, keep it as short as possible. Always have the forward motion of your plot, the flow of the present action, foremost in your mind and in your reader's.

Q: How can I create more conflict between my characters?

A: The most important conflict in romance fiction is the sexual tension between the heroine and the hero. For the sexual tension to build to a tantalizing level, you must create and emphasize strong reasons for the lovers to misunderstand one another and quarrel while you fan the flames of the physical attraction between them.

If you think a scene or chapter lacks conflict, check the problems you've given your heroine and hero. Put huge boulders in their paths, not small pebbles. Make it seem to them that they'll never resolve their differences. Because they are madly in love with one another, this would be a tragedy. They may not have admitted their passionate longing to be together forever, not even to themselves, but the reader knows that the consuming love is there, and is rooting hard for that happy ending.

Well-motivated problems plus strong physical attraction can only equal what the reader thrives on—plenty of sexual tension.

Q: How do I keep from getting bogged down in too much detail?

A: Give only enough detail to sketch a picture in the reader's mind. The reader's imagination will fill the rest. If the heroine is wearing high-but-toned shoes that show off the beauty of her trim ankles and her shapely legs, it's not necessary to describe every button.

If you're going to use a hayloft for a love scene, it's important to describe the sensory details, such as the clean, fragrant smell of the hay, the warmth of the barn, and the feeling of privacy that the loft gives the young lovers. But don't count the pitchforks hanging on the wall unless a jealous suitor is going to take one down and go after the hero.

In selecting details to describe your setting or characters, ask yourself, "What purpose does this serve? Does this detail relate in some way to what my characters are feeling and experiencing? Would another detail work better? Is this detail necessary to set the mood or lay the groundwork for future action?

In describing the fragrant smell of the hay, the warmth of the barn, and the feeling of privacy, we're not surprised when the young lovers, safe from prying eyes, give in to their passions. If we see the pitchfork on the wall, we're not surprised when the villain reaches for it in a jealous rage.

Q: I sold my romance novel on the basis of three chapters and an outline, but now I have new ideas for this book and would like to make changes in the outline. Is this all right?

A: As I've said, outlines are not straitjackets. However, since the editor bought your book on the basis of what you presented, it would be wise to talk to her about any changes you have in mind before you make them.

Your changes may alter the very scenes the editor liked best, or may greatly enhance the appeal of your story. Better to be sure of your editor's reaction before you revise.

Q: What is meant by giving description of setting "in viewpoint"?

A: This means that you should avoid straight narrative description of landscape, the city or town of your setting, or even the objects in a room. Such descriptions stop the story and make it go flat. They just hang there.

The reader is interested in the scenery and interior décor only insofar as they affect the characters. For example, if the heroine is nervously scanning the hero's bedchamber while trying to decide what to do and say next, then what she is feeling and thinking as she notices the dark silk canopy and the heavy mahogany headboard is part of the story.

Try to give all descriptions through the eyes of a character who is thinking or doing something that belongs to the plot and the present action. In using this technique, you'll accomplish two things: You'll be developing your characters and enriching the background of your story at the same time. You won't load your story with big chunks of flat descriptions which the reader will want to skip over to get back to the "interesting part."

"The opening sentence of my first novel was one of a group of 'hook sentences' that were required as a class assignment. When I was encouraged to go on, the first paragraph evolved, then the first chapter and ultimately the entire novel. Nobody was more surprised than I." Marilyn Dickerson, author of Regency romances

---

Q: I start writing, get involved with my characters, get carried away, and write reams of words, only to find I've gone off on tangents I never expected. Once I get started, I can't seem to stop. It's like a snowball rolling downhill. How can I gain better control over my material?

A: Sound familiar to you? I remember clearly the day a student of mine asked this question. Since then she has conquered the problem and has gone on to publish a very nice romance novel.

You cannot write a tight, well-constructed novel without discipline and control. If you don't test your idea and give it structure, and simply write from blind inspiration, you may get carried away and write pages and pages that have little to do with your story. Your description will go on and on, detail piled upon detail, where a few carefully selected words would do.

A writer who can't stop the flow of her words, and who fills up page after page with undirected verbiage, usually has not thought out her plot. When asked, "But what is your heroine's problem? What is the conflict between your heroine and hero? What is motivating them?" She stares blankly.

The cure for writing without control is to follow the suggestions given in this book in the chapter on plotting. Write a short synopsis first. Make short biographies of your main characters. Be sure you can state in a simple declarative sentence the major problem facing your heroine and the motivation for her actions and reactions. With even this much thinking before you start typing, you'll have a solid plan for your novel.

When you find yourself snowballing, you can pull youself up short by referring to your preliminary blueprint. Remember that writing a novel is like going on a journey. You need to know your destination as you travel and have a map close at hand to be sure you get there.

Q: But won't all this planning and calculating cramp my style and kill my inspiration?

A: This question reflects the natural concern of a writer who has not been in the business long. Believe me when I say that those writers who fight hardest against planning out their novels are most enthusiastic about the results of a more organized approach, when they compare the results.

If you are aiming to be a professional writer who produces salable novels, I strongly advise a professional approach to your work.

Q: If I tailor my writing to the romance market, will I spoil my chances of later writing another kind of category novel, such as mystery or science fiction, or even a mainstream novel?

A: Absolutely not. I served my apprenticeship writing confessions. Thanks to that particular kind of writing, I know how to project myself into many viewpoints, and understand the importance of motivation in plotting.

Many successful romance writers came to this genre having written: for literary journals, religious markets, and popular magazines, as well as confession magazines. And more than a few writers manage to write successfully in several categories simultaneously. For example, some of my students write suspense novels right along with their romance novels.

What you learn in one area of writing you can take with you into another. Learning to write sensuously, as you must do if you want to be a romance writer, will help you tremendously in any type of writing. Why? Because sensuous writing creates vivid word pictures, and if you can do that you can write well. Good writing is good writing in any genre.

Q: Is it better to aim for the "best" markets, that is, the highest-paying, and then lower your sights if rejected by those markets?

A: There is nothing wrong with sending your novel first to the publisher that will pay you the most, if you are sure it fits that market. If it doesn't, you're wasting your time and postage.

To send a sweet romance, in which tender kisses and breathless sighs constitute a love scene, to a market requiring a highly explicit story will only earn you a rejection slip.

Write the best novel you can write. Know the specific requirements for that type of book. Select the market that publishes novels like yours. Start with the highest-paying market for that type of novel, and keep mailing until you've exhausted every possibility, unless, of course, editorial reaction shows that you need to do more work on the novel.

Q: Which is more important, to write the way successful romance writers do or to develop your own personal style?

A: In this book, I have shown you how to study the techniques used by writers of romance novels. You certainly need to have such skills. But you are *you*. If a publisher wants to publish a Janet Dailey novel, they'll ask Janet Dailey to write it.

You can learn from others and improve your style through constant reading, but, by all means, develop your own style.

Q: When I told a friend that I had sold a romance novel and was working on another, her response was "Don't you want to be a *real* writer?" I take great pride in mastering the techniques of this craft, and although I am not producing great literature, I hope my romance novels will be good entertainment. Do I have to apologize for that goal?

A: Certainly not. If your friend were involved in writing, publishing, or bookselling, she would have a better understanding of books as a business. As a professional writer, you are aware that writing is hard work and that great skill is needed to produce salable romance novels, and you respect your craft and others who are successful at it.

If some of your friends do not understand what you are doing, think of it this way: if you were doing chemical research, they wouldn't understand that, either.

You are working in a specialized field, too, and probably the only people who will understand completely what you are doing and how you feel about it are your colleagues around the world—other romance writers. The pride and pleasure you take in your profession do not have to be understandable to your friends and neighbors. Take those feelings to the next writers' conference in your area. You'll find plenty of support and appreciation there.

Q: I notice that several romance authors are really two (or more) writers. I am just starting out, and have very little experience as a writer. Would it be a good idea to find someone to collaborate with?

A: Possibly. But think it through carefully before you approach someone. Have you a clear idea of what your own strengths and weaknesses will be as a romance writer? For example, are you interested in writing an historical romance because of a strong interest in history, which gives you good research skills? In that case, you might want to team up with someone who is not so keenly interested in historical details as you are, but who is good at coming up with plot ideas, good characters, and snappy dialogue. You can learn from each other.

What works for some people wouldn't for others. Some collaborators are neighbors who live just a few blocks from each other and spend a great deal of time together working out their stories. Janet Bieber and Joyce Thies, who write as Janet Joyce, make up such a team.

Cornelia Parkinson and Sharon Salvato, who are known as Day Taylor, live in adjoining towns and pass their work back and forth a great deal, editing each other's work.

Another pair of writers live hundreds of miles apart and work almost exclusively on the phone and through the mail. They are Shannon Harper in Georgia and her childhood friend, Madelaine King, in California, who are known collectively as Anna James.

There are even teams of three writers who produce very successful books. For example, "Margaret Ripy" is actually the trio of Patti Moore, Kathleen Daly, and Margaret Daly.

Perhaps the most important thing to consider, though, is this: Can you and she both put *the good of the book* above your individual interests? Can each of you give up a notion if it will not really serve the interests of the novel at hand?

You would work very closely, possibly day and night, with your collaborator. You need to be sure that your egos are not too large for the kinds of compromises you would have to make. Quirks of personality and displays of temperament have no place in a collaboration.

In the end, the question of whether or not to collaborate is a very personal one, and perhaps the only way to find out if it would work for you is to try it. It takes a high degree of professionalism to make it work, and perhaps a good deal of luck to come up with a match of talent and temperament that will produce good books.

If you do decide to collaborate, hire a lawyer to draw up a contract between you as soon as you form your writing partnership. This will keep all questions about division of rights and earnings clear and businesslike from the beginning, and should you die—heaven forbid—your estate would have legal claim to your share of any income from your books.

Q: If I start writing as one half of a writing team, will it be difficult to establish myself later as an author in my own right?

A: No, this should not be a problem. As a collaborator, you will have established a track record, learned to work with an editor and learned to write professionally. If you want to try writing on your own after a few books, start submitting proposals in your name alone. If they are as good as the work you do with your collaborator, there is no reason your editor won't buy them. Several sets of collaborators continue to write together, and write books on their own as well.

Q: Will the romance market really last?

A: Again, I believe it will, in one form or another. A huge romance reader-ship has built up over the last few years. Those readers will go on read-ing, though the specific forms of the romance novel may change over time. In fact, subtle changes in characterization, plotting, and levels of sensuality are taking place all the time. This is why I have advised you to write and talk to editors and agents as much as you can, to update your guidelines often. Romance fiction, like all other fiction, reflects the times we live in. Everything around us is in constant flux; it's called "prog-ress."

The thousands of romance novels being published today fill a basic need. In our coldly technological world, in which sperm banks and test-tube babies are becoming common, women and men hunger for old-fashioned moonlight-and-roses love, for passionate moments. Roman-tic fiction is often a more reliable source of those than life itself.

Think of the number of people who remained glued to their televi-sion sets as Lady Diana wed Prince Charles. The world was captivated by that real-life romance. Will readers remain captivated by romance novels? I would bet on it.

Three generations—
they would know
the splendors of
imperial Russia,
the terror of exile,
the promise of
America, and
the raptures of
forbidden love.

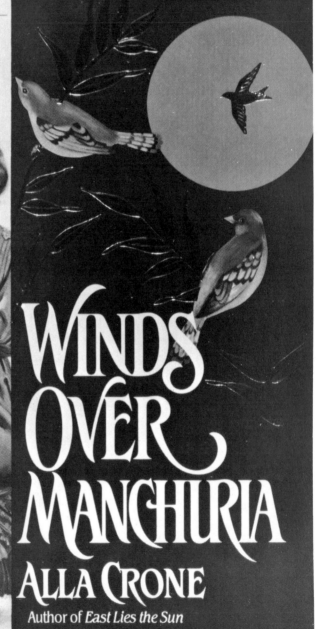

DELL • 18853 • $3.50 U.S. • $4.50 CANADA

WINDS OVER MANCHURIA

ALLA CRONE

Author of *East Lies the Sun*

Chapter **17.**

THE GLORIOUS GLOW OF SUCCESS:
Romance Writers
Tell How
They Did It

Like writers in general, romance writers started out in this genre in different ways. Some had been writing fiction of one kind or another for years. Others had written only nonfiction. Some had always wanted to be writers, and the romance boom gave them the opportunity to make an old dream come true. Others had never thought of telling a story on paper.

Some are young; some are older, with grown children or grandchildren. Some have traveled the world, or have even been born in exotic places; others have hardly left their desks. But they do seem to have a few things in common.

When you read what the authors in this chapter have to say about themselves, you will find nearly all of them were avid readers as children. Books were part of their lives from the start, a love often inherited from their parents.

All of them are excited about romance fiction, and find writing contemporary, historical, or young adult romances exhilarating, satisfying, and rewarding. The careers of all these writers have skyrocketed since they began writing for this genre; in just the last few years, all have developed the special skills needed. And after that first sale in the field, each of these writers has gone on to sell others.

The success of these writers proves the premise of this book: the romance novel is a winner. Established writer and novice alike can feel confident in placing their bets on this genre. What the writers in this chapter have accomplished, so can you. Now let's read what they have to say.

Debbie Gordon, *who writes as Brooke Hastings, author of contemporary romances:*
Until I began writing romances, my writing experience had been almost entirely in the area of nonfiction; political science and educational research, grant proposals, and legislative summaries. The only fiction writing I had done was in high school in Yorktown Heights, New York.

But I think that if someone writes well, she writes well. Doing a novel then becomes a matter of having a good enough imagination and, I suppose, an ability to "get into" your characters.

I wrote my first romance because, like many other people, I'd read a number of contemporary romances, enjoyed them, and decided that I could do as well as some of the authors I'd read.

I sold my first book in 1979, without an agent, and soon after that I started writing romances full time. I went through a very tortured six months or so when I agonized over what I was doing, thinking that I should be writing the Great American Novel, but I finally concluded that I enjoy what I'm doing, that it pays well, and that I'm in no hurry to do anything else just now.

After my fifth book, I turned the business end of things over to an agent. I highly recommend using the expertise of a professional, once your career is under way.

When I run into a period when I don't feel like sitting down at the typewriter, I sit down anyway. I've learned that if I can just get something on paper—anything—I'm okay. It gives me a start, even if it's a bad start. Reading a romance novel or two, sometimes my own, usually someone else's, also helps motivate me.

I regularly read magazines and newspapers, and find that every now and then an article will suggest a story idea. Sometimes the article may concern a specific field that catches my fancy, to use as the background of the story. It may concern dramatic events in the business world, in the area of national politics, or even internationally. It would be very unusual for an article to suggest a whole plot, but an article can give you part of a plot or an important incident in your plot. Since I do contemporary romances, I think it's fun and interesting to be current—even if that means I have to learn something about nuclear physics!

I've written only contemporary novels, varying between 55,000 and 85,000 words in length. I find that the greater lengths give you more room to tell a deeper, more complicated story, and I like that. I tend to create people who take themselves and their work seriously, but not *too* seriously.

Contemporary romances have become far more sophisticated in the last few years. The most welcome change, to me, is the greater use of the male viewpoint. Heroines are older and more confident—not the type of women who will allow themselves to be pushed around or intimidated. Heroes are no longer incomprehensible (except to the extent that men in general are incomprehensible to us women!). They aren't quiche eaters, but they are allowed to have feelings, to make mistakes, to be human.

Contemporary romances by Brooke Hastings:
Playing For Keeps, 1980
Innocent Fire, 1980
Desert Fire, 1980
Island Conquest, 1981
Winner Take All, 1981
Rough Diamond, 1982
A Matter of Time, 1982
An Act of Love, 1983; all Silhouette Romances.
Intimate Strangers, 1982 Silhouette Special Editions.

Alice Morgan, *author of contemporary romances:*
Probably the greatest help to me now as a writer is that I never thought of being a writer until 1980. I was too busy living life to the fullest. Thus, many of the things in my books are things I've done, enjoyed, anguished through,

said, prevaricated about, cried over, laughed at, surreptitiously observed or listened to, with insatiable curiosity about mankind and all its complex diversities.

The idea for my first book, *Sands of Malibu*, came after a four-year stint of reading thousands of romance novels. None had a heroine who was a police officer. Since I had been one, I was familiar with the occupation, and knew that my plot was unique.

I was intensely bored with mild heroes and meek heroines, and with the endless irritation of not knowing whether the hero even *liked* the heroine until page 186 or 187. Numerous conversations with romance readers revealed that many felt as I did.

Filled with endless enthusiasm and confidence, I knew I could write the kind of book I liked to read. I had no past writing experience to fall back on, but for me this was probably best. I wrote without house guidelines, without the pressures of knowing what was or was not acceptable, without knowing that sensuality should be limited in certain ways for certain lines. In fact, I wrote to supply the sensuality I thought was missing in the books I had read. It never entered my mind to wonder what an editor wanted. My sole purpose was to put a passionate love story on paper, one that I could enjoy.

My breaking into the romance market, as with my writing, was accomplished with an equal amount of gall and good luck.

When I finished *Sands of Malibu*, I mailed it directly to Mills & Boon in London, since all Harlequins at that time were reprints of books originally released by that company in England. It was promptly returned with a personal note saying that the book wasn't "on their wave length," at this time. I had no idea what that meant, so I telephoned editor George Glay's office at Harlequin in Toronto. His secretary suggested that I send my manuscript to Dell Candlelight Romances in New York. I did.

After two months, I was climbing the walls, wondering what on earth had happened to my book. Surely no one needed that long to decide! I phoned Dell and asked for "the Candlelight Romance office." When I asked the woman on the other end why I hadn't heard whether they wanted to purchase *Sands of Malibu*, I was informed that, one, it was buried in their slush pile; two, she never had less than sixty manuscripts on her desk at a time, all waiting to be read; and three, two months wasn't all that long anyway.

Then the soft voice informed me that she was no longer buying Candlelight Romances, as she was going to start a new line of more sensual books. I told her I was glad to hear that, since I never liked Candlelight Romances anyhow. By now I was beginning to realize that I was not only talking to a very knowledgeable lady, but to the number-one romance editor in New York at that time, editor-in-chief Vivian Stephens.

Before the end of our long conversation, Vivian told me what she was looking for and I told her what I liked to write. She offered to pull my manuscript from Dell's slush pile, read it, and phone me in one week. I was euphoric. I had actually talked with an editor who would critique my work.

Promptly at eight on the morning promised, Vivian called. Her first words were, "I *cannot* buy your manuscript the way it is." She told me what she liked and what she didn't, and asked me to rewrite it for her. Also, I should double space, use twenty-eight lines per page instead of thirty-seven, start the first chapter halfway down the page, and never, never bind the pages. (I had thought binding would make it easier to read.)

I had overwritten almost everything, my English was the worst she'd seen, the pacing too fast, the hero too ardent. . . but, she liked the plot and the heroine's sensuous underwear, and was intrigued because it was about a policewoman.

Determined to sell her my "cop story," I immediately started revising. I cut up, down, and out, then rewrote the beginning. Within three weeks I had mailed the revised version of *Sands of Malibu* to Vivian, and was offered a contract with a $3,000 advance. I had hoped for $10,000, asked for $6,000, and agreed on $3,000. My new career now began in earnest.

As seems to be the norm with authors, the ending of one book prompted the beginning of another. I could hardly wait to start work on *Impetuous Surrogate. Masquerade of Love* followed a short time later, as did others.

I like to write extremely sensual category romance novels, with the promise of eternal love in a monogamous relationship. With each submission I'm told to tone down my heroes. I keep reminding my editor that they are toned down before I send in the manuscript. It seems unlikely to me that a healthy man in the prime of life, who finally makes contact with the one woman he loves, would be anything other than sensually stirred, passionately aggressive, and tenderly forceful from the first moment of their initial meeting.

In the spring of 1982, I received a phone call from Vivian Stephens telling me that Kathryn Falk, editor of *Romantic Times,* found my writing so sensual that she was giving it the first Pearl Award at the Romantic Book Lovers' Conference in New York. I hurriedly arranged a trip East to receive the beautiful Mikimoto pearl which came with the honor, and this was the ultimate ego trip, going far beyond any dreams I had ever had.

All of the people I have met since I became an author, and those who have written me, I cherish as friends, and that, I find, is the nicest award of all.

Contemporary romances by Alice Morgan:
Sands of Malibu, 1982

Impetuous Surrogate, 1982
Masquerade of Love, 1982; all Dell Candlelight Ecstacy Romances.
Deception for Desire, Harlequin American Romance, 1983.

Dorothy Dowdell, *author of young adult romances, gothic romances, romantic suspense novels, contemporary romance, and historical sagas:* I can't remember a time in my life when I did not want to write. I loved to read as a child, made extensive use of the library, and determined that I, too, wanted to write books someday. My father felt the same urge, and gave me encouragement.

Travel has been an important and helpful source of ideas for my romance novels. Even vicarious travel through reading has yielded ideas. While other writers start with their characters or with plot ideas, I usually start with a setting in mind, and often travel to that place. Sometimes I get two for the price of one, when a trip to one place turns up other backgrounds for other books.

For example, several years ago I went to Hawaii to gather background material for *Roses for Gail,* one of my "career romances." This was originally published by Thomas Bouregy & Co. and reprinted by Dell as an early Candlelight Romance, titled *The Allerton Rose.* (Today, of course, Dell Candlelight Ecstasies are all originals. This was way back at the beginning.)

While I was in Hawaii, I happened to go to the Polynesian Cultural Center there, and unexpectedly became very interested in the island of Samoa. I returned later to collect background for *Hibiscus Lagoon,* a contemporary romance for Dell Candlelight. A year in Munich, Germany, provided the inspiration for *House in Munich,* a Gothic romance, and my childhood travels around Nevada laid the foundation both for *Tahoe,* a romantic suspense novel, and for *Glory Land,* my first historical saga.

I had written several confession stories before I wrote a long novel. The emotions, basic human needs, and conflict important in confessions carried over to the longer form of the romance novel, at least for me.

At the moment, I like best to write historical sagas. Having several interweaving threads about different members of the same family, seeing the interrelationships, and playing these against each other in the plot I find most fascinating of all. I'm at work on another, *A Woman's Empire,* which Fawcett will publish in 1984, about a lumber baron and his family in the mid to late 1800s.

Romance novels by Dorothy Dowdell:

Arctic Nurse, 1969. (Orig. Thomas Bouregy and Co.) Dell Candlelight Romance

Strange Rapture, 1972. (Orig. Thomas Bouregy and Co.) Dell Candlelight Romance

The Allerton Rose, 1972. (Orig. Thomas Bouregy and Co.) Dell Candlelight Romance
Hibiscus Lagoon, 1981. Dell Candlelight Romance
The Impossible Dream, 1981. Gothic romance. Dell Candlelight Romance
Hawk Over Holly Hedge, 1973, and
House In Munich, 1975, both Avon Books.
Tahoe, Playboy Press, 1977, romantic suspense.
Glory Land, Fawcett Gold Medal, 1981, historical saga.
A Woman's Empire, Fawcett Gold Medal, 1984, historical saga.

Janet Bieber *and* **Joyce Thies,** *who write contemporary and historical romances as Janet Joyce:*

> *Joyce:* I had been writing manuscripts and having them rejected for years, until we began collaborating two years ago. I met Jan, who only lives a few blocks away, because a mutual friend knew that I was writing a romance and was having trouble with the historical part of it. She knew Jan, who is a history buff, among other things, and mad for details, and thought we should get together.
>
> *Jan:* I was going to be Joyce's researcher. My great dream was that she would dedicate the book to me when we were finished. But the more we got into *Conquer The Memories,* our first historical, the more it became clear that we needed to write it together.
>
> *Joyce:* While I had the plot well in mind and had no problem keeping the story moving, Jan is very good at knowing what characters are thinking and keeping them from going off on tangents. She's good at describing physical things, too. I'm not. Those are the parts of a book that I skip when I read. I like to get on with the story. Jan has slowed me down, made me focus more on the finer points.
>
> *Jan:* On our early books, Joyce would come up with the bare bones of the plot and I'd flesh that out. Then she would revise what I had done, and I would type it, catching all the last little problems.
> On our latest book, though, we seem to have reversed roles. By now, we've each learned to do everything, I guess. This collaboration works well because we'd both been up front from the beginning. All criticism is constructive. In fact, we go out of our way not to offend each other. Humor and humility help; neither one of us is a prima donna. Whatever is done is done for the good of the work. We haven't had a fight yet. Disagreements, yes. Fights, no.
>
> *Joyce:* We worked on *Conquer* for six months. When we were fin-

ished, we went through *Writer's Market* until we found the name of an agent who took phone queries. Yes, she said, she'd like to see the book. She sent it straight back. "The heroine is unsympathetic, arranged marriages are out, and historicals aren't selling," she wrote. There wasn't even so much as a "good luck" at the end of the letter. We cried, of course. If I had been alone, I might have been defeated at that point. But since there were two of us, we brought each other back to life.

Jan: That agent was right about the heroine. But we found that by changing not *what* she said, but *how* she said it, we could make her much more sympathetic with minimal revision. Then we wrote our crazy query letter to Richard Gallen Publishers.

Joyce: We said we were sending three chapters and an outline, along with excerpts from sensual scenes from the rest of the book. Attached to these, we claimed, were "reader comments," all very positive, of course. Since we live in Columbus, Ohio, the market-research center of the country, we said we had submitted our book to the scientific test used by all romance buyers here, called "scanning for the good parts." It was an outrageous letter.

Jan: When the editor at Gallen called a few days later, we could hear giggles in the background. (We later learned that she had read our letter, read it again, and then gone running around the office shouting, "You gotta read this! You gotta read this!") Her voice, though, was all business. She wanted to see the rest of the manuscript. Was it ready to send? "Oh, yes," we said. We could send it in a few days.

In fact, we had discovered that it was 30,000 to 40,000 words too long. In four days, we cut an average of eighteen words per page out of the book, and I retyped the 120,000-word manuscript. I was packing my fingers in ice: my back and arms were dying. We sent it on Thursday, and they bought it on Tuesday.

Joyce: Our next proposals were all contemporaries, which our editor at Gallen thought would interest Silhouette. At this point, she suggested we get an agent, and gave us four names. The first agent we talked to offered us a two-year contract, but we thought that would be a very long time to be stuck, if things didn't go well between us. Instead we signed with an agent who offers ninety-day contracts, and things have gone beautifully.

Jan: In two years, we've sold nine books (four are for 1984 publication): *Conquer,* five Silhouette Desires, two historicals to Pocket

Books Tapestry line, and a sweet romance to Silhouette. Joyce has just sold a Desire on her own, and I have a proposal out there for one of my own. Together, we always try to have at least two proposals making the rounds, one for a contemporary and one for an historical.

Joyce: As soon as you sell one book, you have to get out another proposal. If you want to maintain a steady income two years from now, you can never have a block of time in the present when you are not writing, i.e., under contract. Now we start by phoning our editor and presenting a few ideas. She might say, "No on the first two. Go with the third." Then we work up a proposal.

Jan: Now the danger is that you can get so bogged down with the promotion of the books, personal appearances, writing workshops, fan mail, and jobber parties that you become a personality instead of a writer. If you stay in your house and never go out, people will continue to buy your books, if you are a good writer. But if you are running around so much that your writing suffers, it will show in the third book, or the fifth book—or sooner or later.

Joyce: Two years ago we didn't anticipate that problem.

Jan: Two years ago we didn't even know each other!

Romance novels by Janet Joyce:
Conquer The Memories, Richard Gallen Publishing Co. (historical), 1982.
Winter Lady, 1983
Man of the House, 1983
Man of Glory, 1983; all Silhouette Desires.
Libertine Lady, Pocket Books, Tapestry (historical).

Emily Hallin, *who writes as Elaine Harper, author of young adult romances:*
I grew up in the Rocky Mountains of Colorado. While I was in high school, my creative writing was often read in class, and one teacher especially encouraged me to go on with it. Later, after college, I was a publicist for a large aircraft corporation. My boss was a top-notch investigative reporter and taught me a lot about how to put things on paper.

Many years later, I was writing children's nature stories when I saw that my friends who wrote romances were getting a lot more fun, profit, and satisfaction out of that. So I decided to try my hand at it. Since I was an experienced children's writer, the young adult lines which were just developing seemed a natural for me.

First of all, I was young once myself. My memories of my own adolescence are very vivid, and although externals may change over the decades, the core of human nature does not. My own three children had just passed through their teens, which gave me the chance to observe and look back on that stage of life.

Also, for the past fifteen years, I have been a counselor to hundreds of young people at a large university. Although they are somewhat older than the characters in my stories, all the types are there; the glamour girls and the grinds, the football players and the flunkouts, the school politicians and the soapbox orators, the Valley Girls, the rockabillies, and the preppies, the punks and the squares, the lead in the school play and the blackboard monitor. They fill my imagination with fabulous riches.

I read teen magazines and books about teens. I save newspaper articles about teen trends. Although they sometimes gag me, I watch TV shows about teens. Teenagers are dynamic, fast-changing people. In my books, they don't stay in one place for long. They're flexible, intense, and fun to write about.

For me, having a job during the day that, on the surface of it, is not related to writing, is very helpful. As a professional university administrator, I can approach my writing career without too much tension or anxiety. If I get burned out on one facet of my life, the other one regenerates me.

Young adult romances by Elaine Harper:
Love at First Sight, 1980
We Belong Together, 1981
Be My Valentine, 1983
Light of My Life, 1983
The Mystery Kiss, October, 1983; all Silhouette, First Love romances.

Alla Crone, *author of historical romances:*
My personal background has played a large role in my writing. I was born of a Russian mother and a German father in Harbin, Manchuria, and grew up there among the White Russian émigrés. I am sure that reading Mark Twain, Jack London, Louisa May Alcott, and other writers from the West, translated into Russian, of course, began my love for stories of adventure and/or love.

My family moved to Shanghai, China, when I was 13, and I went to a French-English convent in the port city of Tsingtao for high school. It was there that I first studied the English language. By the time I was seventeen, I was writing poetry in Russian, and was published in literary magazines in Harbin and Shanghai.

In 1946, I married an American army doctor, and began a life of travel. Over the years we lived in Germany, in Washington, D.C., in San Francisco, and in Seattle. When I first came to America, I did some writing for newspapers in the Northwest, but gave it up to take care of my family, and also to take time perfecting my English.

Finally, I took a two-year correspondence course from the New York School of Writing, which taught me a great deal about techniques used in writing. At first, though, I published nonfiction articles in the *Christian Science Monitor* and the *Michigan Quarterly.*

I had always wanted to base a novel on my mother's experiences in the Ice March across Russia, and at last I began work on my first historical romance, *East Lies the Sun.* I drew a great deal on my memory, did research, spent much time at the Museum of Russian Culture in San Francisco, and tapped into my Russian soul, where seem to be those emotions that appear so often in much Russian literature and music.

It was a great thrill for me when *East Lies the Sun* won the Porgie Award of the West Coast Review of Books, the first-place gold medal for the best paperback original historical book of 1982.

My second book is also set in Russia, Siberia, and China, and I am working on a third, which Dell will publish late in 1984.

Historical romances by Alla Crone:
East Lies the Sun, 1982
Winds Over Manchuria, 1983; both published by Dell.

Phyllis Halldorson, *author of contemporary romances:*
I was born in a small town on the rim of the sandhill country in Nebraska, and three months after I graduated from high school I married my first love, a boy from a neighboring town. Three years later our first child, a daughter, was born; nineteen and a half years after that our last baby, a son, completed our family of three boys and three girls.

During those years of child rearing I washed thousands of diapers and spooned hundreds of jars of pureed vegetables into hungry little mouths. Only when the two youngest children were well established in school did I remember that I was a person in my own right. Not that I hadn't been happy and content in my role of child rearing, but now I had outgrown it. It was time to move on to something else.

I had always been a compulsive reader, and even when the children were small, I managed to find time to read while waiting in the pediatrician's office, standing in line at the supermarket, and during P.T.A. meetings. (Sorry about that.) Also, I'd always had the urge to write, so when I found a creative writing class listed in the Adult Education bulletin here in Sacramento, I enrolled. It was the eighth best decision I ever made. (The other seven were to get married and to have each of our six children.) Helene Barnhart was the teacher.

Under her expert tutelage, I started selling confession stories regularly within two years, and two years after that I sold my first romance to Silhouette. It was titled *Temporary Bride*, and was published four months after the line came on the market. Since then I've sold two more to Silhouette and am working on proposals for several others. So far, I have sold without an agent.

I feel blessed. Now that my children no longer need my personal supervision, I've found a whole new life in my career. It's exciting, financially rewarding, and, best of all, I can spend full time with my husband, who sometimes got lost in the shuffle when there were so many of us around.

I openly and joyously admit to being a hopeless romantic, and have no desire to write in any other genre. My advice to new writers is to learn your craft and then *work* at it. The single most important ingredient in a romance novel is emotion, so don't be afraid to write it. It's almost impossible to put in too much.

Contemporary romances by Phyllis Halldorson:
Temporary Bride, 1980
To Start Again, 1981
Mountain Melody, 1983, all Silhouette Romances.

Irma Walker, *author of mysteries, romantic suspense novels, science fiction, historical and contemporary romances:*
I was a reader long before I became a writer, of course. My mother was an obsessive reader; there were always books around our house, and so reading seemed as natural and reasonable to me as eating or sleeping. Because I was very eager to start school so that I could do my own reading and not have to wait for someone to read those fascinating tales aloud to me, I nagged my mother so shamefully that she finally fibbed about my age and sent me to school a year early.

I sailed through it all beautifully until the end of the year, when a visitor asked my age. Being a truthful little girl, I told her that I was four at home and five at school, and that ended my career of crime. I was probably the only child in Cincinnati, Ohio ever to flunk kindergarten!

Oddly enough, I had no idea of becoming a writer until I was in my thirties, although I was always putting stories together in my mind. I'm an Air Force wife, and we were living at the Air Force Academy in Colorado, which is nine thousand feet above sea level. With so many snowbound days, I needed something to keep me busy. I decided to write a book, and since I loved mysteries, that's what I tried first. The result, *Someone's Stolen Nellie Grey,* was accepted by Abelard-Schuman, and a year later (1964), to my astonishment, I found myself a published writer.

I wrote another mystery and then three romantic suspense novels, in the course of which I discovered that I liked to inject romance into my stories. I've written several more mysteries since then for Raven House Books, plus two science fiction books for Atheneum; another romantic suspense (*Windfall*, published by Playboy Press in 1979 under the pseudonym Andrea Harris) was my first novel to be condensed in *Good Housekeeping Magazine*. My second (*Her Decision*, Love & Life romance published by Ballantine) appeared in the July, 1982 issue.

Usually, my books are built around a premise, an idea that fascinates me. Also, I must always know where the story is heading before I start work on it. Knowing what my main characters will be asked to do helps set them in my mind, and keeps them true to themselves and to the story. Oh, yes, they must change and they do—disconcertingly, sometimes!—but still I must know how it will all turn out in the end.

And because I refuse to read a book that doesn't have a hopeful ending, I also refuse to write one. Not always conventionally happy, but hopeful. Yes, I do insist on that! But the twists and turns between—oh, sometimes they are such a surprise to me! So you can see why I have gravitated to romance writing.

In addition to the four books I've done for Ballantine's Love & Life series, I'm doing a fifth, and I have finished an historical to be published by Dell. I will be doing a longer contemporary romance for Ballantine, which will be a single-title release, and I am working on my first Superromance for Harlequin.

Romantic suspense novels by Irma Walker:
The Murdoch Legacy, 1974
The Lucifer Wine, 1976
The Maunaloa Curse, 1977; all published by Bobbs-Merrill in hardback and
    Ballantine in paperback.
Windfall, Playboy Press, 1979, as Andrea Harris.

Contemporary romances:
Her Decision, 1982
A New Tomorrow, 1982
Surrender, 1983
The Next Step, 1983; all Ballantine Love & Life.

Janet Quin-Harkin, *author of young adult romances:*
I was born in Bath, England and grew up during World War II. Being kept isolated for fear of air raids definitely developed my imagination and capacity to escape into a pretend world. My old blind great-aunt, who lived with us, was a wonderful storyteller and a great companion in my pretending games. I grew up writing poetry and short stories.

After college I worked in the drama department of the BBC in London and had plays of my own broadcast. I met my husband on a visit to Australia and came with him to California in 1966. I have been writing for children ever since, and for the past two years I have concentrated on teenage romances.

I never think of myself as a romance writer—I am a writer who at this moment is writing romance novels for teenagers. My basic ideas for plots come from my own experience, usually emotions that I experienced as a teenager; still being a tomboy when everyone else had grown up, for example. But all the background, the small happenings, and the dialogue come from my own teenage daughters and their friends. I listen to them and steal their conversations quite shamelessly, and that way I keep my stories right up to date. My readers want to read about "now," complete with latest fashions, styles, and vocabulary.

I was lucky to get into writing young adult romance at the beginning of this current boom. My agent got word that Bantam was bringing out a new series, Sweet Dreams, and asked me to write an outline. The outline was accepted and became *California Girl,* one of the first Bantam books to be released and still going strong after eighteen months. To date I have written five more Sweet Dreams books and have contracts for three more. I have also written for Scholastic and for Berkley.

I write quickly, producing one book about every two months. It is very hard work, but the results are worth it, not only in numbers of copies sold (almost a million to date in print) but in the response from teenagers. Letters tell me that I am reaching a lot of first-time readers, girls who have never read a whole book before. Also, girls tell me that my books help them with their fears about the future by giving them a glimpse of the life ahead of them. It is good to know that teenage romances are not just fun to write and to read, but are important tools in the young teenager's emotional and reading development.

Young adult romances by Janet Quin-Harkin:
California Girl, 1981
Love Match, 1982
Ten Boy Summer, 1982
DAYDREAMER, 1983
A Ghost of a Chance, 1984
All Bantam Sweet Dreams
Write Every Day, Scholastic Wildfire, 1982
Tommy Loves Tina, Caprice Romance, Berkley Publishing Group, 1984.

Lynda Ward, *who also writes as Julia Jeffries, author of Regency and contemporary romances:*
I think the books I read as a child gave me a predilection for romances. Our house was always full of books, mostly historical novels and mysteries, and I

read whatever was at hand. I first read *Gone With the Wind*, my mother's favorite book, when I was twelve, and I reread it half a dozen or more times before I married at eighteen.

As a young teenager I read Daphne du Maurier—*Rebecca, Frenchman's Creek, The King's General*—and the historicals of Noel B. Gerson. When I was fourteen I began writing a romantic novel that was a rehash of all I'd read, but after about a hundred pages I tore it up.

I now like to say that the only real dry spell in my career was the eighteen years between my first rejection slip at age thirteen and my first sale, a confession story, when I was thirty-one. All that time, while I was busy raising my three children, I just kept writing. I *had* to write; I knew I had something to offer. Since that first sale, things have gone swimmingly.

I soon wanted to do something a little more challenging than confession stories, and the light romance novel seeemed an obvious and logical progression. I read my first Harlequin in 1978, discovered that I loved the genre, and since then have read thousands of romances.

These days, I prefer to write long contemporary romances with well-defined characters, exotic settings, and a healthy dose of straight (as opposed to perverted) sensuality; in other words, Harlequin Superromances. I have written a couple of period novels, which were well received, but I think I can no longer cope with the realities of Regency or any other past society: the squalor, the violence, and, most especially, the suppression of women.

Though my books have been set in Austria, Italy, and England, I've never been much of anywhere. In my entire live I've never traveled east of the Mississippi, and I lived seventeen years without setting foot outside California.

I always feel slightly fraudulent when people compliment me on how "real" I've made my settings sound. I suppose I have a knack for finding the kind of detail that brings a place to life for the reader. Here's how one such setting evolved.

The idea for *The Touch of Passion* (Harlequin Superromance Library Worldwide) came to me from a fascinating magazine article I read about the Italian town of Pietrasanta and the sculptors who travel there each summer to carve in marble from Michelangelo's very source. By the time I finished reading the article, I knew that I had to write a story about it, and also to learn a lot about Italy.

Actually, I spent less time describing the Italian countryside than I did in explaining the difficulties inherent in making a long-distance call from a pay telephone—a nugget of information I gleaned from a pocket travel guide I found in a bookstore.

One of the most helpful things I did was to read Luigi Barzini's marvelous book, *The Italians*, which gave me a lot of insight into the character of the people. I also used picture books extensively, and kept a map of Italy plastered to the wall over my desk for six months.

I read cookbooks, magazines, newspaper articles. On videotape I watched a number of movies that had Italian settings, and I boned up on the Italian language itself. In the end I had a fairly accurate, albeit superficial, picture of the country and its culture, and I was able to draw on that picture as I wrote.

Regardless of what place I am writing about, I follow pretty much the same procedures in doing my research. If I need to know a specific detail, I use the library and/or the librarians. And if I uncover information about a place or people that I find unflattering or unpleasant, I ignore it. After all, the whole point of these books is to make things sound *romantic!*

Romance novels by Lynda Ward:

The Music of Passion, 1981

The Touch of Passion, 1982; Harlequin Superromance Worldwide Superromances

The Chadwick Ring, 1982

The Clergyman's Daughter, 1983; New American Library Regencies (written as Julia Jeffries).

Jane Peart; author of gothics, romantic suspense, historical, contemporary, and young adult romances:
I always knew I was going to be a writer. I grew up in a family of readers. My father loved the classics, and both Shakespeare's and Dickens' characters were familiar to me before they were required reading in high school. I think it is almost imperative that a writer loves to read and has begun to read early in life.

We lived in the beautiful resort town of Asheville, North Carolina in the Great Smoky Mountains. Since I grew up surrounded by the ever-changing scenery provided by the seasons, I have a deep love of nature in all its many phases. As I was growing up, life there was peaceful, leisurely, and assumed to be otherwise changeless. Southerners revere the past, cherish tradition, value close family ties. I think all this has lingered with me and probably permeates my writing.

I never seem to have any trouble finding ideas for stories. In fact, I have so many I'll never write them all. I do keep a folder into which I put clippings, pictures of people, settings, and interiors, and sometimes an opening paragraph or a sketchy outline of some idea that comes to me while I'm working on another project. This way I don't lose anything, in case the material proves to be the basis for another book.

I am convinced that sometimes a kind of "magic" happens in writing a book. For example, several years ago when I was writing *Vintage Evil,* a romantic suspense (Lancer) set in the wine country of California, I described Chateau Chardonnay, the Adair mansion, the old aging cellars, the orchards, the grounds—before I had *ever* visited Beringer Brothers Winery in Napa. To my amazement, Rhine House, the aging rooms and the grounds were so similar to my descriptions that I could hardly believe it, even to the stained-glass windows and the old oak staircase in the house. It was a form of "déjà vu" for me, since I'd already "seen" it in my imagination.

The same sort of thing happened when I was writing *Spanish Masquerade* (Dell Candlelight). The germ of the story came from something that happened to my niece when she was spending a year in Spain at the University of Madrid. Of course I changed, embellished, romanticized, and enlarged greatly on what had actually taken place. I did extensive research on the country as well.

About halfway through my first draft, she sent me several pages of notes taken from a diary she had kept that year in Spain. Again I was astonished at the similarities between real and fictional descriptions and events. I had a further surprise when the book came out. The girl on the cover looked so much like Anne, my heroine, that she could have been the model who posed for her in my mind.

Romance novels by Jane Peart:
Spanish Masquerade, 1980
Portrait in the Shadows, 1981; Dell Candlelight romances
It's Your Move, Lori, 1982, E.P. Dutton young adult romance

Georgette Livingston, *who writes as Diane Crawford, author of contemporary romances:*
One fateful day several years ago, I picked up a magazine and found a tiny advertisement that said, "Send a sample of your writing." I filled out the coupon and sent it in, and within days a salesman was knocking at my door.

When he finally left, we were seven hundred dollars poorer, and I had to find a typewriter. A corner of the kitchen table became my "office," and peanut butter and jelly invariably landed on the typewriter keys, but I was off and running.

The course took two years to complete, and I was a quiet joke to my family. It wasn't that they didn't believe in me; they were all thinking about that seven hundred dollars that we couldn't afford to toss away.

In fact, the course didn't teach me how to write, but it smoothed out my style and taught me a few of the finer points, which enabled me to consider submitting my work.

A year later, I made my first sale. The $75 seemed like a million. Shortly after that, I sold a story to *Modern Romances* for $300, and my career was launched. For twelve years, I wrote only for *Modern Romances,* having as many as three stories in one issue. Although it wasn't a large income, it certainly helped.

Then for a year or two the well ran dry, until one day I read in the newspaper about three successful romance writers in my area. I decided writing romances couldn't be all that different from writing a confession story.

My first two attempts were rejected. The third, two years later, was accepted by Jove's Second Chance at Love, and then I sold two more to them. I've recently sold my first longer romance to Harlequin Superromances (1984 release), and again my career has gone in a new and exciting direction. I've also acquired a wonderful agent. I think having an agent is a matter of personal preference, but I know I couldn't get along without mine.

Almost all my contemporary romances have been set in foreign locations—Samoa, Brazil, and Africa. Two in progress, long reads, are set in the New Zealand high country (South Island) and in the South Pacific. I handle exotic locations by doing a tremendous amount of research, and actually prefer them because of the challenge.

I spend eight to ten hours at my typewriter each day. It's a private life of total dedication to the craft, in which life becomes just you, your typewriter, and your characters. All you need is ability to tell an exciting, passionate story and the capacity to take the rejections, as they will surely come, and still keep right on creating.

Contemporary romances by Diane Crawford:
Sapphire Island, 1982
Savage Eden, 1982; both Jove, Second Chance at Love

Helen Santori, *who writes as Helen Erskine, author of contemporary and young adult romances:*
When I found myself widowed at an early age, I became a full-time confession writer, and earned a comfortable living at it for some thirty years. The time comes when a writer wants to move on, however, and so in 1980 I decided to try my hand at writing a romance novel. Luckily for me this coincided with the time when the romance market began to explode. Harlequin was no longer the only game in town. One publisher after another was putting out a romance line. Applying all I had learned in my previous writing, I sold my first romance, *Fortunes of Love,* to Silhouette in 1981.

Since then I've sold to Harlequin, and have also sold young adult romances to Silhouette. When I was interviewed on television recently, the host narrowed his gaze and asked me if I had any trouble capturing the viewpoint of these teenage girls and young women who were experiencing the first throes of love. (He was referring, of course, to the fact that my own youth was obviously far behind me.)

I told him I had no problem at all writing about young women in love, pointing out that everything we've ever experienced remains with us. I can close my eyes and become a teenage girl on her way home from high school, dizzy with the excitement of being in love for the first time. I can remember my first day on a new job, looking across the office and meeting a pair of interested male eyes. Everything we have ever been, or experienced, remains with us as long as we live.

The elements that make up a love story do not change either. My first little love story, published almost forty years ago, could be refurbished, updated, and expanded, and have a chance in today's market because *love itself does not change.* It's still the mysterious, magic emotion that drew Romeo and Juliet together. The basic story ingredients are the same in today's romance market as they were in the love pulps and confessions. In current romances, you must have a sympathetic heroine, the type of young woman the reader cares about and eagerly identifies with. She may have some flaws, if they're not the kind of faults that would turn the reader against her. She must also have a problem, but she doesn't wring her hands helplessly while waiting for somebody else to come along and solve it for her. She strikes out bravely to overcome all obstacles to her ultimate happiness.

None of this is new. None of these basic ingredients has changed, or ever will. The romance stories of today are sexier and more sophisticated, the heroines more career-minded. But today's heroines have the same emotional needs women have always had.

In learning to write romance novels, you'll be learning a skill that will last you a lifetime, for no matter how much the market may seem to change from month to month, year to year, or even decade to decade, the really important elements of romance fiction remain the same.

Romance novels by Helen Erskine:

Kate Herself, Silhouette First Love, 1981 (young adult)

Fortunes of Love, Silhouette Romance

Best-selling author of SAVAGE SURRENDER

NATASHA PETERS

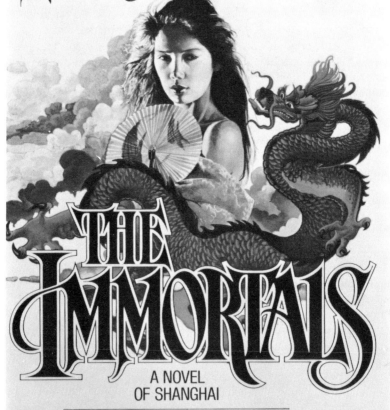

THE IMMORTALS

A NOVEL
OF SHANGHAI

UNFORGETTABLE MEN AND WOMEN
DRIVEN BY RAGING DESTINIES

FAWCETT
COLUMBINE

90041-1/**$6.95** in USA • $8.95 in Canada

Chapter **18.**
TO YOU, WITH LOVE

Art work copyright Elaine Gignilliat, 1983. Used by permission of Silhouette Books.

Before you close this book, I'd like to share my personal thoughts on what it means to be a romance writer and to belong to the writing profession.

We've talked about the exciting monetary rewards awaiting you as a published romance fiction writer, and I'd like to add to that the happy news that even as this book goes to press, many new romance lines are being planned by such established publishers as Harlequin, Bantam, Silhouette, Jove, and Dell.

Harlequin will soon launch a new line of *American Romances* with a promotional budget of $5 million. Bantam will introduce its new *Loveswept* series. Silhouette plans *Intimate Moments* and a line of inspirational or religious romances. Jove will follow up the success of *Second Chance* with *To Have and To Hold,* stories of romance *within* marriage. Other publishers are following suit as well with additions to their already-established lines. There is no doubt in my mind that you have a good chance to realize your writing goals and to make money for yourself in this lucrative market.

We've covered the techniques you need to master to write professionally: plotting, characterization, viewpoint, motivation, and all the other elements that make up a *salable* romance novel. You now know how to write for money.

This brings us to the other part of romance writing suggested in the title of this book—*writing for love.*

Writing For and With Love

There is nothing wrong with writing for money. To expect to be paid for your efforts is normal, healthy, and professional.

It is my conviction, however, that you need something more than a desire for fame and fortune to fulfill the promise of your talent. You may have spectacular success for a while, if you hit a certain market at just the right time with a fresh idea. You may ride high on the crest of that wave and even make several more sales to that market.

Eventually, though, your luck may seem to run out; you may not make another sale for a long time. This sort of thing happens to most writers.

It is at that point in your writing life—when income is down and luck is running low—that you will need something more than your professional ambition to sustain you. That something is the *love* of writing.

From the day you decide to become a professional writer, you also enter into what should be a lifetime love affair. Like the heroines in your romance novels, you are obsessed with a goal. Your heroine's goal is the attainment of love with a very special man, Mr. Right. How much easier it would be for our heroine if she'd settle for Mr. Almost Right, but this she will never do. She must have that one man, and she'll fight to get him.

With the same determination, you go after your goal, your dream. Next to your love for your real-life hero and your family is your love of and dedication to the talent you've been given—a talent for setting down words that transport your reader into another world.

The joy you experience in the act of writing is unlike any other. It has nothing to do with contracts and sales. It does relate to being published, since you wouldn't be sharing your imagined worlds with readers if you were not published. But the same sense of accomplishment and elation comes regardless of the size of the check. It is there, even when there is no check. *Writers are in love with the process of writing.*

Writing is a high-risk occupation. Dry spells will come in spite of your talent and your determination. Sometimes sales will be few and far between. But if you love the act of writing, you'll survive those periods. You'll persevere, keep writing, and keep submitting, and eventually you'll find your market again.

Love of writing, dedication, obsession, whatever you wish to call it, must be present even when great success comes to you. Wealth and fame are not enough. Writers who have made huge profits for their efforts keep on writing. Is it really to gain larger fortunes? I'll wager that Janet Dailey, Rosemary Rogers, and all other highly successful writers are captives of their calling along with the rest of us. They keep chaining themselves to their typewriters or word processors for long hours of hard work. Why? Because in spite of the many changes that success has brought into their lives, they're still caught up in that same old romance—the thrill of putting words on paper.

In addition to the indefinable happiness that comes as you sit alone, creating fictional worlds, come other rewards that make up for all the disappointments and frustrations of being a writer. The next time you have an attack of writer's block, or feel the blues of rejectionitis, think of the following advantages that are yours as a writer:

1. If you write well and have something significant to say, you'll have the opportunity to reach out and touch not just *one* somebody, but thousands—your readers today, tomorrow, and even beyond your time on this planet. Your writing is your immortality.

   Would you give up that possibility for the security of a nine-to-five job with its regular paycheck on the first and the fifteenth? Not likely.

2. Isn't it nice to realize that you won't be grounded at age sixty? (You would be if you were an airline pilot.) Ernest Gann, author of the memorable *The High and the Mighty,* is retired from commercial flying, but he's still writing. Fred Astaire can no longer dance professionally, but he can write about his

life and the love affair he had with his other profession. If your mind is still clicking, you can go on writing until you are ninety, if you choose to.

Unlike most other professions, in which age brings voluntary or forced retirement, writing has no such limits. As you learn your craft, and as the words you write become better and better over the years, you'll grow *more* valuable to your publisher, not less. And you'll build up a faithful following, a readership that will be yours as long as you live, and longer.

3. Whatever kind of writing you do now or in the future, every day is an educational experience, which broadens your interests and keeps your mind expanding. I'm sure it is the constant flow of new ideas that keeps writers young and alive, seeing the world and the people in it with curiosity and fascination.

In fact, I sense a kind of eternal youth in writers. Whenever they come together at big conferences, age is forgotten in the exciting exchange of ideas and the kindling of new dreams. Tongues wag continually, eyes light up, and excitement fills the air. Age, backgrounds, special interests are no barrier to communication among people who share the love of writing.

These are just a few of the rewards that come to all writers. To the author of romances comes another special return, not always experienced by other kinds of writers.

As a romance writer, you will relive the days of your own romance over and over again. Writing romance fiction keeps you not only mentally alive, but young in heart. And, as you write sensuously of love and create a fictional world for your reader, you will find your own senses sharpened to the beauty of the real world. The grass will be greener outside your writing-room window, the sky bluer. Your romance-colored glasses will give you new vision, so that when you see people you will take in things that you once ignored. Look at that older couple at the next table to yours in the restaurant—she with the beautiful cloud of silvery hair, and he with that tender gleam in his eye. They gaze at each other across their small candlelit table, and lean toward each other as they talk. They're in love! Can you imagine them as they were thirty or forty years ago? Would those imagined people make a hero and heroine in your next book?

That thirtyish couple at another table—notice the recent tears in her eyes and the drawn look about his mouth as he tries earnestly to explain something to her. Perhaps these two have both known love before, lost it, and are now about to find it again with each other. Do they inspire an idea for a pair of lovers?

What about the girl and the boy who walk past your house every day on the way home from high school? They're holding hands and smiling into each other's eyes. They're oblivious of you at the window and of all the world around them. Is it time to write a story of first love?

Strange how much love there is around you, now that you are more aware of it.

It is said that romance fiction satisfies the need for fantasy, and this is certainly true. But fantasy alone would soon wear thin. Romance fiction is popular because it is based on the truth, spoken in the word of the old song; *it's love that makes the world go 'round.*

In real life, love may not conquer all obstacles, but it makes many of them seem smaller.

As a romance writer, you will touch other lives, expanding other minds with information you've carefully researched and with stimulating ideas born in your imagination. You'll be privileged to touch the human heart, stirring it to new awareness. In writing romantic tales in which love always wins the day, you are saying, "All is right with the world." These days, who isn't cheered by such a message?

If one beautifully written love scene awakens one reader to feelings long forgotten, you have added pleasure to the world. If you realize that as many as 300,000 people could read your novel, you can't take lightly your responsibility as a romance writer.

Again you ask, "But will the romance market last?" You are concerned that so many romance lines by so many publishers will glut the market. Personally, I don't think this need be a worry for good romance writers.

As I've said, new lines appear in answer to reader response. What readers like in romance fiction will prevail and last, and there will always be a demand for the heart-warming love story in one form or another. Write with skill and style and with love in your heart, and you'll find an editor who will say, "We've read your romance novel. We like it, and we'd like to publish it."

If after reading this book, you have any questions, I'll be happy to try to answer them. You can write me in care of Writer's Digest Books. I wish you the very best of luck in your writing of romance fiction.

What others have done, you can and will do. Dreams always come true in romance fiction, and quite often they come true in real life, too.

The End

Appendix 1 ▲

READING TO PUT YOU IN A ROMANTIC MOOD

Everything You Always Wanted to Know about Sex and Were Afraid to Ask by Dr. David Reuben, Bantam, 1971.

How to Make Love to a Man by Alexandra Penney, Crown, 1981. Paperback.

How to Make Love to a Woman by Michael Morgenstern, Crown, 1982; Ballantine paperback, 1983.

The Sensuous Man by "M," Lyle Stuart. Paperback: Dell, 1982.

The Sensuous Woman by "J," Lyle Stuart, 1970. Dell paperback, 1982.

The Sensuous Couple by Robert Chartham, Ballantine, 1981.

The Joy of Sex by Alex Comfort, Crown, 1972.

Sensual Pleasure: A Woman's Guide by Eva L. Margolies, Avon, 1981.

My Secret Garden; Women's Sexual Fantasies by Nancy Friday, Trident Press, 1973.

Forbidden Flowers; More Women's Sexual Fantasies by Nancy Friday, Pocket Books, 1975.

Men in Love; Men's Sexual Fantasies; The Triumph of Love Over Rage by Nancy Friday, Delacourt, 1980. Dell paperback, 1981.

Your Erogenous Zones by Dr. Wayne Dyer, T. Y. Crowell, 1976. Avon paperback, 1977.

The Lessons of Love; Secrets of the World's Most Glamorous Dating Servce by Abbey Hersch and Susan Dooley, William Morrow, 1983.

The Gift of Touch by Helen Colton, G. P. Putnam's Sons, 1983.

Love by Dr. Leo Buscaglia, Charles B. Slack Co., 1972, paperback, Fawcett, 1978.

Personhood by Dr. Leo Buscaglia, Charles B. Slack, 1978, Fawcett paperback, 1982.

Living, Loving, and Learning by Dr. Leo Buscaglia, Charles B. Slack Co., 1982.

Vogue Complete Beauty by Deborah Hutton, Harmony Books, 1982.

The Miss Universe Beauty Book by Susan Duff, G. P. Putnam's Sons, 1983.

World's Great Romances Walter J. Black, Inc. First printing, 1929.

Bring Back Romance by Natalie Willner, Berkley Publishing Co.

Appendix 2 ▲

ROMANCE NEWSLETTERS TO SUBSCRIBE TO

Boy Meets Girl
Vivien Lee Jennings
Rainy Day Books
2812 West 53rd St.
Fairway, Kansas 66205

Affaire De Coeur
Barbara Keenan
5660 Roosevelt Place
Fremont, California 94538

Romance Writers Report
Romance Writers of America
5206 FM 1960 West, Suite 207
Houston, Texas 77069

Romantic Times
Kathryn Falk
163 Joralemon Street
Suite 1234
Brooklyn Heights, New York 11201

Heartline
Terri Busch
140 Schoolhouse Lane
Brookhaven, Pennsylvania 19015

Barbra Critiques
2710 Mize Road
Independence, Missouri 64057

Romance Books and Reviews
3744 Charlemagne
Long Beach, California 90808

Publishers Weekly
Subscription Dept.
R.R. Bowker Co.
P.O. Box 13710
Philadelphia, Pennsylvania 19101

The Writer
8 Arlington St.
Boston, Massachusetts 12116

Writer's Digest
Subscription Dept.
205 West Center St.
Marion, Ohio 43306

Appendix 3 ▲

ENDURING ROMANCE TITLES

Compiled by Vivien Lee Jennings

©1983 by Vivien Lee Jennings

What causes certain romance stories to rise above all the others in an especially crowded market? Fresh, original treatments of the traditional, beloved elements of the love story.

The following is a bibliography of books that are proven reader favorites. They represent some of the best of a particular line or series or subcategory of romance fiction. As you read this sampling, you'll note certain common elements, elements that worked together to make these stories both initially popular and still memorable.

Look for particularly skillful executions of humor and wit, dialogue, drama, sexual chemistry, and the identification of a compelling romantic fantasy.

Sadly, some of the stories listed here are no longer in print. The shelf life of paperback romance is often brief. However, many bookstores that carry used paperbacks have extensive collections of romance, collections which may include many of these titles. Public libraries have begun to save some of the best of the genre. The books listed here are also the foundation for many private romance collections.

Contemporary category romances:

1. *Sweet Compulsion*
   Victoria Woolf
   Harlequin Romance
2. *Bewildered Haven*
   Helen Bianchin
   Harlequin Romance
3. *A Frozen Fire*
   Charlotte Lamb
   Harlequin Presents
4. *A Secret Sorrow*
   Karen Van der Zee
   Harlequin Presents

5. *Confirmed Bachelor*
   Roberta Leigh
   Harlequin Presents
6. *Jake Howard's Wife*
   Anne Mather
   Harlequin Presents
7. *Witchstone*
   Anne Mather
   Harlequin Presents
8. *Irish Thoroughbred*
   Nora Roberts
   Silhouette Romance
9. *For the Love of God*
   Janet Dailey
   Silhouette Romance
10. *After the Rain*
    Linda Shaw
    Silhouette Special Edition
11. *Captive of Desire*
    Alexandra Sellers
    Worldwide Library-Superromance
12. *Infidel of Love*
    Casey Douglas
    Worldwide Library-Superromance
13. *Friends and Lovers*
    Diana Palmer
    Silhouette Desire
14. *Experiment in Love*
    Rita Clay
    Silhouette Desire
15. *Gentle Pirate*
    Jayne Castle
    Dell Candlelight Ecstasy
16. *The Game Is Played*
    Amii Lorin
    Dell Candlelight Ecstasy
17. *Love Beyond Reason*
    Rachel Ryan
    Dell Candlelight Ecstasy
18. *The Golden Touch*
    Robin James
    Jove-Second Chance at Love

19. *Relentless Desire*
    Sandra Brown
    Jove-Second Chance at Love
20. *Forsaking All Others*
    LaVyrle Spencer
    Jove-Second Chance at Love
21. *Torn Asunder*
    Ann Cristy
    Jove-Second Chance at Love
22. *Summer Storm*
    Joan Wolf
    New American Library-Rapture
23. *A Love for All Time*
    Dorothy Garlock
    Bantam-Loveswept
24. *Silver Miracles*
    Fayrene Preston
    Bantam-Loveswept
25. *The Testimony*
    Tom and Sharon Curtis
    Jove-To Have and To Hold
26. *Tomorrow's Promise*
    Sandra Brown
    Harlequin American Romance

Full-length contemporary romance—
single title releases:
1. *Chasing Rainbows*
   Esther Sager
   Jove
2. *The Sapphire Sky*
   Kristin James
   Richard Gallen Books
3. *Gifts of Love*
   Charlotte Vale Allen
   New American Library

Full-length historical romance:
1. *Caroline*
   Cynthia Wright
   Ballantine
2. *The Flame and the Flower*
   Kathleen Woodiwiss
   Avon

3. *The Fulfillment*
   LaVyrle Spencer
   Avon
4. *The Rainbow Season*
   Lisa Gregory
   Jove

Mainstream/crossover:
1. *The Tiger's Woman*
   Celeste DeBlasis
   Dell
2. *To Love Again*
   Danielle Steel
   Dell
3. *This Calder Sky*
   Janet Dailey
   Pocket Books
4. *Deceptions*
   Judith Michael
   Pocket Books

Regency:
1. *Alicia*
   by Elizabeth Neff Walker
   Dell
2. *Love's a Stage*
   Laura London
   Dell
3. *The Nabob's Widow*
   Elsie Lee
   Dell
4. *A Kind of Honor*
   Joan Wolf
   New American Library

5. *The Rebel Bride*
   Catherine Coulter
   New American Library

Gothic/romantic mystery and suspense:
1. *Moonraker's Bride*
   Madeleine Brent
   Fawcett
2. *Black Rainbow*
   Barbara Michaels
   Fawcett
3. *The Defector*
   Evelyn Anthony
   New American Library
4. *Solo Blues*
   Paula Gosling
   Ballantine
5. *Summer of the Dragon*
   Elizabeth Peters
   Fawcett
6. *Crocodile on the Sandbank*
   Elizabeth Peters
   Fawcett

Young adult:
1. *Popularity Plan*
   Rosemary Vernon
   Bantam-Sweet Dreams
2. *Kate Herself*
   Helen Erskine
   Silhouette-First Love

Appendix 4 ▲
RESEARCH SOURCES

America's Front Page News
edited by Emery, Schuneman and
Emery
Doubleday
100 Park Ave., New York, NY
10017

This Fabulous Century
Time-Life Books
Time-Life Bldg.
Rockefeller Center, New York

Poole's Guide to Periodical Literature
Available in your library

Subject Collections
guide to special book collections in
library
R.R. Bowker Co.
1180 Ave. of the Americas
New York 10036

Subject Guide to Major U.S. Gov. Publications
Entries arranged by subject matter
under Library of Congress headings.
American Library Assoc.
50 E. Huron St.
Chicago, IL 60611

Reference Books: A Brief Guide
Enoch Pratt Free Library
400 Cathedral St.
Baltimore, MD 21201

The Encyclopaedia Britannica
or others

Webster's Biographical Dictionary

Webster's New International Dictionary
unabridged

Costume Through the Ages
James Laver
available in paperback

Lovejoy's College Guide and American Universities and Colleges
Topics by subject, and college
named where the subject matter is
catalogued. Research programs listed. Write to colleges named for bibliographies, or for their catalog of
books in print.

Directory of Special Libraries and Info. Centers
Tells where special collections of papers and sources are available.
Gale Research Company
Detroit, Michigan

Writer's Research Handbook
Keith M. Gottam and Robert W. Pelton
Barnes & Noble

Writer's Resource Guide
edited by Bernadine Clark
Writer's Digest Books
9933 Alliance Rd.
Cincinnati, OH 45242
Toll-free number: 1-800-543-4644

Writer's Encyclopedia
edited by Kirk Polking
Writer's Digest Books
Address and phone number same as above.

Writer's Market
Published yearly by Writer's Digest Books. More than 4,000 listings of markets for writers.

Writer's Yearbook
Published by Writer's Digest. An annual magazine for writers with how-to articles on writing and lucrative markets for all types of manuscripts.

Additional Sources of Research Information
Almanacs
Biographies
Catalogs
Dictionaries
Encyclopedias
Maps and Atlases
Newspapers
Newspaper Indexes
Pamphlets
Periodical Indexes
Picture Files
Journals and Diaries

Magazines
Architectural Digest
House Beautiful
Home & Garden
Woman's Day
Family Circle
Cosmopolitan
Antique Magazines
Ladies Home Journal
Goodhousekeeping
Redbook
Sunset Magazine
Travel magazines
Hobby magazines

Appendix 5 ▲

PUBLISHERS OF ROMANCE FICTION

*indicates a romance line or series. Guidelines are available on request.

Ace/Tempo (See Berkley/Jove)

Avalon Books
22 East 60th Street
New York, New York 10022
(Imprint includes Thomas Bouregy & Co.) Hardcover, contemporary and gothic romance, romantic suspense.

Avon Books
959 8th Avenue
New York, New York 10019
Paperback. Contemporary, historical and Regency romance.
*Finding Mr. Right—short, sensual contemporary romantic series.

Bantam Books, Inc.
666 5th Avenue
New York, New York, 10019
Paperback. Contemporary, historical and gothic romance.
*Sweet Dreams young adult romance line (See Cloverdale Press).

*Loveswept romances, line of short, sensual contemporary romances.

Ballantine Books
Division of Random House
201 East 50th Street
New York, New York 10022
Paperback. Contemporary, historical and Regency romance.
*Love & Life, series of short contemporary romances with older heroines.

Berkley/Jove/Ace/Tempo
Berkley Publishing Group
200 Madison Avenue
New York, New York 10016
Paperback. Contemporary, historical and Regency romances.
*Jove, Second Chance At Love, line of short, sensual contemporary romances.
*Jove, To Have and To Hold, line of short, sensual contemporary romances featuring married heroines and heroes.
*Ace/Tempo Caprice romances for young adults.

Bethany Fellowship, Inc.
6820 Auto Club Road
Minneapolis, Minnesota 55438
Paperback. Inspirational romance.

Bookcraft, Inc.
1848 W. 2300 South
Salt Lake City, Utah 84119
Hardcover, publishes a few contemporary and historical romances per year.

Bradbury Press, Inc.
2 Overhill Road
Scarsdale, New York 10583
Hardcover. Looking for "realistic" romances. Short list.

Cloverdale Press
133 5th Avenue
New York, New York 10003
Packagers of Sweet Dreams young adult romances for Bantam Books.

Dell Publishing Co., Inc.
1 Dag Hammarskjold Plaza
New York, New York 10017
Hardcover and paperback. Contemporay and historical romances; sagas.
*Dell Candlelight Ecstasy, lne of short, sensual contemporary romances.
*Dell Ecstasy Supreme, line of longer sensual contemporary romances.
Dell Young Love books for young adults.

Dodd, Mead & Company, Inc.
79 Madison Avenue
New York, New York 10016
Hardcover. Some historical romance

E. P. Dutton Publishers
2 Park Avenue
New York, New York 10016
Hardcover.
*Heavenly romances for young adults.

Doubleday and Co., Inc.
245 Park Avenue
New York, New York 10017
Hardcover. Starlight romances, imprint for contemporary and historical romances.

Fawcett Gold Medal
1515 Broadway
New York, New York 10036
Paperback. Contemporary and historical romance, family sagas, and teen romance.

Harcourt Brace Jovanovich
757 3rd Avenue
New York, New York 10017
Hardcover and paperback. Romance for young adults.

Harlequin Enterprises, LTD.
Paperback. Harlequin Romance and Harlequin Presents lines, short sweet contemporary romances.

Mills & Boon
15-16 Brook's Mews
London WIA IDR England
Harlequin Worldwide Library Superromance line, longer, sensual contemporary romance.

Harlequin Books
220 Duncan Mills Road
Don Mills, Ontario
Canada M3B 3J5

Harlequin Books
919 Third Avenue
New York, New York 10022
*Harlequin American Romance, line of longer, sensual contemporary romance with American hero, heroine and setting.

Harvey House Publishers
20 Waterside Plaza
New York, New York 10010
Hardcover. Young adult romance.

Highway Bookshop
Highway 11N
Cobalt, Ontario, Canada P0J 1C0
Paperback. Publishes a few contemporary, historical and gothic romances per year.

Holiday House, Inc.
18 East 53rd Street
New York, New York 10022

William Morrow and Company, Inc.
105 Madison Avenue
New York, New York 10016
Hardcover. Highest quality romance.

New American Library
1633 Broadway
New York, New York 10019
Hardcover and paperback. Contemporary and historical romance.
*Rapture romances, line of short, sensual contemporary romances.
*Signet/Vista young adult romances.
*Signet Regency Romances.

Pocket Books
(Division of Simon & Schuster)
1230 Avenue of the Americas
New York, New York 10020
Paperback. Contemporary, historical and gothic romance.

*Tapestry, line of medium length historical romances.

Pinnacle Books, Inc.
1430 Broadway
New York, New York 10018
Paperback. Contemporary, historical, and gothic romance.

Seal Books, McClelland and Stewart-Bantam Ltd.
60 St. Clair Avenue E.
#601, Toronto, Canada M4T 1N5
Paperback. Contemporary, historical and gothic romance.

St. Martin's Press
175 Fifth Avenue
New York, New York 10010
Hardcover and paperback. Contemporary, historical, gothic and Regency romance.

Silhouette Books
Simon & Schuster Bldg.
1230 Avenue of the Americas
New York, New York 10020
Paperback.
*Silhouette romance, short, sweet contemporary romance.
*Silhouette Desire, short, sensual contemporary romance.
*Silhouette Special Edition, longer, sensual contemporary romances.
*Silhouette Intimate Moments, highly sensual longer contemporary romances.
*First Love from Silhouette, young adult romance.

Scholastic Book Services
50 West 44th Street
New York, New York 10036
Paperback.
*Wildfire and *Windswept romances for young adults.

Tandem Publishers
Box 237
Tannersville, Pennsylvania 18372
Paperback. Publishes a few contemporary, historical and gothic romances a year.

Vesta Publications, Ltd.
Box 1641
Cornwall, Ontario, Canada K0H 5V6
Hardcover and paperback. Publishes a few contempoary, historical and gothic romances a year.

Walker and Co.
720 5th Avenue
New York, New York 10019
Hardcover. Regency romances.

Warner Books
75 Rockefeller Plaza
New York, New York 10019
Hardcover and paperback. Some long contemporary, historical romances and sagas.

Zebra Books
475 Park Avenue South
New York, New York 10016
Hardcover and paperback. Contemporary, historical, gothic romance and sagas.
*Leather and Lace, historical/western romances.
*Hourglass, short, sensual contemporary romances.

INDEX

ABC's "20/20," 7
Abelard-Schuman, 237
Accents, 133-136
Ace Books, 2, 7
Ace Tempo Books, 28, 60
Act of Love, A, 227
Adult education, 206
Adult westerns, 9
Advances, 2, 6, 8, 215
Affaire de Coeur, 206
Age of heroine, 4
Agents, 189-190, 214, 215
   correspondence with, 50-51
Alexander, Megan, 24, 185
Aliveness of characters, 62-65
Allerton Rose, The, 231
Amber Wine, 165
American contemporary, 3
American Romances, Harlequin, 9,
   24, 230
Americans, The, 28
American settings, 3
Ames, Winter (aka Phyllis Taylor
   Pianka), 116
Analytical reading, 32
Annual income, 2
Annual sales, 8
Antihero, 57
Antique & Collectors Mart, 48
Antique Monthly, 48
Antique Reader Weekly, 48
Antiques Magazine, 48
Aphrodite's Legend, 109

Architectural Digest, 48
Arctic Nurse, 231
Art on cover, 12
Articles on romance writing, 51
Austen, Jane, 1
Author. *See* Writer
Authors Guild, 206
Avon Books, 9, 73, 81, 188, 231
   Finding Mr. Right, 8, 24

Background of characters, 217
   professional, 38, 83-86
Balkin, Richard, 200
Ballantine Books, 8, 237
   Love & Life, 8, 24, 97, 237
Bantam Books, 7, 8, 9, 15, 73, 238,
   246
   Circle of Love, 7, 8
   Loveswept, 9, 24, 130
   Sweet Dreams, 28, 74, 238
   Windswept, 28
Barzini, Luigi, 239
Beckman, Charles, 15
Beckman, Patti, 15, 23, 110
Beginnings, 35
Beginning writers, 214
Believability
   of ending, 164
   vs. realism, 62
Be My Valentine, 234
Berkley/Jove Publishing Group, 5
Berkley Publishing Group, 238
Better Homes and Gardens, 48

Bianchi, Jacqui, 8, 49, 149
Bibliography, 50
Bieber, Janet (one half of Janet Joyce), 231-233
Biographies of characters, 60-62, 69, 186
Bitter Victory, 110
Black Swan, The, 134
Block, 207-210
Bobbs Merrill, 237
"Bodice rippers," 3, 20, 27
Bonds, Parris Afton, 122
Bookstore promotion, 204
Boy Meets Girl, 206
Browning, Dixie, 23
Brown, Sandra, 192
Business, 51

California Girl, 238
Candlelight series. *See* Dell
Caprice Romances, 60, 238
Career information, 46
Cartland, Barbara, 3, 6, 15
Castle, Jayne (aka Stephanie James, Jane Frentz), 6, 52, 92, 167
Category fiction vs. category romance, 21
Category romances, 1, 29
See also Contemporary romances
vs. category fiction, 21
hero and heroine in, 56-58
secondary characters in, 58-59
sensual, 21, 22, 24-26
setting in, 78-81
sex in, 150-155
shifts viewpoint in, 111-112
sweet, 21, 22, 23
Cavanagh, Helen, 189
Chadwick Ring, the, 240
Changes by editors, 196
Chapters
folders for, 48-49
sample, 186-187
Characterization, 175-176
dialogue for, 121-123

Characters, 35-36, 45-46, 186, 216
See also Hero; Heroine
aliveness of, 62-65
background of. *See* Background of characters
basic aspects of lives of, 61
biographies of, 60-62, 69, 186
building of, 68-69
death of, 168
secondary, 25, 58-59
stereotypes in, 58
tagging of, 65-68, 69
Christian Science Monitor, 235
Circle of Love, Bantam, 7, 8
Cirillo, Andrea, 32
Clergyman's Daughter, The, 240
Cliches, 138
Climax, 96-98
Clothing, 46
Collaborations, 221, 222
College lectures and workshops, 206
Collins, Susanna, 80
Colloquial expressions, 137
Competition, 2
Complications, 36-37, 90-91
Comworld, 7
Conference funds, 206
Conflict, 36-37, 217
Conquer the Memories, 233
Contemporary romances, 21
See also Category romances
American, 3
category. *See* Category romances
series vs. lines, 21
viewpoint in, 109-111
Contract for Marriage, 24, 185
Contracts, 2
Correspondence, 50-51
Cover art, 12
Cover letter with manuscript, 187
Crawford, Diane (aka Georgette Livingston), 111, 152, 241-242
Credit page, 187
Cristy, Ann (aka Helen Mittermeyer), 103

Crone, Alla, 15, 73, 234-235
Cuddy, Page, 188, 196
Curtis, Richard, 200
Curtis, Tom, 164

Dailey, Janet, 3, 6, 7, 15, 20, 155
Dark moment, 98
Daydreamer, 238
Day, Jocelyn, 62, 65, 67
Deadlines, 199-201
Deaths of characters, 168
Deception for Desire, 230
Dell 5, 7, 8, 9, 56, 73, 134, 235,
   237, 246
   Candlelight, 4, 6, 7, 23, 24, 79,
      92, 125, 228, 229, 230, 231,
      241
   guidelines from, 57, 58
   Supreme, 24
   Young Love Books, 28
Demand for romance fiction. *See*
   Market
Description
   of places, 216
   vs. plot, 78
   of setting, 218
Desert Fire, 227
Desire line. *See* Silhouette
Desk, 51-52
Details, 26, 78, 218
Deveraux, Jude, 210
Dialects, 133-136
Dialogue, 38-39, 120-139, 177-178
   building sexual tension with, 123-
      126
   for characterization, 121-123
   hearing, 121
   in historical romance, 122, 134
   humorous, 131-133
   punctuation of, 126-130
   in young adult romances, 122,
      136-137
Dickerson, Marilyn, 219
Doctor Anne, 2
Donahue, Phil, 7, 24

Doubleday, 8
Douglas, Anne, 7
Dowdell, Dorothy, 27, 77, 92, 94,
   230-231
Doyle, Emily (aka Betty Henrichs,
   Amanda Kent), 139
Drafts, 50
Drake, Bonnie, 125, 128, 131
Drugstore promotion, 204
Dude Ranch Nurse, 2
Du Maurier, Daphne, 239
Dutton young adult romances, 241
Duvall, Aimee, 61

Earnings. *See* Income
East Lies the Sun, 73, 235
Ecstasy Supremes, Dell, 9
Editorial changes, 196
Editorial correspondence, 50
Editorial guidelines, 45, 51
Editorial package, 184-187
Editor-writer relationship, 193, 198,
   200
Education, 14
   adult, 206
Edwardian romances, 21
Edwards, Ellen, 8, 58
Embers of Dawn, 73
Endings, 164-171, 178-179
   believable, 164
   happy, 164
   for historical romances, 168
   planning of, 164-167
E.P. Dutton young adult romances,
   241
Erskine, Helen (aka Helen Santori),
   74, 82, 96, 99, 170, 242-243
Escapist fantasy, 4
Exclusive multibook contracts, 2
Eye appeal of manuscript, 182

Fairfax, Lynn, 73, 109
Falk, Kathryn, 229
Family Circle, 48
Family sagas, 20

Fantasy, 4
Faulkner, William, 1, 2
Fawcett Gold Medal, 27, 94, 112, 231
File basket, 53
File cabinet, 49-51, 206
File cards, 40-41
File tray, 53
Filing system, 52, 53
Final check before mailing manuscript, 174
Final scene of passion, 167-170
Financial returns, 13
Finding Mr. Right, Avon, 8, 24
First books, 13, 17
First Love. *See* Silhouette
Flamenco Nights, 80
Folders
  chapter, 48-49
  for ongoing business, 51
Food, 47
Forbes, 8, 17
Forever Amber, 1
Formula romances. *See* Contemporary romances
Fortunes of Love, 243
Frenchman's Creek, 239
Frentz, Jane (aka Jayne Castle, Stephanie James), 52, 167
Freud, Sigmund, 5
Friends who are writers, 209
Fund for conferences, 206
Furnishings, 48
Future-novel ideas, 51

Garlock, Dorothy, 130
Gentle Pirate, 6
Gerson, Noel B., 239
Ghost of a Chance, A, 238
Gisonny, Anne, 7, 8
Glitter Girl, 62, 65
Glory Land, 94, 231
Golden Girl, 74, 82
Golden Touch, The, 131
Gone With the Wind, 1
Good Housekeeping, 7, 48, 237

Goodman, Irene, 208
Gordon, Debbie (aka Brooke Hastings), 23, 73, 133, 142, 226-227
Gothics, 2, 20, 29
Grunder, Robin, 234, 185
Guarded Moments, 73
Guidelines, 21, 45, 56
  Dell's, 57, 58
  editorial, 45, 51
Guinness Book of World Records, 3

Hall, Donald, 1
Halldorson, Phyllis, 23, 235-236
Hallin, Emily (aka Elaine Harper), 137, 233-234
Hampson, Anne, 23, 149
Happy endings, 164
Harlequin, 2, 3, 4, 6, 7, 8, 9, 16, 23, 145, 246
  American Romances, 9, 24, 230
  Superromances, 24, 168, 185, 239, 240, 242
Harlequin Presents, 7, 8, 24, 149
Harper, Elaine (aka Emily Hallin), 137, 233-234
Harper, Shannon, 94, 120
Harris, Andrea, 237
  Harvesters, The, 15
Hastings, Brooke (aka Debbie Gordon), 23, 73, 133, 142, 226-227
Hawk Over Holly Hedge, 231
Hawthorn Books, 200
Hearing dialogue, 121
Hella, Christine, 72
Henrichs, Betty (aka Amanda Kent, Emily Doyle), 139
Her Decision, 97, 98, 100, 237
Hero, 186
  See also Characters
  brief shifts into viewpoint of in category romance, 111-112
  in category romances, 56-58, 111-112
  in historical romances, 59

professional background of, 38, 72

in young adult romances, 60

Heroine, 38, 186

See also Characters

age of, 4

in category romances, 56-58

in historical romances, 59

professional background of, 72

in young adult romances, 60

Hibiscus Lagoon, 231

Historical romances, 3, 8, 9, 20, 26-27, 29

characters in, 59

dialogue in, 122, 134

endings for, 168

multiple viewpoint in, 112-114

research for, 75

series of, 28

setting in, 73, 81-82

sex scenes in, 155-157

viewpoint in, 112-114

Historical sagas, 27-28

Hold Fast to Love, 197

Hospital on Wheels, 2

Houghton Mifflin, 200

Hourglass, Zebra Books, 24

House Beautiful, 48

House in Munich, 231

Houston, Henrietta (aka Prudence Lichte, Prudence Martin), 144

How To Be Your Own Literary Agent, 200

Humorous dialogue, 131-133

Ideas for novels, 40, 51

Impetuous Surrogate, 229, 230

Impossible Dream, The, 231

Income, 1. 17, 215

annual, 2

Index file, 52

Innocent Fire, 227

Inspirational (religious) romances, 22

Intimate Moments, 246

Intimate Moments, Silhouette, 24

Intimate Strangers, 73, 227

Investing in your business, 205-207

Island Conquest, 227

Italians, The, 239

It's Your Move, Lori, 241

I've Got a Crush on You, 114

James, Robin, 131

James, Stephanie (aka Jayne Castle, Jane Frentz), 52, 167

Jane Eyre, 3

Jeffries, Julia (aka Lynda Ward), 79, 146, 238-240

Jennings, Vivien Lee, 1

Jove, 6, 8, 143, 246

Regency, 26

Second Chance at Love, 5, 6, 8, 9, 24, 62, 73, 80, 109, 131, 146, 147, 242

To Have and To Hold, 8, 24

Joyce, Janet (team of Janet Bieber and Joyce Thies), 73, 150, 231-233

Kate Herself, 96, 170, 243

Kendrick, Walter, 16

Kent, Amanda (aka Betty Henrichs, Emily Doyle), 139

King's General, The, 239

Kingston, Meredith, 73

Ladies' Home Journal, 48

Learning to write romance, 14

Leather & Lace, Zebra Books, 9, 26

Lectures, 206

Leigh, Roberta, 23

Lesbian romances, 22

Libertine Lady, 233

Librarian promotion, 204

Lichte, Prudence (aka Prudence Martin, Henrietta Houston), 144

Light of My Life, 234

Lines

vs. contemporary series, 21

vs. series, 25

Livingston, Georgette (aka Diane

Crawford), 111, 152, 241-242
Love for All Time, A, 130
Love Comes to Annie, 74
Love at First Sight, 137, 234
Love & Life, Ballantine, 8, 24, 97, 237
Love Match, 238
Love Once in Passing, 197
Lover from the Sea, 125, 128, 131
Loveswept, Bantam, 9, 24, 130
Love's Wildest Fires, 3
Lucifer Wine, The, 237

MacFadden Romances, 7
Magazine subscriptions, 206
Man of Glory, 233
Man of the House, 233
Manuscript
  cover letter with, 187
  eye appeal of, 182
  final check before mailing, 174
  typing of, 182-184
Market, 2, 16, 223
  open, 13
Marriage Contract, The, 112
Martin, Prudence (aka Prudence
  Lichte, Henrietta Houston),
  144
Masquerade of Love, 229, 230
Mather, Anne, 23
Matter of Time, A, 227
Matthews, Clayton, 15
Matthews, Patricia, 15, 20, 27, 73, 96
Maunaloa Curse, The, 237
McBain, Laurie, 73, 81, 169
Michigan Quarterly, 235
Midnight Magic, 72, 73
Midnight Whispers, 15
Mills & Boon, 2, 8, 228
Mittermeyer, Helen (aka Ann Cristy), 103
Modern Romances, 242
Morgan, Alice, 159, 228-230, 230
Mountain Melody, 236

Multibook contracts, 2
Multiple viewpoint, 108-109
  in historical romance, 112-114
Murdoch Legacy, The, 237
Music of Passion, The, 79, 240
Mystery Kiss, The, 234

NAL. *See* New American Library
National Enquirer, 7
National League of American Pen
  Women, 206
"NBC Magazine," 7
New American Library (NAL), 8, 142
  Rapture Romance, 24
  Regencies, 26, 240
  Signet Regency, 26
Newspapers
  promotion through, 204
  subscriptions to, 206
New Tomorrow, A, 237
New York Times, 7
Next Patient, 2
Next Step, The, 237
Nichols, Carolyn, 8, 9, 62, 175
Nielsen, Virginia, 112
Nurse with a Dream, 2
"Nurse novels," 2

Occult romances, 22
Office, 49-53
Office supplies, 206
Ongoing-business folder, 51
Opening, 130-131
Open market 13
Oppenheimer, Joan L., 157
Organization, 34, 174-175
Originality, 2
Outlines, 186-187, 218
  working, 102-103
Overall organization, 34, 174-175
*Oxford Book of American Literary
  Anecdotes, The,* 1

Pacing, 100-101

Passion, final scene, 167-170
Peake, Lilian, 23
Pearl Award, 229
Peart, Jane, 79, 240-241
Pen names, 190-191
Perfect Stranger, 73
Personal library, 206
Pianka, Phyllis Taylor (aka Winter
    Ames), 116
Place descriptions, 216
Planning, 220
    of endings, 164-167
    of plot, 101-102
    of sex scenes, 144-148
Plant and animal life, 48
Playboy Press, 231, 237
Playing for Keeps, 227
Plot, 36, 176-177
    climax of, 96-98
    vs. description, 78
    planning of, 101-102
Plotting, 90-103
Plunge opening, 130-131
Pocket Books, 4, 6, 7, 8, 155
    Tapestry, 8, 26, 233
Porgie Award, 235
Portrait in the Shadows, 241
Post Office, 188
Power Seekers, The, 15
Professional background of heroine
    and hero, 38, 72, 83-86
Promotion, 204, 205, 207
Proposals, 207
Publicizing, 204, 205, 207
Publishers Weekly, 200, 206
Punctuation of dialogue, 126-130

Quin-Harkin, Janet, 237-238

Radio station promotion, 204
Random House, 28
Rape, 155
Rapture Romances, 8
    sex scenes in, 142
RCA, 9

Reader reaction, 33
    analyzing of, 34
Reading, 12, 29
    analytical, 32
    as help in writer's block, 210
    for pleasure, 12
Realism vs. believability, 62
Real people as models, 216
Rebecca, 3, 239
Regencies, 7, 21, 29
    sex in, 143
Rejection, 191-193
Religious (inspirational) romances,
    22
Renaissance Man, 167
Research, 26, 48, 74-77
    for historical romances, 75
Resolution, 98-100
Response of reader, 33, 34
Revision, 196
Rhapsody Romance, 7
Richard Gallen Books, 6, 8, 232,
    233
River of Desire, 73
Rogers, Rosemary, 20, 26, 27, 102,
    174
Romance Theater, 7
Romance Writers of America, 7, 206
Romance Writers' Report, 206
Romantic Book Lovers' Conference,
    New York, 229
Romantic resolution, 98-100
Romantic suspense, 22
Romantic Times, 206, 229
Ross, Dana Fuller, 28
Rough Diamond, 227
Royalties, 2, 215

Saal, Jocelyn, 74
Sagas, 29
    family, 20
    historical, 27-28
Sales
    annual, 8
    first, 13

Sample chapters, 186-187
Sands of Malibu, 228, 230
Santori, Helen (aka Helen Erskine),
    74, 82, 96, 99, 170, 242-243
Sapphire Island, 242
Saturday Review, 6
Savage Eden, 242
Savage Surrender, 3
Scariano, Margaret, 209
Scholastic, 157
    Wildfire, 74, 114, 143, 238
School promotion, 205
Secondary characters, 25
    in category romances, 58-59
    in historical romances, 59
Second Chance, 246
Second Chance at Love. *See* Jove
Seger, Maura, 17, 57
Senior citizen romances, 8
Sensual category romances, 21, 22,
    24-26
Sensuality, 5
Sensuousness, 23, 39
Series, 29
    contemporary, 21
    historical, 28
    vs. lines, 25
Setting, 37, 47, 72, 73, 176
Setting
    American, 3
    bringing to life of, 77-78
    in category contemporary ro-
        mances, 78-81
    description of, 218
    in historical romances, 73, 81-82
    of sex scenes, 158-160
    of workplace, 44-53
    of young adult romances, 73, 74,
        82-83
Sex scenes, 2, 4, 23, 39, 42, 178,
    187
    in category romances, 150-155
    in historical romances, 155-157
    planning of, 144-148
    in Rapture Romances, 142

in Regencies, 143
setting of, 158-160
in Silhouette romances, 142
in sweet romances, 149-150
in young adult romances, 143,
    157-158
Sexuality spectrum in romance fic-
    tion, 148-158
Sexual tension, 91-96, 144
    building of with dialogue, 123-126
Sherwood, Valerie, 27
Shifts of viewpoint, 108, 111-112
Silhouette, 4, 7, 8, 15, 23, 165,
    227, 236, 243, 246
    Desire, 7, 8, 73, 111, 167, 233
    First Love, 28, 74, 96, 137, 234,
        243
    Intimate Moments, 24
    sex scenes in, 142
    Special Edition, 7, 8, 24, 73, 110,
        168, 227
Simon, Jo Ann, 197
Simon & Schuster, 4
Single-title releases, 21
Single viewpoint, 108
Slang, 137, 138
Small, Beatrice, 27
Small index file, 52
Solem, Karen, 107, 198
Someone's Stolen Nellie Grey, 237
Spanish Masquerade, 79, 241
Speech tags, 126-130
Special Edition. *See* Silhouette
Stanley, Carol, 114
Starlight romance series, 8
Steel, Danielle, 20
Steno pad, 52-53
Stephens, Vivian, 7, 8, 40, 229
Stereotypes in characters, 58
Strange Rapture, 231
Structure, 34, 174-175
Style, 40, 179, 221
Subscriptions, 206
Sunset, 48
Supermarket promotion, 204

Superromances. *See* Harlequin
Supplies, 206
Surrender, 237
Suspense, 92
  romantic, 22
Sweet category romances, 3, 21, 22,
  23
  sex in, 149-150
Sweet Dreams, Bantam, 28, 74, 238
Synopsis, 40, 185-186

Tagging
  of characters, 65-68, 69
  of speech, 126-130
Tahoe, 231
Tapestry, Pocket Books, 8, 26, 233
Taylor, Abra, 73
Taylor, Day, 134
Tears of Gold, 73, 81, 169
Teen romances, 7, 8, 22
  See also Young adult romances
Temporary Bride, 236
Temptation line, 9
Ten Boy Summer, 238
Tension. *See* Sexual tension
Thies, Joyce (one half of Janet Joy-
  ce), 148, 199, 231-233
This Calder sky, 155
This Loving Torment, 3
Thomas Bouregy and Co., 231
Thornton, Carolyn, 45
Time needed for writing romances,
  13
Tip sheets. *See* Guidelines
Title page, 33
To Have and To Hold, 246
To Have and To Hold series, Jove,
  8, 24
Tommy Loves Tina, 238
To Start Again, 236
Touch of Passion, The, 239, 240
Town and Country, 48
Trusting Hearts, 74
"20/20," ABC, 7
Typewriters, 206

Typing of manuscript, 182-184
Typists, 206

Victorian romances, 21
Viewpoint, 38, 106-117, 177, 218
  in contemporary category ro-
    mances, 109-111
  defined, 106
  multiple, 108-109, 112-114
  shifts in, 108, 111-112
  single, 108
  in young adult romance, 114-116
Village Voice, The, 16
Vintage Books, 28
Vintage Evil, 241
Vogue, 48
Voices of Julie, The, 157

Wagered Weekend, 92
Wagons West, 28
Waldenbooks, 9
Walker, Irma, 35, 97, 236-237
Walk Softly, Doctor, 2
Wallace, Pamela, 73
Ward, Lynda (aka Julia Jeffries), 79,
  146, 238-240
Warner, 7
Warner, Lucille S., 74
We Belong Together, 234
West Coast Review of Books, 235
Westerns, 9
Wicked Loving Lies, 26
Wilde, Jennifer, 15
Wilson, Fran, 165
Windfall, 237
Winds Over Manchuria, 235
Windswept, Bantam, 28
Windward Crest, 149
Winner Take All, 227
Winspear, Violet, 23
Winter Lady, 73, 111, 150, 233
Winter Love Song, 73
Woman's Day, 48
Woman's Empire A, 27, 231
Women's club promotion, 205

Woodiwiss, Kathleen, 20
Word processors, 206
Working outline, 102-103
Workplace setting, 44-53
Workshops, 206
Worldwide Library, 6, 24
Write Every Day, 238
Writer credit page, 187
Writer-editor relationship, 193, 198,
    200
Writer-friends, 209
Writer's block, 207-210
Writer's clubs, 206
Writer's Digest, 200, 206
Writer's Digest School of Writing, 12
Writer's group promotion, 205

*Writer's Guide to Book Publishing,
    A,* 200
Writer's Market, 200
Writer tip sheets. *See* Guidelines

Young adult romances, 22, 28-29
    See also Teen romances
    dialogue in, 122, 136-137
    heroine and hero in, 60
    setting of, 73, 74, 82-83
    sex in, 143, 157-158
    viewpoint in, 114-116
Young Love Books, Dell, 28

Zebra Books, 8
    Hourglass, 24
    Leather & Lace, 9, 26

Other Writer's Digest Books

General Writing Books
  Beginning Writer's Answer Book, edited by Polking, et al $9.95
  How to Get Started in Writing, by Peggy Teeters $10.95
  International Writers' & Artists' Yearbook, (paper) $10.95
  Law and the Writer, edited by Polking and Meranus (paper) $7.95
  Make Every Word Count, by Gary Provost (paper) $6.95
  Teach Yourself to Write, by Evelyn A. Stenbock $12.95
  Treasury of Tips for Writers, edited by Marvin Weisbord (paper) $6.95
  Writer's Encyclopedia, edited by Kirk Polking $19.95
  Writer's Market, edited by P.J. Schemenaur $18.95
  Writer's Resource Guide, edited by Bernadine Clark $16.95
  Writing for the Joy of It, by Leonard Knott $11.95
Magazine/News Writing
  Complete Guide to Marketing Magazine Articles, by Duane Newcomb $9.95
  Craft of Interviewing, by John Brady $9.95
  Magazine Writing: The Inside Angle, by Art Spikol $12.95
  Magazine Writing Today, by Jerome E. Kelley $10.95
  Newsthinking: The Secret of Great Newswriting, by Bob Baker $11.95
  1001 Article Ideas, by Frank A. Dickson $10.95
  Stalking the Feature Story, by William Ruehlmann $9.95
  Write On Target, by Connie Emerson $12.95
  Writing and Selling Non-Fiction, by Hayes B. Jacobs $12.95
Fiction Writing
  Creating Short Fiction, by Damon Knight $11.95
  Fiction Writer's Help Book, by Maxine Rock $12.95
  Fiction Writer's Market, edited by Jean Fredette $17.95
  Handbook of Short Story Writing, by Dickson and Smythe (paper) $6.95
  How to Write Best-Selling Fiction, by Dean R. Koontz $13.95
  How to Write Short Stories that Sell, by Louise Boggess $9.95
  One Way to Write Your Novel, by Dick Perry (paper) $6.95
  Secrets of Successful Fiction, by Robert Newton Peck $8.95
  Writing Romance Fiction—For Love And Money, by Helene Schellenberg Barnhart $14.95
  Writing the Novel: From Plot to Print, by Lawrence Block $10.95
Special Interest Writing Books
  Cartoonist's & Gag Writer's Handbook, by Jack Markow (paper) $9.95
  The Children's Picture Book: How to Write It, How to Sell It, by Ellen E. M. Roberts $17.95
  Complete Book of Scriptwriting, by J. Michael Straczynski $14.95
  How to Make Money Writing . . . Fillers, by Connie Emerson $12.95
  Confession Writer's Handbook, by Florence K. Palmer. Revised by Marguerite McClain $9.95
  Guide to Greeting Card Writing, edited by Larry Sandman $10.95
  Guide to Writing History, by Doris Ricker Marston $9.95
  How to Write and Sell Your Personal Experiences, by Lois Duncan $10.95
  How to Write and Sell (Your Sense of) Humor, by Gene Perret $12.95
  How to Write "How-To" Books and Articles, by Raymond Hull (paper) $8.95
  Mystery Writer's Handbook, edited by Lawrence Treat (paper) $8.95
  Poet and the Poem, revised edition by Judson Jerome $13.95
  Poet's Handbook, by Judson Jerome $11.95
  Sell Copy, by Webster Kuswa $11.95
  Successful Outdoor Writing, by Jack Samson $11.95

TV Scriptwriter's Handbook, by Alfred Brenner $12.95
Travel Writer's Handbook, by Louise Purwin Zobel $13.95
Writing and Selling Science Fiction, by Science Fiction Writers of America (paper) $7.95
Writing for Children & Teenagers, by Lee Wyndham. Revised by Arnold Madison $10.95
Writing for Regional Publications, by Brian Vachon $11.95
Writing to Inspire, by Gentz, Roddy, et al $14.95

The Writing Business

Complete Handbook for Freelance Writers, by Kay Cassill $14.95
How to Be a Successful Housewife/Writer, by Elaine Fantle Shimberg $10.95
How You Can Make $20,000 a Year Writing, by Nancy Hanson (paper) $6.95
Jobs for Writers, edited by Kirk Polking $11.95
Profitable Part-time/Full-time Freelancing, by Clair Rees $10.95
The Writer's Survival Guide: How to Cope with Rejection, Success and 99 Other Hang-Ups of the Writing Life, by Jean and Veryl Rosenbaum $12.95

To order directly from the publisher, include $1.50 postage and handling for 1 book and 50¢ for each additional book. Allow 30 days for delivery.

Writer's Digest Books, Department B
9933 Alliance Road, Cincinnati OH 45242
Prices subject to change without notice.